ESSENTIALS OF NURSING LEADERSHIP AND MANAGEMENT

ESSENTIALS OF NURSING LEADERSHIP AND MANAGEMENT

RUTH M. TAPPEN, EdD, RN, FAAN
Christine E. Lynn Eminent Scholar and Professor
College of Nursing
Florida Atlantic University
Boca Raton, Florida

SALLY A. WEISS, EdD, RN
Associate Professor of Nursing
Broward Community College
Pembroke Pines, Florida

DIANE K. WHITEHEAD, EdD, RN
Department Head, Nursing
Broward Community College
Davie, Florida

 F. A. DAVIS COMPANY • Philadelphia

F. A. Davis Company
1915 Arch Street
Philadelphia, PA 19103

Printed in the United States of America

Last digit indicates print number: 10 9 8 7 6 5 4 3

Acquisitions Editor: Joanne P. DaCunha
Developmental Editor: Melanie Freely
Production Editor: Jessica Howie Martin
Cover Designer: Louis J. Forgione

As new scientific information becomes available through basic and clinical research, recommended treatments and drug therapies undergo changes. The authors and publisher have done everything possible to make this book accurate, up to date, and in accord with accepted standards at the time of publication. The authors, editors, and publisher are not responsible for errors or omissions or for consequences from application of the book, and make no warranty, expressed or implied, in regard to the contents of the book. Any practice described in this book should be applied by the reader in accordance with professional standards of care used in regard to the unique circumstances that may apply in each situation. The reader is advised always to check product information (package inserts) for changes and new information regarding dose and contraindications before administering any drug. Caution is especially urged when using new or infrequently ordered drugs.

Library of Congress Cataloging-in-Publication Data

Tappen, Ruth M.
    Essentials of nursing leadership and management / Ruth M.
Tappen, Sally A. Weiss, Diane K. Whitehead.
        p. cm.
    Includes bibliographical references and index.
    ISBN 0-8036-0244-8 (pbk.)
    1. Nursing services—Administration. 2. Leadership. I. Weiss,
Sally A., 1950–   . II. Whitehead, Diane K., 1945–   . III. Title.
    [DNLM: 1. Nursing. 2. Nursing Services—organization &
administration—United States. 3. Leadership. WY 16 T175e 1998]
RT89.T357 1998
362.1′73′068—dc21
DNLM/DLC
for Library of Congress   97-39633
                                                                      CIP

To our teachers, students, colleagues, and mentors, who continue to enrich our lives.

Preface

*E*ssentials of Nursing Leadership and Management is designed to help the new graduate make the transition to professional nursing practice. The content, examples, and diagrams were designed with this reader in mind.

This textbook focuses on the staff nurse as a vital member of the health-care team and manager of patient care. As a manager of care, the staff nurse must have the knowledge and skills necessary to make decisions on setting priorities, delegation, quality improvement, legal parameters of nursing practice, and ethical issues confronting nursing today. These issues are presented with up-to-date information and relevant examples.

This book also provides comprehensive, practical information on developing a nursing career. Workplace issues such as change, conflict management, safety, stress, burnout, and cultural diversity are addressed in an easy-to-understand style.

It is our hope that this textbook will assist new graduates in developing their professional roles in the ever-changing healthcare environment.

We would like to thank the people at F. A. Davis for their assistance and all of the reviewers for their helpful suggestions.

Ruth M. Tappen
Sally A. Weiss
Diane K. Whitehead

Reviewers

Anne D'Antuono, RN, PhD, CS
Program Coordinator
Catholic Medical Center
Woodhaven, New York

Karen T. Braswell, RNC, MSN
Instructor
Asheville-Buncombe Technical
Community College
Asheville, North Carolina

Lorraine M. Clarke, RN, EdD
Professor
University of Vermont
Burlington, Vermont

Robbie Joy Conger, RN, MSN
Chair, Division of Nursing
Abraham Baldwin College
Tifton, Georgia

Carmel Esposito, RN, EdD
Nurse Educator/Coordinator
Trinity Health System
Steubenville, Ohio

Roberta Fruth, RN, PhD, CCRN
Assistant Professor
Rush University
Chicago, Illinois

Bruce Garrett, RN, MBA, CNA
Clinical Instructor
New Mexico State University
Alamogordo, New Mexico

Patricia A. Girczyc, RN, MPH, FNP
Professor
College of the Redwoods
Eureka, California

Eleanor Green, RN, MSN
Instructor
Bucks County Community College
Newtown, Pennsylvania

Esther P. Haloburdo, RN, PhD
Professor
St. Joseph College
West Hartford, Connecticut

Martha Harrop, RN
Professor
Florida International University
Fort Lauderdale, Florida

Pamella E. HoSang, RN, EdD
Associate Professor
Medgar Evers College
New York, New York

Dr. Vivian Lilly, RN, PhD, CNS
Collin County Community College
Division of Health Sciences
McKinney, Texas

Diane MacLaughlin, BSN, MS
Associate Professor
Erie Community College
Buffalo, New York

Susan Mudd, MSN
Associate Professor
Elizabethtown Community College
Elizabethtown, Kentucky

Patricia Newland, MS, BS
Associate Professor
Broome Community College
Binghamton, New York

Victoria Poole, RN, DSN
Assistant Professor
University of Alabama
Birmingham, Alabama

Patricia Porterfield, MSN, BSN
Instructor
St. Charles County Community College
St. Peters, Missouri

Marcia Shannon, RN, MSN
Professor
Saginaw Valley State University
University Center, Michigan

Judith Turbanic, RN, BSN, MA
Assistant Professor
Fairmont State College
Fairmont, West Virginia

Sylvia H. Womack, MSN
Assistant Professor
Macon College
Macon, Georgia

Linda E. Wrynn, RN
Instructor
Big Bend Community College
Moses Lake, Washington .

Contents

UNIT I

Introduction to Leadership and Management

CHAPTER 1

Keys to Effective Leadership and Management

OBJECTIVES   *After reading this chapter, the student will be able to:*

◆ Define leadership and management.

◆ Distinguish between leadership and management.

◆ Discuss the qualities and behaviors that contribute to effective leadership.

◆ Discuss the qualities and behaviors that contribute to effective management.

The study of leadership and management is essentially the study of how to work with other people. Nurses usually work alongside a great number of other professional and nonprofessional personnel: physicians, therapists, social workers, psychologists, technicians, aides, unit managers, and couriers, to name just a few. Many nurses are also expected to manage staffs that include a wide variety of personnel. Some of these people have healthcare skills; others do not.

In this chapter, we define leadership and management, look at the differences between the two, and discuss the qualities and behaviors that make an effective leadership and nurse manager.

■ The Difference between Leadership and Management

• • • • • • • • • • • • • • • • • •

LEADERSHIP DEFINED

The essence of leadership is the ability to influence other people. Stephen R. Covey, author of several popular books on leadership, says that a leader "enables people to work more effectively together in a state of interdependence" (1992, p. 267). Max DePree, chairman of the board of a well-known American manufacturer, defines the art of leadership as "liberating people to do what is required of them in the most effective and humane way possible" (1989).

Effective nurse leaders are the ones who can inspire others to work together in pursuit of a shared goal. This goal may be providing excellent patient care, designing a cost-saving procedure, or challenging the ethics of a new advanced directives policy. We discuss the qualities and behaviors of an effective leader in the next section of this chapter.

MANAGEMENT DEFINED

There are two schools of thought about what management is. In 1916, Henri Fayol defined management as planning, organizing, commanding, coordinating, and controlling the work of a given set of employees (Wren, 1972). This definition has influenced thinking in management, including nursing management, for years. However, Mintzberg (1989) says that Fayol's list of management functions does not really describe what managers do. Instead, the manager's function is to do whatever is necessary to make sure that employees do their work and do it well. This includes interpersonal, informational, and decisional actions. We consider Mintzberg's list of management functions in more detail in the section on effective nursing management.

Effective managers, according to Covey, are able to elicit from each employee "his or her deepest commitment, continued loyalty, finest creativity, consistent excellent productivity, and maximum potential contribution toward . . . continuous improvement of process, product, and service" (1992, p. 276). The effective nurse manager is responsible for ensuring not only that patient care is given but also that it is given in the most effective and efficient manner possible.

ARE YOU READY TO BE A LEADER OR MANAGER?

You may be thinking, "I'm just beginning my career in nursing. Aren't leadership and management capabilities an expectation of the experienced nurse?" This is partly correct. It is true that new nurses should not be given managerial responsibility under most circumstances. New graduates need time to develop their own clinical skills and are not ready to help others in this development process. The breadth and depth of their experience are insufficient for the fulfillment of a managerial role right after graduation.

On the other hand, new graduates can function as leaders within their new nursing roles.

Billie Blair Thomas is a new staff nurse at Green Valley Nursing Home. After orientation, she was assigned to a very active subacute unit with high admission and discharge rates. Billie noticed that the handling of resident admissions and discharges was rather haphazard. Anyone who was "free" at the moment was directed to handle them. Sometimes nursing aides were assigned to these tasks. Billie felt that using aides was inappropriate because they have no training in discharge planning and their assessment skills are usually quite limited.

Billie thought there was a better way to handle admissions and discharges but was not sure that she should suggest it because she was so new. "Maybe they've already thought of this," she said to a former classmate. "It's such an obvious solution." They began to talk about what they had learned in their leadership course before graduation. "I just keep hearing our instructor saying, 'There's only one manager, but anyone can be a leader if they act on their good ideas.' " "To be a leader, you have to act on your idea," her friend said. "Maybe I will," Billie responded.

Billie decided to speak with her nurse manager, an experienced long-term care nurse who seemed approachable and open to new ideas. "I have been so busy getting our new computer system in place before the surveyors come that I overlooked that," the nurse manager told her. "I'm really happy you brought it to my attention."

Billie's nurse manager raised the issue at the next executive meeting, giving credit to Billie ("our newest nurse") for having brought it to her attention. The other nurse managers had the same reaction: "We were so focused on that new computer system that we overlooked that. We need to take care of this situation as soon as possible. That Billie Blair Thomas has real leadership potential."

COMPARISON OF LEADERSHIP AND MANAGEMENT

The terms "leadership" and "management" are often confused, although the differences between them are quite straightforward. The fundamental differences between leaders and managers are (1) managers have formal authority to direct the work of a given set of employees and (2) managers are formally responsible for the quality and cost of that work. Neither of these is necessary to be a leader. On the other hand, to be an effective manager, you do need to be a good leader (Table 1–1).

Leadership is an essential part of effective management, but the reverse is not true: you do not have to be a manager to be a leader. You can be the youngest, newest, or even the least experienced nurse and yet still have opportunities to be a leader, as the Billie Blair Thomas example illustrates. These opportunities will increase as your experience increases, as will your readiness to assume managerial responsibility.

■ *What Makes a Person a Leader?*

• • • • • • • • • • • • • • • • • • • •

LEADERSHIP THEORIES

There are many different opinions or theories about how a person becomes a leader and what type of leader is most effective. Although quite a lot of research has been done on this subject, no theory has emerged yet as the clear winner. The result is that we do not have a theory that provides the single best answer to our question: what makes a person a leader? The reason for this may be

TABLE 1–1
DIFFERENCES BETWEEN LEADERSHIP AND MANAGEMENT

Leadership	Management
Based on influence	Based on authority and influence
An informal designation	A formally designated position
An achieved position	An assigned position
Part of every nurse's role	Usually responsible for budgets, hiring and firing people
Independent of management	Improved by the use of effective leadership skills

that different qualities and behaviors are most important in different situations faced by leaders. In nursing, for example, some situations require quick thinking and fast action. Others require some time to figure out the best solution to a complicated problem. Different leadership qualities and behaviors are needed in these two different situations.

We now look at some of the most prominent leadership theories and consider the many qualities and behaviors of an effective nurse leader (Dunham-Taylor, 1995; Manske, 1989; Montebello, 1994; Tappen, 1995).

Trait Theories

At one time or another, you've probably heard someone say that "leaders are born, not made." This saying claims that some of us are born with the qualities required of a leader and others are not. This is not true. Although leadership may come more easily to some of us than to others, every one of us can be a leader if we develop the necessary knowledge and skill.

Many research studies have been done in an attempt to identify the qualities (or traits) that distinguish a leader from a nonleader. The most common traits noted were:

◆ Intelligence

◆ Initiative

Other characteristics that are frequently cited as leadership traits are:

◆ Excellent interpersonal skills

◆ High self-esteem

◆ Creativity

◆ Willingness to take risks

◆ Ability to tolerate the consequences of taking risks

Behavioral Theories

Although the trait theories were concerned with what a leader *is*, the behavior theories are concerned with what the leader *does*. One of the most influential of these behavioral theories is concerned with *leadership style* (White & Lippitt, 1960) (Table 1–2). The three styles are:

◆ **AUTHORITARIAN (AUTOCRATIC, DIRECTIVE, CONTROLLING).** The authoritarian leader gives orders, makes decisions for the group as a whole, and bears most of the responsibility for the outcomes. Although this is an efficient way to run things, it usually stifles creativity and may inhibit motivation. Authoritarian leadership may be either punitive or benign.

◆ **DEMOCRATIC (PARTICIPATIVE).** In contrast to the authoritarian leader, the democratic

TABLE 1–2
COMPARISON OF AUTHORITARIAN, DEMOCRATIC, AND LAISSEZ-FAIRE LEADERSHIP STYLES

	Authoritarian	Democratic	Laissez-Faire
Degree of freedom	Little freedom	Moderate freedom	Much freedom
Degree of control	High control	Moderate control	No control
Decision making	By the leader	Leader and group together	By the group or by no one
Leader activity level	High	High	Minimal
Assumption of responsibility	Primarily the leader	Shared	Abdicated
Output of the group	High quantity, good quality	Creative, high quality	Variable, may be poor quality
Efficiency	Very efficient	Less efficient than authoritarian	Inefficient

Source: Adapted from White, R.K., & Lippitt, R. *Autocracy and Democracy: An Experimental Inquiry.* New York: Harper & Row.

leader shares the planning, decision making, and responsibility for the outcomes with other members of the group. Although this is often a less efficient way to run things, it is more flexible and more likely to foster motivation and creativity. Democratic leadership is characterized by guidance rather than control.

► **LAISSEZ-FAIRE (PERMISSIVE, NONDIRECTIVE).** The laissez-faire ("let it alone") leader does very little planning or decision making and fails to encourage others to participate in either. In fact, laissez-faire leadership is really a lack of leadership. The laissez-faire leader often leaves people feeling confused and frustrated because there is no goal, no guidance, and no direction. Some mature individuals enjoy laissez-faire leadership because they need little guidance. Most people, however, flounder under this kind of leadership.

Another important distinction in leadership style is the one between an emphasis on the *task* to be done and an emphasis on the *relationships* between the people who are working (Blake, Mouton, & Tapper, 1981). Some leaders emphasize the task (e.g., keeping the nurses station neat and clean) and fail to realize that interpersonal relationships (e.g., attitudes of physicians toward nurses and vice versa) have considerable impact on the morale and motivation of employees. Others focus on the interpersonal aspects and ignore the quality of the job being done as long as people get along with each other. The most effective leader is able to balance the two, making sure that both the task and the relationship aspects of working together are attended to.

Situational Theories

A more complex set of theories has evolved since the introduction of the trait and behavioral theories. These situational theories recognize the complexity of work situations and encourage the leader to consider a number of factors when deciding what action to take. One of the most important of these situational factors is the type of organization

in which the leader works (discussed in Chap. 6).

The following is an illustration of how just one factor can affect people's response to an organizational change:

> Two nurse managers were talking before the nursing administration council meeting began. "How did your staff react to the new 6 AM to 2 PM times for the day tour?" Jennifer Chinn asked her friend Esther Cabriollo.
>
> "They love it," said Esther.
>
> "Really?" said Jennifer. "My staff are so upset. They said it was an inhuman schedule, that they have to be at work before the birds get up in the morning. You should hear their complaints."
>
> "Most of my staff think it's just the opposite," said Esther. "Many have young children. With this new schedule, their spouse can take the children to school in the morning, and they can be home in time to meet the school bus. They said it's the most humane change the administration has made."
>
> "That explains it," said Jennifer. "Most of my staff have older children who have a lot of activities in the evening, and they're all having trouble getting up an hour earlier in the morning. Their situation is entirely different."

Every situation is different. A change that is welcomed by one group of people may be hated by another group. Situational theories emphasize the importance of understanding all of the factors that affect a particular group of people in a particular environment, including the type of leadership approach that is being used.

TRANSFORMATIONAL LEADERSHIP

Although the situational type of theory was a major step in the right direction in terms of recognizing how complex the process of influencing others really is, there was still a sense that something was missing. Meaning, inspiration, and vision had not been given enough attention in the earlier theories. Although these are not the only factors involved in transformational leadership, they are the outstanding features of this theory.

According to the transformational theory of leadership, people need a sense of mission that goes beyond good interpersonal relationships or the appropriate reward for a job well done. This is especially true in nursing. Caring for people, sick or well, is the goal of our profession, not manufacturing widgets. Most of us chose nursing to do something for the good of humankind. This is our vision, and one goal of nursing leadership is to guide us toward achievement of that vision.

Transformational leaders can describe this goal of nursing in a manner that is so meaningful and exciting that it inspires commitment in the people with whom they work (Trofino, 1995). If successful, the goals of the leader and staff will "become fused, creating unity, wholeness, and a collective purpose" (Barker, 1992, p. 42). Effective leadership is defined as the accomplishment of the goals shared by leaders and followers.

QUALITIES OF AN EFFECTIVE LEADER

Integrity, courage, initiative, energy, optimism, perseverance, balance, the ability to handle stress, and self-awareness are some of the qualities nurses who wish to be effective leaders should try to develop in themselves (Fig. 1–1).

◆ **INTEGRITY.** Integrity is expected of professional people. Our clients, colleagues, and employers all expect nurses to be honest, law-abiding, and worthy of their trust. Adherence to both a code of personal ethics and a code of professional ethics (like the American Nurses Association Code for Nurses in Appendix 1) is expected of every nurse. Would-be leaders who do not exhibit these characteristics cannot expect them of their followers either.

◆ **COURAGE.** Sometimes being a leader means taking some risks. In the story of

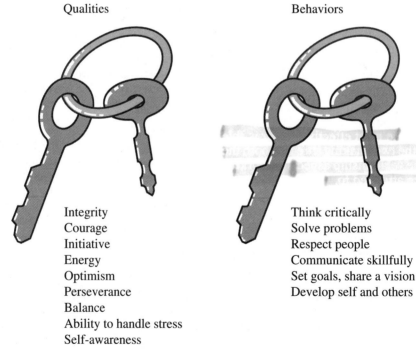

Qualities

Integrity
Courage
Initiative
Energy
Optimism
Perseverance
Balance
Ability to handle stress
Self-awareness

Behaviors

Think critically
Solve problems
Respect people
Communicate skillfully
Set goals, share a vision
Develop self and others

FIGURE 1–1 Keys to effective leadership.

Billie Blair Thomas, for example, Billie needed some courage to speak to her nurse manager.

◆ **INITIATIVE.** Good ideas are not enough. To be a leader, you must *act* on those good ideas. This requires some initiative on your part.

◆ **ENERGY.** Leadership also requires energy. Both leadership and management are hard but satisfying work that requires effort on your part. Of course, it is also important that you use your energy wisely.

◆ **OPTIMISM.** When the work is difficult and one crisis seems to follow another in rapid succession, it is easy to become discouraged. However, it is important not to let discouragement keep you and your coworkers from seeking ways to resolve your difficulties. In fact, the ability to see a problem as an opportunity is part of the optimism that makes a person an effective leader. Like energy, optimism is "catching." An optimistic leader can remotivate a discouraged group. Holman (1995) calls this being a *winner* instead of a *whiner* (Table 1–3).

◆ **PERSEVERANCE.** Perseverance is another related characteristic of effective leaders. Effective leaders do not give up easily. Instead, they persevere. They continue their efforts when their coworkers are tempted to give up the struggle. This perseverance often pays off in success.

◆ **BALANCE.** In our effort to become the best nurses we can be, we may forget that other aspects of life are equally important. As important as our clients and colleagues are to us, family and friends are important too. Although school and work are meaningful activities, cultural, social, recreational, and spiritual activities have meaning too. The most effective leaders and managers have found a balance among work, reflection, and play in their lives.

◆ **ABILITY TO HANDLE STRESS.** There is some stress in almost every job. Coping with stress in as positive and healthy a manner as possible helps you conserve your energy and be a model for others. We talk more about maintaining balance and handling stress in Chapter 9.

◆ **SELF-AWARENESS.** Knowing, understanding, and accepting yourself as a thinking, feeling human being who interacts with other thinking, feeling people is an extremely important leadership quality. People who do not know themselves are limited in their ability to understand the motivations of other people. They are also far more likely to fool themselves than are people who are self-aware. For example, it is much easier to be fair with a coworker you like than with one you do not like. Recognizing that you like some people better than others is the first step in preventing unfair treatment based on your own personal likes and dislikes.

TABLE 1–3
WINNER OR WHINER—WHICH ARE YOU?

A winner says . .	A whiner says . . .
We have a real challenge here.	This is really a problem.
I'll give it my best.	Do I have to?
That's great!	That's nice. I guess.
We can do it.	Impossible. It can't be done.
Yes!	Maybe . . .

Source: Adapted from Holman, L. (1995). *Eleven Lessons in Self-Leadership: Insights for Personal and Professional Success.* Lexington, Ky: A Lessons in Leadership Book.

BEHAVIORS OF AN EFFECTIVE LEADER

As mentioned earlier, leadership requires action. The effective leader not only takes action but chooses the action carefully. Some of the most common leadership behaviors are thinking critically, solving problems, respecting the individual, listening to others and communicating skillfully, setting goals and a vision for the future, and developing oneself and coaching others.

◆ **THINKING CRITICALLY.** Critical thinking is reflective, reasoned analysis that focuses on thinking before deciding what to believe or do (Miller & Malcolm,

1990). The essence of critical thinking is questioning and analyzing ideas, suggestions, habits, routines, common practices, and policies before deciding to accept or reject them. It is a way to avoid falling prey to the assumptions and biases of oneself and others.

It is not always easy to be a critical thinker. Critical thinkers sometimes make other people uncomfortable because they challenge their assumptions and upset the status quo. Nevertheless, critical thinkers often ask the questions that need to be asked and raise issues that need to be raised. This is not without risk, but it is part of being a leader.

SOLVING PROBLEMS. Client problems, paperwork problems, people problems: these and others occur frequently and need to be solved. The effective leader helps people to identify problems and to work through the problem-solving process to find a reasonable, workable solution.

RESPECTING THE INDIVIDUAL. Although we all have much in common with each other as thinking, feeling human beings, each of us has different wants and needs and has had different life experiences. For example, some people really value the psychological rewards of helping others. Other people are most concerned about earning a decent salary. There is nothing wrong with either of these points of view; they are simply different. The effective leader recognizes these differences in people and helps them find the rewards of their work that mean the most to them.

LISTENING TO OTHERS AND COMMUNICATING SKILLFULLY. The only way to find out people's individual wants and needs is to observe them and to listen to what they tell you. It is amazing how often leaders and managers fail simply because they did not listen to what other people were trying to tell them.

We have separated listening from communicating with other people just to emphasize that communication involves *both* giving and receiving information, not just giving out information.

Skillful communication includes the following:

- **Encouraging the Exchange of Information.** Many misunderstandings and mistakes occur because people failed to share sufficient clear information with each other. The leader's role is to make sure that the channels of communication remain open and that people use them.

- **Providing Feedback.** Everyone needs some information about the effectiveness of their performance. Frequent feedback, both positive and negative, is needed so that people can continually improve their performance. Some nurse leaders find it difficult to give negative feedback, fearing that they will upset the other person. How else can a person know where improvement is needed? Objective negative feedback can be given in a constructive, helpful manner that is neither hurtful nor resented by the individual receiving it. In fact, it is often appreciated.

  Other nurse leaders forget to give positive feedback, assuming that co-workers will know when they are doing a good job. This is a mistake: everyone appreciates positive feedback. In fact, for some people, it is the most important reward they get from their jobs.

SETTING GOALS AND A VISION FOR THE FUTURE. Just as each one of us is unique in terms of our experiences, needs, and wants, we are also likely to have unique goals for ourselves and others. The task of the leader is to find the common threads in all of those goals and to help the group reach a consensus about its goals. This may require considerable discussion in some groups.

The effective leader also has a vision of the future that is shared with and by the group. Communicating this vision to the group and involving everyone in working toward that vision of the future are the inspiration that keeps people going when things become difficult.

DEVELOPING ONESELF AND COACHING OTHERS. Learning does not end with leaving school. In fact, experienced nurses may tell you that school is just the beginning, that it only prepares you to continue learning throughout your career. As new and better ways to care for clients are discovered, it is your responsibility as a professional to critically analyze these new approaches and decide whether they would be better for your clients than current approaches to care.

Finally, effective leaders not only continue to learn themselves but also encourage others to do the same. Sometimes leaders function as teachers. Other times their role is primarily to encourage and guide others to seek more knowledge. Observant, reflective, analytical practitioners know that learning takes place every day if one is open to it. The true value of experience as a registered nurse is in the amount of learning that has taken place.

■ *What Makes a Person a Manager?*

• • • • • • • • • • • • • • • • • • •

MANAGEMENT THEORIES

Although there are quite a few management theories, just as there are many leadership theories, we focus primarily on the two opposing schools of thought in management: the human relations approach to management and scientific management. As you will see, one emphasizes the relationship aspects of managing people, and the other emphasizes the task aspects of management.

Scientific Management

Frederick Taylor is usually credited with the development of the scientific management approach (Lee, 1980; Locke, 1982). Almost 100 years ago, Taylor argued that most jobs could be done more efficiently if they were thoroughly analyzed and that most workers could work more efficiently given a properly designed task and sufficient incentive to get the work done. For example, Taylor encouraged paying people "by the piece," that is, by the number of "widgets" made (in health care, it could be by the number of clients bathed or fed) rather than by the number of

hours worked. This would be an incentive to get the most work done in the least amount of time, Taylor said.

The work itself was also analyzed to improve efficiency. In health care, for example, there has been a lot of discussion regarding the time it takes to bring patients to the x-ray or electrocardiogram (ECG) department versus bringing the x-ray or ECG equipment to the patient. The current emphasis on eliminating excess staff and increasing the productivity of remaining employees is based on the same kind of thinking (Lublin, 1992).

A nurse manager working under the principles of scientific management emphasizes the task aspects of providing health care. Considerable attention is paid to the type of care provided by the unit, the equipment needed to provide this care efficiently, and the procedures that would facilitate accomplishment of these tasks. This nurse manager probably keeps careful records of the amount of work accomplished by each staff member and rewards those who accomplish the most in a day.

Human Relations-Oriented Management

McGregor's Theory X and Theory Y are a good example of the difference between scientific management and human relations–oriented management. Theory X, says McGregor (1960), reflects a very common attitude among managers that most people really do not want to work very hard and that the manager's job is to see that they do work hard. According to Theory X, employees need strict rules, constant supervision, and the threat of punishment (in the form of reprimands, withheld raises, and threats of job loss) to make them careful, conscientious workers.

Theory Y, which McGregor proposes, takes an opposite viewpoint. Theory Y managers believe that the work itself can be motivating and that people will work hard if their managers provide an atmosphere in which they are supported and encouraged to do so. A Theory Y manager would emphasize guidance rather than control, development rather than close supervision, and reward rather than punishment (Fig. 1–2).

A very different emphasis from that of scientific management is found in the human

Work is something
to be avoided

People want to do as
little as possible

Use control-supervision-
punishment

The work itself can be
motivating

People really want to do
their job well

Use guidance-development-
reward

FIGURE 1–2   Theory X versus Theory Y. (Adapted from McGregor, D. [1960]. *The Human Side of Enterprise*. New York: McGraw-Hill.)

relations–oriented manager. This nurse manager would be concerned with keeping employee morale and motivation as high as possible, assuming that satisfied, motivated employees will do the best work. Employees' attitudes, opinions, hopes, and fears would be important to this type of nurse manager. Considerable effort would be expended to work out conflicts and promote mutual understanding among the staff to provide an atmosphere in which people can do their best work.

QUALITIES OF AN EFFECTIVE MANAGER

The most effective nurse manager possesses a combination of qualities: leadership, clinical expertise, and business sense. None of these alone is enough; it is the combination that prepares an individual for the complex task of managing a group or team of health-care providers.

There is some controversy over the amount of clinical expertise versus business sense that is needed to be an effective nurse manager. Some argue that a person can be a "generic" manager, that the job of managing people is the same no matter what tasks they perform. Others argue that the manager must understand the tasks better than anyone else in the work group. Our position is that both are needed, along with excellent leadership skills. Let's look at each of these briefly:

- **LEADERSHIP.** Managers manage people. All of the people skills of the leader are essential to the effective manager. While they may not be sufficient by themselves, they are the fundamental

core of skills needed to function as a manager.

- **CLINICAL EXPERTISE.** It is very difficult to either help others develop their skills or evaluate how well they have done this without possessing clinical expertise oneself. It probably is not necessary (or even possible) to know everything every other professional on the team knows, but it is important to be able to assess the effectiveness of their work in terms of patient outcomes.

- **BUSINESS SENSE.** Nurse managers also need to be concerned with the "bottom line," that is, with the *cost* of providing the care that is given, especially in comparison with the benefit received from that care. In other words, nurse managers need to be able to assess and analyze how much is spent to provide a given amount of client care and how effective that client care has been. This is a very complex task, one that requires knowledge of budgeting, staffing, and measurement of patient outcomes, all subjects beyond the scope of this textbook.

BEHAVIORS OF AN EFFECTIVE MANAGER

Now it is time to consider all of the things an effective manager does over and above the behaviors of an effective leader, which are also a part of the behavior of an effective manager but will not be repeated here.

Mintzberg's list, mentioned earlier, provides us with a useful outline of managerial roles and responsibilities. As you will recall,

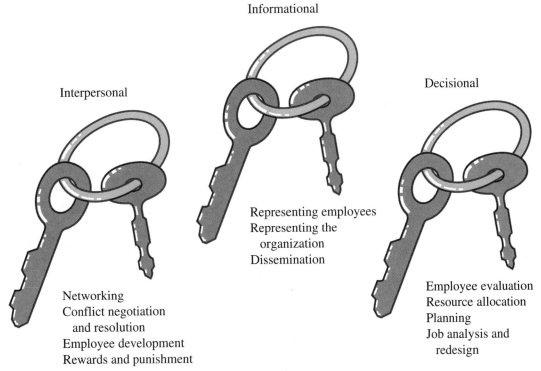

FIGURE 1–3 Keys to effective management.

Mintzberg (1989) divides the manager's activities into three categories: interpersonal, informational, and decisional. We will use these categories but have taken some liberties with them, rearranging them a little and adding some activities suggested by other authors (Dunham-Taylor, 1995; Montebello, 1994) and by our own observations of nurse managers (Fig. 1–3).

Interpersonal

The interpersonal area is one in which leaders and managers have similar responsibilities. However, the manager has some additional responsibilities seldom given to leaders. The following are some of the most important interpersonal skills for nurse managers:

◆ **NETWORKING.** The position of nurse managers in the hierarchy provides them with many opportunities to develop positive working relationships with other disciplines, departments, and units within the organization.

◆ **CONFLICT NEGOTIATION AND RESOLUTION.** Managers often find themselves occupied with resolving conflicts between employees, between clients and staff members, and between staff members and administration.

◆ **EMPLOYEE DEVELOPMENT.** Providing for the continuing learning and upgrading of skills of employees is a managerial responsibility that overlaps with managers' informational responsibilities.

◆ **REWARDS AND PUNISHMENTS.** Managers are in a position to provide both tangible (e.g., salary, time off) and intangible (e.g., praise, public announcements) rewards as well as punishments.

Informational

Nurse managers often find themselves in central positions within the organizational hierarchy where they acquire much information that is not available to their work group and have much information about the work group that is not readily available to the administration. This is, as you can see, a strategic position in the information web of any organization. The effective manager uses this position for the benefit of both the work group and the organization. The following are some examples:

◆ **SPOKESPERSON.** Managers frequently represent their work group or department at meetings. They often speak for administration when relaying and interpreting information to staff members. Likewise, they speak for staff members when relaying and interpreting information to administration.

◆ **MONITORING.** Nurse managers monitor the activities of their units or work groups. This may include the number of clients seen, infection rates, fall and injury rates, and so forth. They also monitor the staff (e.g., absentee rates, tardiness, unproductive time) and the budget (e.g., money spent, money left to spend in comparison with money needed to operate the unit).

◆ **DISSEMINATION.** Nurse managers share information with their clients, staff members, and employers. This information could be related to the results of their monitoring efforts, new developments in healthcare, policy changes, and so forth.

Decisional

◆ **EMPLOYEE EVALUATION.** Managers are responsible for conducting formal appraisals of their staff members.

◆ **RESOURCE ALLOCATION.** In decentralized organizations, nurse managers are often given a set amount of money for running their units or departments and must allocate these resources wisely, especially when they are very limited.

◆ **HIRING AND FIRING EMPLOYEES.** Most nurse managers participate in or do the hiring and firing for their units or departments.

◆ **PLANNING FOR THE FUTURE.** Even though the day-to-day operation of most units is a complex and time-consuming respon-

sibility, nurse managers must also look to the future and prepare themselves and their units for future changes in budgets, care priorities, and patient populations.

◆ **JOB ANALYSIS AND REDESIGN.** In a time of extreme cost consciousness, nurse managers are frequently being called on to analyze and redesign the work of their units or departments to make them as efficient and cost-effective as possible.

As you can see, nurse managers have very complex, responsible positions within healthcare organizations. Ineffective managers may do harm to their employees and to the organization, but effective managers can help their staff members grow and develop as healthcare professionals while providing the highest quality care to their clients.

■ *Conclusion*

The essentials or key elements of leadership and management have been discussed in this chapter. Every registered nurse needs leadership skills to be most effective as a practitioner and colleague. Many of the leadership qualities and behaviors mentioned in this chapter are discussed in more detail in later chapters. Nurses who assume management positions still need their leadership skills as well as an additional set of management skills.

? *Study Questions*

1. What is the difference between leadership and management? In what ways are they alike?

2. Compare and contrast the authoritarian, democratic, and laissez-faire styles of leadership. List alternative names for each of these styles. What effect does each style have on followers?

3. Why do nurse managers need business sense? Under what circumstances would clinical expertise be more important than

business sense? When would it be less important?

4. Select an individual whose leadership skills you particularly admire. What qualities and behaviors does this individual display? In what ways could you emulate this person?

5. Describe the ideal nurse manager.

Critical Thinking Exercise

Joe Garcia is an operating room nurse. He was often on call on Saturday and Sunday, but he enjoyed his work and knew that he would not be called unless he was really needed. When the hospital he worked for was bought by a large healthcare corporation, Joe was pleased because he thought that this would increase his opportunities for advancement.

A multicar accident on the interstate highway occurred on the second weekend after the hospital had been purchased. Most of the clients were taken to the city-owned hospital, but two were taken to the emergency room of the hospital where Joe worked. One was critically injured; the other had minor cuts and bruises. Joe was called in to prepare for emergency surgery. When he arrived, he was told that the client had died. As usual, Joe requested payment for the time spent traveling to and from the hospital on the emergency call.

Joe was not paid for this time on his next paycheck. When he asked about it, his nurse manager told him that he would not be paid because he did not do any work. "That's not fair," he said, "I'm going to speak with the director about this." "The last person who did that was fired," the nurse manager warned him. "I can't believe that," said Joe, "The director has always been fair with all of us." "No more," said the nurse manager. "The old director has been replaced by a real authoritarian. This is no longer the fair, employee-centered organization we used to work for. With this new management, your protest, however

justified it is, will be criticized and you might be punished. The choice is up to you."

Joe decided that he did not want to work in such an institution. With his 5 years of operating room experience, he quickly found another operating room position in an organization with a more humanistically oriented management.

1. What style of leadership and school of management thought seem to be preferred by Joe Garcia's employer?

2. What style and school of thought were preferred in the past?

3. What effect did the change in approach have on Joe Garcia?

4. Which qualities and behaviors of leaders and managers did this nurse manager display? Which ones did the nurse manager not display?

5. If you were Joe, what would you have done? If you were the nurse manager, what would you have done? Why?

REFERENCES

Barker, A.M. (1992). *Transformational Nursing Leadership: A Vision for the Future*. New York: National League for Nursing Press.

Blake, R.R., Mouton, J.S., & Tapper, M. (1981). *Grid Approaches for Managerial Leadership in Nursing*. St. Louis: C.V. Mosby.

Covey, S.R. (1992). *Principle-Centered Leadership*. New York: Simon & Schuster.

DePree, M. (1989). *Leadership is an Art*. New York: Dell.

DePree, M. (1992). *Leadership Jazz*. New York: Dell.

Dunham-Taylor (1995). Identifying the best in nurse executive leadership. *J Nurs Adm*, 25(7/8), 24–31.

Holman, L. (1995). *Eleven Lessons in Self-Leadership: Insights for Personal and Professional Success*. Lexington, KY: A Lessons in Leadership Book.

Lee, J.A. (1980). *The Gold and the Garbage in Management Theories and Prescriptions*. Athens, OH: Ohio University Press.

Locke, E.A. (1982). The ideas of Frederick Taylor: An evaluation. *Academy of Management Review*, 7(1), 14.

Lublin, J.S. (1992, February 13). Trying to increase worker productivity, more employers alter management style. New York: *Wall Street Journal*.

Manske, F.A. (1987). *Secrets of Effective Leadership*. Memphis, TN: Leadership Education and Development.

McGregor, D. (1960). *The Human Side of Enterprise*. New York: McGraw-Hill.

Miller, M.A., & Malcolm, N.S. (1990). Critical thinking in the nursing curriculum. *Nursing and Health Care, 11*(2), 67–73.

Mintzberg, H. (1989). *Mintzberg on Management: Inside Our Strange World of Organizations.* New York: Free Press.

Montebello, A. (1994). *Work Teams that Work.* Minneapolis: Best Sellers Publishing.

Tappen, R.M. (1995). *Nursing Leadership and Management: Concepts and Practice.* Philadelphia: F.A. Davis.

Trofino, J. (1995). Transformational leadership in health care. *Nursing Management, 26*(8), 42–47.

White, R.K., & Lippitt, R. (1960). *Autocracy and Democracy: An Experimental Inquiry.* New York: Harper & Row.

Wren, D.A. (1972). *The Evolution of Management Thought.* New York: Ronald Press.

CHAPTER 2

Getting People to Work Together

OBJECTIVES   *After reading this chapter, the student will be able to:*

- Define the basic listening sequence.
- Discuss the importance of effective communication.
- Make appropriate assignments to team members.
- Develop a system for organizing and delivering client care.
- Deliver an effective and informative change-of-shift report.

Inez has been working on a busy on-cology floor for several years. Although she usually has a caseload of 8 to 12 clients on her shift, she feels that she provides safe, competent care to her clients.

While Inez was on her way to medicate a client suffering from cancer of the bone, a colleague called to her, "Inez, come with me, please." Inez responded, "I need to medicate Mr. J. in Room 203. I will come right after that. Where will you be?" "Never mind!" her colleague answered. "I'll find someone who's more helpful. Don't ask me for help in the future."

This was not the response Inez had expected. She thought she had expressed both an interest in her client and a willingness to help her colleague. What was the problem?

After Inez gave Mr. J. his pain medication, she went back to her colleague. "Sonja, what's the matter?" she asked. Sonja replied, "Mrs. V. fell in the bathroom. I needed someone to stay with her while I got her walker." "Why didn't you tell me it was urgent?" asked Inez. "I was so upset about Mrs. V. that I wasn't thinking about what else you were doing," answered Sonja. Inez said, "And I didn't ask you why you needed me. I guess we need to work on our communication, don't we?"

In the busy and sometimes chaotic world of nursing practice, nurses work continuously with all sorts of people, which makes the work dynamic and challenging. Just when it appears that things have settled down, something else happens requiring immediate attention. All of these busy people need to communicate effectively with each other. They also must responsibly delegate tasks to others, or the workload will be insurmountable. This chapter is designed to help new nurses communicate more effectively with their colleagues, work with people of all kinds, and share the workload equitably, even in situations filled with multiple demands and constant change.

■ *Communication*

Historically, the process of communication between two people has been viewed as consisting of five elements (Berlo, 1960). The first element is the *encoder*, or sender. The second element is the *message*, or the information that needs to be conveyed. The third is the *sensory channel* or method of sending the communication to the fourth element, or *decoder*. The decoder receives the message. The last element is the *feedback* or return. This feedback to the sender indicates the degree of understanding of the message. A more contemporary model of communication views the process as a circular one affected by many factors. Communication in this model has both a content and relationship context in which the activity is continuous, mutually interdependent, and influenced by the behaviors of each communicator. Cultural influences, communication abilities, values, needs, goals, and previous experiences all affect the content of the communication (Arnold & Boggs, 1995; Fontaine & Fletcher, 1995) (Fig. 2–1).

People often assume that communication is simply giving information to another person. Communication involves not only the spoken word but also the nonverbal message, the emotional state of people involved, and the cultural background that affects their interpretation of the message (Fontaine & Fletcher, 1995).

There are two basic channels of communication, verbal and nonverbal:

◆ **VERBAL.** Verbal communication uses words to communicate messages. Communication is achieved by writing or speaking in a code or language that is mutually understood. Talking is the verbal or spoken mode. Written communication translates a thought or spoken word into printed form.

◆ **NONVERBAL.** Nonverbal communication is a set of behaviors that conveys messages without words. It often supplements verbal communication. Most nonverbal communication is done unconsciously and is more difficult to control than verbal communication. Often discrepancies exist between verbal and nonverbal communication. What is

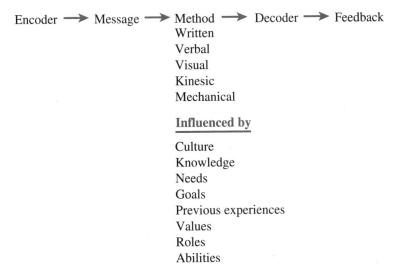

Encoder → Message → Method → Decoder → Feedback
Written
Verbal
Visual
Kinesic
Mechanical

Influenced by

Culture
Knowledge
Needs
Goals
Previous experiences
Values
Roles
Abilities

FIGURE 2–1 Communication elements. (Adapted from Fontaine, K.L., & Fletcher, J.S. [1995]. *Essentials of Mental Health Nursing* [ed. 3]. Redwood City, Calif: Addison-Wesley.)

stated is not necessarily felt or believed. It is important for nurses to observe nonverbal behavior when communicating with colleagues and clients and to try to make their own nonverbal behavior congruent with their verbal communications. Telling people you understand their problem when you appear thoroughly confused or inattentive is an example of incongruence between verbal and nonverbal communication. The way people move their bodies or parts of their bodies while communicating is called *body language*. People use body language as a way of presenting themselves to the world (Vacarolis, 1994).

Paralanguage is the nonverbal component of *spoken* language. This includes the rhythm of speech, pitch, stress, intonation, rate, and volume (Fontaine & Fletcher, 1995), all of which affect the interpretation of the message communicated.

THE BASIC LISTENING SEQUENCE

Listening is the most critical of all communication skills. You indicate to another person that you are listening through attending behaviors such as eye contact, attentive body language, vocal qualities, and verbal tracking.

Eye contact requires the listener to look at the speaker. This indicates interest in what is being conveyed. Although expected in the American culture, direct eye contact may be considered disrespectful in other cultures. Members of some cultures look away when being spoken to and have direct eye contact only when speaking. When one is interacting with colleagues or clients who are culturally different, this needs to be understood and not misinterpreted as disinterest or rudeness on the part of the other person.

Attentive body language conveys interest and openness. Leaning forward, having open arms, and maintaining an interested expression on one's face indicate that the listener is actively involved in the interaction and open to the other person's ideas. Sitting back, folding the arms across the chest, and looking away indicate disinterest in what is occurring or unwillingness to accept what the other person is saying.

Vocal qualities include pitch, volume, and rapidity of speech. When people are hurried, annoyed, angry, anxious, or distracted by other thoughts or activities, vocal qualities change. Speech may become rapid and choppy or slow and halting. The pitch, or highness, of the voice may change. This occurs during surprise or anxiety. Volume changes when individuals are annoyed or angry. A listener needs to be aware of chang-

Box 2–1 Basic listening sequence
- Listening
- Eye contact
- Attentive body language
- Vocal qualities
- Verbal tracking

ing pitch and volume when responding during a communication.

Verbal tracking is paying attention to what is being said. To verbal-track accurately, one must actively listen to what is being said. Often summarizing and paraphrasing parts of the conversation indicate to the speaker that what is being said has been heard (Box 2–1).

COMPONENTS OF EFFECTIVE COMMUNICATION

To communicate effectively with others, consider the following seven principles (Table 2–1):

1. Information giving alone is not communication. As stated before, communication requires the *sharing* of information. Sharing the information means that the person receiving it understands both the content of the message,

the feelings communicated in the message, or both.

2. The sender is responsible for clarity. Making messages clear to the others involved in the communication decreases frustration and confusion. It is up to the sender to be sure that the message is understood. Asking for feedback from the receiver helps to clarify any confusion. Help the sender to communicate more effectively by bringing focus to the interaction. This can be accomplished by repeating key words or phrases as questions or using open-ended questions. For example: "You have been telling me that Susan is not providing safe care to her patients. Can you tell me specifically what you have identified as unsafe care?"

3. Use simple but precise language. Whether written or spoken, messages should be stated clearly and concisely in language that is easily understood by all involved.

4. Feedback should be encouraged. This is the best way to help people understand each other and work together better. Remember that feedback may not be complimentary and the ideas of the receiver and sender may be in conflict. It is always important to evaluate feedback and deal with it in a constructive manner.

5. The sender must have credibility. Both the personal and professional credibility of the sender is important. If the receiver does not perceive the sender as credible, it is not likely that the message will be given importance.

6. Acknowledgment of others is essential. Sometimes it may be difficult to give others credit for their contributions. Everyone wants to feel that they have individual worth.

7. Direct channels of communication are best. The more individuals who are involved in filtering messages, the less likely the message is to be received appropriately. As in the game "Whispering down the Lane," messages sent through a variety of senders become distorted. Most of the time, face-to-face communication is preferable to telephone or written communication because people can see nonverbal be-

TABLE 2–1
SEVEN PRINCIPLES OF COMMUNICATION

Principle One:	Information giving is not communication.
Principle Two:	The sender is responsible for clarity.
Principle Three:	Use simple and exact language.
Principle Four:	Feedback should be encouraged.
Principle Five:	The sender must have credibility
Principle Six:	Acknowledgment of others is essential.
Principle Seven:	Direct channels of communication are best.

Source: Tappen, R.M. (1995). *Nursing Leadership and Management: Concept and Practice* (ed. 3). Philadelphia: F.A. Davis, with permission.

haviors and ask for immediate clarification. Information that is controversial or may elicit negative responses should definitely be delivered in a manner that allows the receiver to ask questions or receive further clarification. A memo delivered "To all nursing staff" in which cutbacks in personnel are discussed will deliver a different message from a meeting in which all staff members are allowed to verbalize feelings and ask questions.

ASSERTIVENESS IN COMMUNICATION

Assertiveness describes behaviors that people can use to stand up for themselves and their rights without violating the rights of others. One can be assertive without being aggressive (Tappen, 1995). Aggressiveness describes behaviors that people use to force their wishes or ideas on others. In assertive communication, an individual's position is stated clearly and firmly using "I" statements. For example:

> The nurse manager noticed that Steve's charting has been of less than the expected quality during the past few weeks. She rescheduled her lunch break to have some time to speak with him. After her break, the nurse manager said to Steve, "JCAHO surveyors are coming in several months. I have been reviewing records. I noticed that on several of your charts there is some pertinent information missing. I have scheduled time today and tomorrow from 1 to 2 PM for us to review the charts. Then you can make the necessary corrections and return them to me."

By using "I" statements, the nurse manager is confronting the issue without being accusatory. Assertive communication always requires congruence between verbal and nonverbal messages. If she were shaking her finger close to Steve's face or using a loud voice, the nurse manager might think she was being assertive when in reality her manner was aggressive.

Many misconceptions exist regarding assertive communication. The first is that all communication is either aggressive or passive. Actually, communication may be passive, aggressive, passive-aggressive, or assertive. Passive communication happens when someone does not voice opinions about an issue. Aggressive individuals express their opinions in a direct and often hostile manner that infringes on others' rights. These people feel that they must be the "winner" in all communications. Passive-aggressive communication is aggressive communication presented in a passive way. There is very little verbal communication, and incongruence is present between the verbal and nonverbal behaviors.

The second misconception is that those who communicate assertively always get what they want. Being assertive involves both rights and responsibilities. Assertive communicators have the right to speak up, but they also must be prepared to listen to the response.

The third misconception about assertiveness is that it is unfeminine. Often women are taught to withdraw rather than be assertive. Learning to be assertive is part of effective nursing action. Nurses who continue patterns of either nonassertive or overly aggressive behaviors may have a negative impact on themselves and the nursing profession (Arnold & Boggs, 1995).

The fourth misconception is that assertiveness and aggressiveness are synonymous. To be assertive is not to be aggressive. Assertiveness does not force agreement between participants but permits them to disagree while promoting clarification of each other's position. Developing assertive behavior may decrease stress as individuals respond appropriately and at the appropriate time.

EFFECTIVE COMMUNICATION IN THE WORKPLACE

Many times people are unwilling or unable to accept responsibility or perform a specific task because they do not fully understand what is expected of them. As the professional nurse, you will be required to communicate client information to other members of the nursing team. Although this sounds easy enough, potential barriers to communication exist. These barriers may be physical, psychological, or semantic.

Physical Barriers

Physical barriers include extraneous noise, too much activity, or physical separation of people trying to engage in verbal interaction.

Psychological Barriers

Communication can be impeded by social values, emotions, judgments, and cultural influences. Previous life experiences and preconceived ideas about other cultures may influence how we communicate.

Semantic Barriers

Semantic refers to the meaning of words. Sometimes, no matter how hard one tries, the message just does not get across. For example, words such as "neat," "cool," or "bad" may convey meanings other than those intended. Many individuals have learned English as a second language and therefore understand only literal translations of certain words. For example, to many people, "cool" means interesting, unique, clever, or even sharp (e.g., "This is a cool way to find the vein"). To someone for whom the word "cool" refers only to temperature (e.g., "It is cool outside"), the preceding statement would make very little sense.

COMMUNICATION WITH COLLEAGUES

Members of the nursing team include administrators, directors of nursing, supervisors, clinical specialists, nurse managers, and ancillary personnel. Each of these individuals is involved with client care in different ways.

Communication among team members is enhanced by promoting trust and sincerity. Congruency between your words and deeds will promote trust. If team members feel you are trustworthy and sincere, they will be more likely to ask questions and seek clarification if they are uncertain of something. Box 2–2 gives guidelines for facilitating communication among team members.

To manage client care effectively, it is important to keep the lines of communication open on all levels. Using active listening skills and assertive behavior supports clear communication.

> **Box 2–2 Guidelines for facilitating good communication**
>
> - Practice active listening.
> - Communicate genuine interest and concern.
> - Provide the employee with adequate information.
> - Use the team members' ideas in the plan of action.
> - Maximize feelings of self-respect.
> - Focus on the team members' ability to help themselves.
> - Do not minimize the value of time allowed to learn.
> - Praise competent performance.
> - State expectations clearly and identify key points.
> - Be willing to look at alternatives that others may feel are important.
> - Demonstate respect for the values and dignity of all team members.
> - Depersonalize potential conflict situations.

Telephone Etiquette

Nurses spend a significant amount of time on the phone, gathering and relating information. Using telephone etiquette takes into account the needs of both senders and receivers. The courtesy and clarification that you would use in a face-to-face contact are just as important in a telephone contact.

Information Systems

Communication through the use of computer technology is rapidly growing in nursing practice. A study conducted by KPMG-Peat Marwick of healthcare systems that were using their bedside terminals found that medication errors and use of client call bells were decreased, whereas nurse productivity was increased. Additional benefits of computerized systems for health care are listed in Box 2–3 (Arnold & Pearson, 1992).

Box 2–3 Potential benefits of computer-based client information systems

- Increased hours for direct patient care
- Patient data accessible at bedside
- Improved accuracy and legibility of data
- Immediate availability of all data to all members of team
- Increased safety related to positive patient identification, improved standardization, and quality
- Decreased medication errors
- Increased staff satisfaction

Source: Adapted from Arnold, J., & Pearson, G. (eds.) (1992). *Computer Applications in Nursing Education and Practice.* New York: National League for Nursing.

■ *Delegation of Client Care*

Delegation is not a new concept. In the Old Testament, Moses was instructed to identify 70 elders "so they will share with you the burden of this nation and you will no longer have to carry it by yourself" (Numbers 11:16–17).

Regardless of where you work, you cannot assume that only those in the higher levels of the organization will delegate work to other people. You too will probably be delegating some of your work to another nurse, to technical personnel, or to another department. Often this responsibility causes some difficulty for new nurses. Knowing each person's capabilities and job description can help you decide which personnel can assist with a task.

COORDINATING ASSIGNMENTS

For new nurses, one of the most difficult tasks to master is coordinating daily activities. Often you not only have a group of clients for whom you are expected to provide direct care but you must also supervise the work of others. Although care plans, critical (or clinical) pathways, and computer information sheets are available to help identify client needs, these items do not provide a mechanism for coordinating the actual delivery of care. To do this, you can develop personalized worksheets that organize tasks in order of their priority for each client.

On the worksheet, tasks are prioritized on the basis of client need, not nursing convenience. For example, an order states that a client is to receive continuous tube feedings. Although it may be convenient for the nurse to fill the feeding bag with enough supplement to last 6 hours, it is not good practice and not safe for the client. Instead, the nurse should to plan to check the tube feeding every 2 hours.

The following are some tips for organizing your work on personalized worksheets (Tappen, 1995):

- Some activities must be done at a certain time, and their timing may be out of your control. Plan your time around these activities.
- High-priority activities must be done first.
- Some activities are best done in a cluster.
- You are still responsible for activities delegated to others.
- Consider your peak energy time when scheduling optional activities.

Figure 2–2 is an example of a personalized worksheet.

See Chapter 5 for a complete discussion of time management.

SAFE DELEGATION

Healthcare institutions often use unlicensed personnel to perform certain client care tasks (Huber et al., 1994). Although some of these people may be certified (e.g., certified nursing assistant [CNA]), it is important to remember that certification differs from licensure. When a task is delegated to an unlicensed person, the professional nurse remains personally responsible for the outcomes of these activities. The American Nurses Association (ANA) Code for Nurses states, "The nurse exercises informed judg-

Nurse/Team_____DNR 4580/35 Code 61

Room #_____Name_____Age_____

Allergies_____Weight/Height_____

Dx_____Restrictions_____

Activity_____

Diet_____

Fluids_____

Assessment_____

Monitor_____

Treatments_____

4_____

5_____

6_____

7_____

8_____

9_____

10_____

Misc._____

FIGURE 2–2　Personalized client worksheet.

ment and uses individual competence and qualifications as criteria in seeking consultation, accepting responsibilities, and delegating nursing activities to others" (1985). To delegate tasks safely, nurses must delegate appropriately and supervise adequately (Barter & Furmidge, 1994).

The use of the registered nurse (RN) to provide all of the care a client needs may not be the most efficient or cost-effective use of professional time. As the use of licensed practical nurses (LPNs) or client care extenders increases, the nurse's focus will be on diagnosing client care needs and carrying out complex interventions (Conger, 1994). The ANA cautions against delegating nursing activities that include the foundation of the nursing process and require specialized knowledge, judgment, or skill (ANA, 1994). On the other hand, non-nursing functions (Hayes, 1994) such as clerical/receptionist, trips or errands off the unit, cleaning floors, making beds, collecting trays, and ordering supplies should not be carried out by the highest paid and most educated member of the team.

The ANA has developed a definition of unlicensed assistive personnel:

> Unlicensed assistive personnel are individuals who are trained to function in an assistive role to the registered nurse in the provision of patient/client care activities as delegated by and under the supervision of the registered professional nurse. (ANA, 1994)

Nurses who are delegating tasks to unlicensed assistive personnel should evaluate the activities being considered for delegation (Herrick et al., 1994). The American Association of Critical Care Nurses (AACN) (1990) recommends consideration of five factors affecting the decision to delegate: potential for harm, complexity of task, problem solving and innovation necessary, unpredictability of outcome, and level of interaction required with the client (Box 2–4).

It is the responsibility of the RN to be well acquainted with the state nurse practice act

---

Box 2–4 Criteria for determining which client care activities can be delegated to other personnel

- Potential for harm to the patient
- Complexity of the nursing activity
- Extent of problem solving and innovation required
- Predictability of the outcome
- Extent of interaction

Source: Adapted from American Association of Critical Care Nurses (AACN) (1990). *Delegation of Nursing and Non-Nursing Activities in Critical Care: A Framework for Decision Making.* Irvine, Calif: AACN.

---

and regulations issued by the state board of nursing regarding unlicensed assistive personnel. State laws and regulations supersede any publications or opinions set forth by professional organizations. However, the *American Nurses Association's Documents on Nursing: A Social Policy Statement* (1980), *The Standards of Clinical Nursing Practice* (1991), and *Registered Professional Nurses and Unlicensed Assistive Personnel* (1994) may provide guidance for the practicing RN in delegating to unlicensed assistive personnel.

Licensed practical nurses (LPNs) are trained to perform specific tasks such as basic medication administration, dressing changes, and personal hygiene tasks. In some states, with additional training, the LPN may start and monitor intravenous (IV) infusions and administer certain medications.

CRITERIA FOR DELEGATION

The purpose of delegation is not to assign tasks to others that you do not want to do yourself. When you delegate to others effectively, you should have more time to perform the tasks that only a professional nurse is permitted to do.

When you delegate, you must consider both the *ability* of the person to whom you are delegating and the *fairness* of the task to the individual and the team (Tappen, 1995). In other words, you need to consider both the *task aspects* of delegation (Is this a complex task? Is it a professional responsibility? Can this person do it safely?) and the *interpersonal aspects* (Does the person have time to do this? Is the work evenly distributed?).

TASK-RELATED CONCERNS

The primary task-related concern in delegating work is whether the person assigned to do the task has the ability to do that task. Team priorities and efficiency are also important considerations.

Ability

To make appropriate assignments, the nurse needs to know the knowledge and skill level, legal definitions, role expectations, and job description for each member of the team. It is equally important to be aware of the different skill levels of caregivers within each discipline, as ability differs with each level of education. Additionally, different individuals within each level of skill will possess their own particular strengths and weaknesses. Prior assessment of the strengths of each member of the team will assist in providing safe and efficient care to clients.

People should not be assigned a task they are unable to do, regardless of their professional level. Many times people are reluctant to admit that they cannot do something. Instead of seeking help or saying they do not feel comfortable with the task, they may avoid doing it, delay starting it, do only part of it, or even bluff their way through it, a risky choice in health care.

Regardless of the length of time they have been in a position, employees need orientation when assigned a new task. Those who seek assistance and advice are showing concern for the team and the welfare of their clients. Requests for assistance or additional explanations should not be ignored, and the person should be praised, not criticized, for seeking guidance (Tappen, 1995).

Priorities

You have probably noticed that the work of a busy unit rarely ends up going as expected. Dealing with sick people, their families, physicians, and other team members all at the same time is a difficult task. Setting priorities for the day should be based on client needs, team needs, and organizational and community demands. The values of each may be very different, even opposed. These differences should be discussed with team members so that decisions can be made based on team priorities.

One way to determine patient priorities is to base your decisions on Maslow's (1954) hierarchy of needs (see Chap. 8, Fig. 8–2). Maslow's hierarchy is frequently used in nursing to provide a framework for prioritizing care to meet client needs. The basic physiological needs come first because they are necessary for survival. Oxygen and medication administration, IV fluids, and enteral feedings are included in this group.

Identifying priorities and deciding the needs to be met first help in organizing care and in deciding which other team members can meet client needs. For example, nursing assistants can meet many hygiene needs, allowing licensed personnel to administer medications and enteral feedings in a timely manner.

Efficiency

The current healthcare delivery environment demands efficient, cost-effective care. Delegating appropriately can increase efficiency and save money.

Maintaining continuity is one action to consider. Keeping the same staff members on the unit all the time, for example, allows them to develop familiarity with the physical setting and routines of the unit and the types of clients the unit services. Time is lost when staff members are reassigned frequently to different units. Although physical layouts may be the same, client needs, unit routines, and use of space are often different, as is the availability of supplies. Time spent to orient reassigned staff members takes away from time for the delivery of client care.

Efficiency means that all members of the team know their jobs and responsibilities and work together like gears in a well-built clock. They mesh together and keep perfect time!

Appropriateness

Appropriateness is another task-related concern. Nothing can be more counterproductive than floating a coronary care nurse to labor and delivery. More time will be spent on teaching the skills necessary than on safe mother-baby care. Assigning an educated, licensed staff member to perform non-nursing functions to protect safety is also poor use of personnel.

RELATIONSHIP-ORIENTED CONCERNS

Relationship-oriented concerns include fairness, opportunities for learning, health concerns, compatibility, and staff preferences.

Fairness

Fairness means evenly distributing the workload in terms of both the physical requirements and the emotional investment in providing health care. The nurse who is caring for a dying client may have less physical work to do than another team member, but in terms of emotional care to the client and family, he or she may be doing double the work of another staff member. Fairness also means considering equally all requests for special considerations. There is no quicker way to alienate members of your team than to be unfair. It is important to discuss with team members any decisions you have made that may appear unfair to others. Allow the team to participate in making decisions regarding assignments. Their participation will decrease resentment and increase cooperation. In some healthcare institutions, team members make these decisions as a group.

Learning Opportunities

Including assignments that stimulate motivation and learning and assisting team members to learn new tasks and take on new challenges is part of the role of the RN.

Health

Some aspects of caregiving jobs are more stressful than others. Rotating team members through the more difficult jobs may decrease stress and allow empathy to increase among the members. Special health needs such as family emergencies or special physical problems of team members also need to be addressed. If other team members have difficulty accepting the needs of others, the situation should be discussed with the team, bearing in mind the employee's right to privacy when discussing sensitive issues.

Compatibility

No matter how hard you may strive to get your team to work together, it just might not happen. Some people work together better than others. Helping people develop better working relationships is part of team building. Creating opportunities for people to share and learn from each other will increase the overall effectiveness of the team.

As the leader, you may be forced to intervene in team member disputes. Many individuals find it difficult to work with others they do not like personally. It sometimes becomes necessary to explain that liking another person is a plus but not a necessity in

the work setting and that personal problems have no place in the work environment. Take the example of Laura:

> Laura had been a labor and delivery room supervisor in a large metropolitan hospital for 5 years before she moved to another city. Because a position similar to the one she left was not available, she became a staff nurse at a small local hospital. The hospital had just opened its new birthing center. The first day on the job went well. The other staff members seemed cordial enough.
>
> As the weeks went by, however, Laura began to have problems getting other staff to help her. No one would offer to relieve her for meals or a break. She noticed that certain groups of staff members always went to lunch together, but she was never invited to join them. She attempted to speak to some of the more approachable coworkers, but she did not get much information. Disturbed by the situation, Laura went to the nurse manager.
>
> The nurse manager listened quietly while Laura related her experiences. She then asked Laura to reflect back on some of the events of the past weeks, particularly the last staff meeting. Laura realized that she had alienated the staff during that encounter because she had monopolized the meeting and kept saying that in "her hospital" things were done in a particular way. Laura also realized that, instead of asking for help, she was in the habit of demanding it. Laura and the nurse manager discussed the difficulties of her changing positions, moving to a new place, and trying to develop both professional and social ties. Together they came up with several solutions to Laura's problem.

Preferences

Considering the preferences of individual team members is important but should not supersede the other criteria for delegating responsibly. Allowing team members to always select what they want to do may cause

Box 2–5 Basic rights of women in the health professions

- You have the right to be treated with respect.
- You have the right to a reasonable workload.
- You have the right to an equitable wage.
- You have the right to determine your own priorities.
- You have the right to ask for what you want.
- You have the right to refuse without making excuses for feeling guilty.
- You have the right to make mistakes and be responsible for them.
- You have the right to give and receive information as a professional.
- You have the right to act in the best interest of the patient.
- You have the right to be human.

Source: Adapted from Chevernet, M. (1988). *STAT, Special Techniques in Assertiveness Training for Women in Healthcare Professions* (ed. 2). St Louis, Mosby.

the less assertive members' needs to be unmet.

It is important to explain the rationale for decisions made regarding delegation so that all team members may understand the needs of the unit or organization.

Box 2–5 outlines basic rights for professional healthcare team members. Although written originally for women, the concepts are applicable to all professional healthcare providers.

■ *Communicating Client Care Needs*

• • • • • • • • • • • • • • • • • • • •

DEVELOPING THE CHANGE-OF-SHIFT REPORT

It is important to understand exactly how your day at work will begin. Regardless of

the shift one works, some things never change. Throughout nursing history, nurses have traditionally given one another "the report." The change-of-shift report has become

Box 2–6 Information for change-of-shift report.

- Identify the client, including the room number and bed.
- Include the client diagnosis.
- Account for the presence of the client on the unit. If the client has left the unit for a diagnostic test, surgery, or just to wander, it is important for the oncoming staff members to know the client is off the unit.
- Provide the treatment plan that specifies the goals of treatment. The goals and critical pathway steps either achieved or in progress should be discussed. Personalized approaches can be developed during this time and client readiness for those approaches evaluated. It is helpful to mention the client's primary care physician. Include new orders and medications and treatments currently prescribed.
- Document client responses to current treatments. Is the treatment plan working? Evidence for or against this should be presented. Pertinent lab values should be included as well as any untoward reactions to medications or treatments. Any comments the client has made regarding the hospitalization or treatment plan that the oncoming staff members need to address should be discussed.
- Omit personal opinions and value judgments about clients as well as personal/confidential information not pertinent to providing client care. If using computerized information systems, make sure that you are knowledgeable in how to present the material accurately and in a concise manner.

the accepted method of communicating client care needs from one nurse to another. During report, pertinent information related to events that occurred are given to the individuals responsible for providing continuity of care (Box 2–6). Although historically the report has been given face-to-face, there are also newer ways to share information. Many heathcare institutions use audiotaping and computer printouts as mechanisms for information sharing. These mechanisms allow the nurses from the previous shift to complete their tasks and those coming on to make inquiries for clarification as necessary.

The report should be organized, concise, and complete with relevant details. Not every unit uses the same system for giving a change-of-shift report. The system is easily modified according to the pattern of nursing care delivery and the types of clients serviced. For example, many intensive care units, because of their small size and the greater acuity of their clients, use *walking rounds* as a mechanism for giving the report. This system allows nurses to discuss the client situation as it exists and to set goals for the next several hours. Together the nurses gather objective data as one ends the shift and the other begins. In this way, there is no confusion as to what the client's status was at that time. This same system is often used in emergency departments and labor and delivery units. Larger client care units may find the walking report time-consuming and an inefficient use of resources.

It is helpful to take notes or create a worksheet while listening to the report. This worksheet helps organize the work for the day (Fig. 2–3). As specific tasks are mentioned, the nurse coming on makes a note of the activity in the time slot. Medications and treatments can also be added. Any changes from the previous day should be noted, particularly if the nurse is familiar with the client. This counteracts the tendency to remember what one did the day before and repeat it, often without checking for new orders. During the day, the worksheet acts as a reminder of the tasks that have been completed and those that still need to be done.

PRESENTING THE INFORMATION

When presenting information in a report, certain things must be included. The report should begin with the identification of the client and the admitting as well as current diagnoses. Include the expected treatment plan and the client's responses to the treatment. For example, if the client has had multiple antibiotics and a reaction occurred, that is important information to relay to the next nurse. Value judgments and personal opinions about the client are not pertinent to the report (Fig. 2–4).

Reporting skills improve with practice. In an interdisciplinary team conference, all individuals involved in client care share information through verbal and written communication. The team conference begins by giving the client's name, age, and diagnoses. Each member of the interdisciplinary team then explains the goal of that discipline, the interventions, and the outcome. Effectiveness of treatment, development of new interventions, and setting new goals are then discussed. The key is to present the information in a clear and concise manner.

■ *Communicating with Other Disciplines*

• • • • • • • • • • • • • • • • • • •

In many settings, nurses are the client care managers. Ultimately integration, coordination, and communication among all disciplines delivering care to a specific client are the responsibility of the nurse care manager. Nurses spend time with the client on a day-to-day basis and therefore are in a particularly advantageous position to observe the client's responses to treatments. For example:

> Mr. Richards is a 75-year-old man who was in a motor vehicle accident. He had right-sided weakness and dysphagia. The speech therapy, physical therapy, and social services departments were called in to see Mr. Richards. A speech therapist was working with Mr. Richards to assist him with swallowing. He was to receive pureed foods for the second day. The RN assigned an LPN to feed Mr. Richards. The LPN reported that, although Mr. Richards had done well the previous

day, he had difficulty swallowing to day. The nurse immediately notified the speech therapist, and a new treatment plan was developed.

The role of the professional nurse in relation to their clients' physicians is to communicate changes in the client's condition, share other pertinent information, discuss modifications of the treatment plan, if necessary, and clarify physician orders. This can be stressful for a new graduate who still has some role insecurity. Using good communications skills and having the necessary information at hand are helpful when discussing client needs.

Before calling a physician, make sure that all the information you need is available. The physician may want more clarification. If you are calling to report a drop in a client's blood pressure, for example, be sure that the list of the client's medications, vital signs, and blood pressure trends is at hand.

Sometimes nurses call physicians, and they do not return the call. It is important to document all physician contacts in the client's record. Many units have physician calling logs. The date, time, and reason for the call should be entered in the log. The time the physician returns the call is also entered.

Nurses or their delegates are responsible for accepting, transcribing, and implement-

NAME_____ ROOM # _____ ALLERGIES: _____

3:00 P.M.	4:00 P.M.	5:00 P.M.	6:00 P.M.	7:00 P.M.	8:00 P.M.	9:00 P.M.	10:00 P.M.

NAME:_____ ROOM # _____ ALLERGIES:_____

3:00 P.M.	4:00 P.M.	5:00 P.M.	6:00 P.M.	7:00 P.M.	8:00 P.M.	9:00 P.M.	10:00 P.M.

NAME_____ ROOM # _____ ALLERGIES: _____

3:00 P.M.	4:00 P.M.	5:00 P.M.	6:00 P.M.	7:00 P.M.	8:00 P.M.	9:00 P.M.	10:00 P.M.

FIGURE 2–3 Organization and time management schedule for client care.

ing physicians' orders. Two main types of orders exist: written and verbal. Written orders are dated and placed on the appropriate institutional form. Verbal orders are given directly to the nurse either by telephone or face to face. A verbal order needs to be written on the appropriate institutional form, timed and dated, and signed as a verbal order by the nurse. It is later cosigned by the physician. When receiving a verbal order, it is necessary to repeat it for clarification. If the physician is speaking too rapidly, ask him or her to speak more slowly, and then repeat the information for clarification.

Room#_____ Patient Name_____ Diagnoses_____

Diet_____ Activity_____

3:00	8:00
4:00	9:00
5:00	10:00
6:00	11:00
7:00	Misc.

FIGURE 2–4   Client information report.

Professionalism and a courteous attitude on both sides are necessary ingredients in maintaining collegial relationships with physicians and other healthcare professionals.

■ Conclusion

• • • • • • • • • • • • • • • • • •

The responsibility for delivering and coordinating client care is an important part of the role of the professional nurse. To accomplish this, nurses need good communication skills and an ability to safely delegate tasks to others. Being assertive without being aggressive and conducting interactions in a professional manner enhance the relationships nurses develop with colleagues, physicians, and other members of the interdisciplinary team.

Perhaps if Inez and her colleague had known more about communication, especially how to ask for help, their day would not have been so difficult. A cool head and good communication skills demonstrate professionalism and an ability to work with others.

? Study Questions

1. Role-play a situation between a client and a nurse. Have a third student make a list of the different attending skills you used with the client during the interaction.

2. What are the responsibilities of the professional nurse when delegating tasks to an LPN and a CNA? What factors do you need to consider when delegating tasks?

3. This is your first position as an RN, and you are working with an LPN who has been on the unit for 20 years. Your first day on the job she says to you, "The only difference between you and me is the size of the paycheck." Demonstrate how you would respond to this statement using assertive communication techniques.

4. A physician orders, "Vit K 10 mg. IVP." You realize that this is a dangerous order. How would you approach the physician?

Critical Thinking Exercise

Eric worked the evening shift. Every day when he got the report from Yvonne, he heard how difficult the day had been, what a "pain" certain patients were, and excuses as to why so many things had been left for him to do. Eric quietly listened to this and continued to pick up after Yvonne. He did not discuss the situation with anyone but felt very anxious because he was always behind before he could begin. One afternoon Eric became annoyed and yelled, "What is your problem? Everything is left for me to do, and all you give me are excuses. Besides complaining, what do you do all day?"

1. What type of communicator is Eric?

2. Identify the behavior Eric exhibited that enabled Yvonne to continue her behavior.

3. How could Eric have handled this situation with Yvonne in a more constructive manner?

4. If you were the team leader, how would you handle this situation?

REFERENCES

American Association of Critical Care Nurses (AACN). (1990). *Delegation of Nursing and Non-Nursing Activities in Critical Care: A Framework for Decision Making*. Irvine, Calif: AACN.

American Nurses Association (ANA). (1985). *Code for Nurses*. Washington, DC: ANA.

American Nurses Association (ANA) (1994). *Registered Professional Nurses and Unlicensed Assistive Personnel*. Washington, DC: ANA.

Arnold, E. & Boggs, K. (1995). *Interpersonal Relationships* (2nd ed.). Philadelphia: W.B. Saunders.

Arnold, J., & Pearson, G. (eds.). (1992). *Computer Applications in Nursing Education and Practice*. New York: National League for Nursing.

Barter, M., & Furmidge, M. (1994). Unlicensed assistive personnel. *J Nurs Adm, 24*(4), 36–40.

Berlo, D.K. (1960). *The Process of Communication*. San Francisco: Reinhart Press.

Chevernet, M. (1988). *STAT, Special Techniques in Assertiveness Training for Women in Health Professions* (2nd ed.). St. Louis: C.V. Mosby.

Conger, M. (1994). The nursing assignment decision grid: Tool for delegation decision. *Journal of Continuing Education in Nursing, 25*(4), 21–27.

Fontaine, K.L., & Fletcher, J.S. (1995). *Essentials of Mental Health Nursing* (3rd ed.). Redwood City, Calif: Addison-Wesley.

Hayes, P. (1994). Non-nursing functions: Time for them to go. *Nursing Economics, 12*(3), 120–125.

Herrick, K., Hansten, R., O'Neill, L., Hayes, P., & Washburn, M. (1994). My license is on the line: The art of delegation. *Nursing Management, 25*(2), 48–50.

Huber, D., Blegan, M., & McCloskey, J. (1994). Use of nursing assistants: Staff nurse opinions. *Nursing Management, 25*(5), 64–68.

Maslow, A. (1954). *Motivation and Personality*. New York: Harper.

Vacarolis, E.M. (1994). *Foundations of Psychiatric-Mental Health Nursing*. Philadelphia: W.B. Saunders.

Tappen, R.M. (1995). *Nursing Leadership and Management: Concepts and Practice* (3rd ed.). Philadelphia: F.A. Davis.

CHAPTER 3

Giving and Receiving Feedback

OBJECTIVES   *After reading this chapter, the student will be able to:*

◆ Provide positive and negative feedback in a constructive manner.

◆ Respond to feedback in a constructive manner.

◆ Evaluate the conduct of performance appraisals.

◆ Participate in formal peer review.

In good weather, Herbert usually played basketball with his kids after dinner. Yesterday, however, he told them he was too tired. This evening he said the same thing. When they urged him to play anyway, he snapped at them and told them to leave him alone. "Herbert!" his wife exclaimed, "Why did you do that?" "I don't know," he responded. "I'm just so uptight these days. My annual review was supposed to be today, but my nurse manager was out sick. I have no idea what she is going to say. I can't think about anything else."

If Herbert's nurse manager had been providing informal feedback to staff on a regular basis, Herbert would have known where he stood. He would have had a good idea what his strengths and weaknesses were and would not be afraid of an unpleasant surprise during the review. He would also be looking forward to the review as an opportunity to review his accomplishments and make plans for further developing his skills with his manager. He could have been disappointed that she was unavailable, but he would not have been so stressed by it.

The process of giving and receiving evaluative feedback is an essential leadership responsibility. Done well, it is very helpful. Done poorly, as in Herbert's case, it can be stressful, even injurious. In this chapter, we consider the dos and don'ts of giving and receiving feedback, how to share constructive positive and negative evaluative comments with your coworkers, and how to respond constructively when you are on the receiving end of such comments.

■ *Feedback Is Essential*
• • • • • • • • • • • • • • • • • • • •

Why do people need feedback? The following are just a few of the reasons why evaluative feedback is such an important leadership responsibility. Done well, evaluative feedback:

◆ Reinforces constructive behavior. Positive feedback lets people know which behaviors are the most effective and encourages continuation of these behaviors.

◆ Discourages unproductive behavior. Correction of inappropriate actions begins with provision of negative feedback.

◆ Provides recognition. The power of praise (positive feedback) in motivating people to work even harder is often underestimated (Glaser, 1994).

◆ Develops employee skills. Feedback helps people to identify their strengths and weaknesses and guides them in seeking opportunities to further develop their strengths and manage their weaknesses (Rosen, 1996).

■ *Guidelines for Providing Feedback*
• • • • • • • • • • • • • • • • • • • •

Done well, evaluative feedback can reinforce motivation, strengthen teamwork, and improve the quality of care given. When poorly done, evaluation can reinforce poor work habits, increase insecurity, and destroy motivation and morale (Table 3–1).

Evaluation involves making judgments and communicating these judgments to oth-

TABLE 3–1
DOS AND DON'TS OF PROVIDING FEEDBACK

Do. . . .	Don't. . . .
Be objective	Let personalities intrude
Be specific when correcting someone	Be vague
Treat everyone the same	Play favorites
Include positive comments	Focus only on the negative
Correct people in private	Correct people in front of others

Source: Adapted from Gabor, D. (1994). *Speaking Your Mind in 101 Different Situations.* New York: Stonesong Press (Simon and Schuster).

(Box 3–1).

Box 3–1 Tips for providing helpful feedback

- Provide both positive and negative feedback.
- Give immediate feedback.
- Provide frequent feedback.
- Give negative feedback privately.
- Be objective.
- Base feedback on observable behavior.
- Communicate effectively.
- Include suggestions for change.

ers. People make judgments all the time about all types of things. Many times these judgments are based on opinions, preferences, and inaccurate or partial information.

Subjective, unfair, biased judgments offered as objective feedback have given evaluation a bad name. Poorly communicated feedback has an equally negative effect. In fact, you will find that many of the people who are threatened by evaluation have been the recipients of subjective, biased, or poorly communicated evaluations in the past.

Evaluative feedback is most effective when it is given immediately, frequently, and privately. To be constructive, it must be objective, based on observed behavior, and skillfully communicated. The feedback message should include the reasons why a behavior has been judged good or poor. If the message is negative, it should be nonthreatening and include suggestions and support for change and improvement (Box 3–1).

PROVIDE BOTH POSITIVE AND NEGATIVE FEEDBACK

Leaders and managers often neglect to provide positive feedback. If questioned, people who do not give positive feedback explain that, "If I don't say anything, that means everything is okay." Unfortunately, they do not realize that some people assume that everything is *not* okay when they receive no feedback. Others assume that no one is aware of how much effort has gone into their work

unless it is acknowledged with positive feedback.

Most people want to do their work well. They also want to know that their efforts are recognized and appreciated; it is a real pleasure to be able to share the satisfaction of a job well done with someone else. Kron (1981) calls positive feedback a "psychological paycheck." She points out that it is almost as important to people as their actual paycheck.

Some say that nurses do not do enough to support each other as colleagues. Whether that is true or not, giving positive feedback is an important way to support your colleagues.

Negative feedback is just as necessary as positive feedback but probably more difficult to convey well. Too often, negative feedback is critical rather than constructive. It is easier just to tell people that something has gone wrong or could have been done better than it is to make the feedback a learning experience for the receiver by suggesting ways to make the needed changes or working together to develop a strategy for improvement. It is also easier to make broad, critical comments (e.g., "You're too slow") than it is to describe the specific behavior that needs improvement (e.g., "Waiting in Mr. D.'s room while he finishes brushing his teeth takes up too much of your time") and then add a suggestion for change (e.g., "You could get your bath supplies together while he finishes").

Providing no negative feedback at all is the easiest but least effective solution to the problem of being too critical. Unsatisfactory work must be acknowledged and discussed with the people involved. The "gutless wonder" (Del Bueno, 1977) who silently tolerates poor work encourages it to continue and undermines the motivation of the whole team.

GIVE IMMEDIATE FEEDBACK

The most helpful feedback, positive or negative, is given as soon as possible after the behavior has occurred. There are several reasons for this. Immediate feedback is more meaningful to the person receiving it. If it is delayed too long, the person may have forgotten the incident altogether or assumed that your silence indicated approval.

Like other confrontation situations, problems that are ignored often get worse, and a lot of frustration and anger can build up in the meantime. When feedback is given as soon as possible, there is no time for this buildup.

PROVIDE FREQUENT FEEDBACK

Feedback should not only be immediate but also frequent. Frequent constructive feedback keeps motivation and awareness levels high and avoids the possibility that problems will grow larger and more serious before they are confronted. It also becomes easier with practice. If giving and receiving feedback are a frequent and integral part of team functioning, feedback will be easier to give and less threatening to most people. It becomes an ordinary, everyday occurrence, one that happens spontaneously and is familiar to everyone on the team.

GIVE NEGATIVE FEEDBACK PRIVATELY

Giving negative feedback privately rather than in front of others prevents embarrassment. It also avoids the possibility that those who overhear the discussion may misunderstand it and draw erroneous conclusions from it. One management authority suggests that a manager should praise staff in public but punish (correct) them in private (Matejka, Ashworth, & Dodd-McCue, 1986).

BE OBJECTIVE

It can be very difficult to be objective when giving feedback to others. First of all, people should be evaluated on the basis of job expectations and not compared, favorably or unfavorably, with other staff members (Gellerman & Hodgson, 1988). Another way to increase objectivity is to always give a reason why you have judged a behavior as good or poor. Reasons should be given for both positive and negative messages. For example, if you tell a coworker, "That was a good patient interview," you have told that person nothing except that the interview pleased you. However, when you add to the message, "because you asked many open-ended questions that encouraged the client to explore

personal feelings," you have identified the specific behavior that made your evaluation positive and reinforced this specific behavior.

Finally, use broad and generally accepted standards for making judgments as much as possible to avoid basing evaluation on your own personal likes and dislikes. Objectivity can be increased by using standards that reflect the consensus of the team, the organization, the community, or the nursing profession. Formal evaluation should always be based on agreed-on, written standards of what is acceptable behavior. Informal evaluation, however, is based on unwritten standards. If these standards are based on personal preferences, the evaluation will be highly subjective. The following are some examples:

- A team leader who describes a female social worker as having a professional appearance because she wears dark suits instead of bright dresses to work is using a personal standard to evaluate that social worker.

- A supervisor who asks an employee to stop wearing jewelry that could get caught in the equipment used at work is applying a more generally accepted standard of safety in making the evaluative statement.

- The nursing home administrator who insists that staff members include every resident in the weekly birthday party game is applying a narrower and more personal standard than the administrator who insists that staff members offer every resident the opportunity to participate in weekly activities.

BASE FEEDBACK ON OBSERVABLE BEHAVIOR

An evaluative statement should describe observed behavior, not personality traits or attitudes that involve interpretation of behavior. The observation is much more likely to be factual and accurate than is the interpretation. It is also less likely to evoke a defensive response. For example, saying, "You were impatient with Mrs. G. today" is an interpretive comment. Saying, "You interrupted Mrs. G. before she finished explaining her problem" is based on observable behavior. It is more specific and may be more accurate because the caregiver may have been trying to redirect the conversation to more immediate concerns rather than feeling impatient. The second statement is more likely to evoke an explanation than a defensive response.

COMMUNICATE EFFECTIVELY

An evaluative statement is a form of confrontation. Any message that contains a statement about the behavior of a staff member is confronting that staff member with information. All of the guidelines given in Chapter 2 about the appropriate ways to communicate with another person or group apply to giving evaluative feedback.

The leader who gives evaluative feedback needs to be prepared to receive feedback in return and to engage in active listening. Active listening is especially important because the person receiving the evaluation may respond with disagreement and high emotion. The following is an example of what may happen:

> You point out to Mr. S. that his clients need to be monitored more frequently. Mr. S. responds emotionally about doing everything possible for the clients and not having a free moment all day for one extra thing. In fact, Mr. S. tells you about never even taking a lunch break and going home exhausted. Active listening and problem solving with this coworker aimed at relieving his overloaded time schedule are a must in this situation.

When you give negative feedback, allow time for the individuals to express their feelings and for problem solving to find ways to improve a situation. This is particularly important if the problem has been ignored long enough to become serious (Box 3–2).

Box 3–2 Be TACTFUL: Guidelines for providing negative feedback

T = Think before you speak
A = Apologize quickly if you've made a mistake
C = Converse, don't be patronizing or sarcastic
T = Time your comments carefully
F = Focus on behavior/not on personality
U = Uncover hidden feelings
L = Listen for feedback

Source: Gabor, D. (1994). *Speaking Your Mind in 101 Difficult Situations.* New York: Stonesong Press (Simon and Schuster).

INCLUDE SUGGESTIONS FOR CHANGE

When you give feedback that indicates some kind of change in behavior is needed, it is helpful to suggest alternative behaviors. This is easier to do when the change is a simple one.

When complex change is needed (as with Mr. S.), you may find that the person is aware of the problem but does not know how to solve it. In such a case, oversimplified solutions are inappropriate, but an offer to engage in searching for the solution is appropriate. A willingness to listen to the other person's side of the story and assist in finding a solution indicates that your purpose is to help rather than just to criticize the individual.

COMMUNICATE IN A NONTHREATENING MANNER

When the feedback is negative, the focus of the message should be on the specific behavior, not on the person as a whole, which devalues the person and threatens self-esteem. Highly threatening messages reduce motivation and inhibit learning by diverting people's energies into activities aimed at reducing the threat. Although a small degree of anxiety may increase learning, too much fear immobilizes people. The ultimate purpose for providing informal evaluation is, after all, to improve the function of the team and its individual members.

Negative feedback may contain hints of dire consequences, probably in the mistaken belief that it will increase the person's motivation to change. The following are some common examples:

> ◆ "You're not going to last long if you keep doing that."
>
> ◆ "People who want to do well here make sure their assignments are done on time."
>
> ◆ "Don't argue with the doctors; they'll report you to the nursing office."

When a person's behavior actually does threaten job security, a formal evaluation stating this fact directly and proposing needed changes is appropriate.

You may have assumed that people in the ranks above you (e.g., manager, head nurse, supervisor, director) could not be threatened by feedback from you. This is not true. They are all human and as susceptible to feeling threatened as you are. You need to follow the same guidelines in giving feedback to people above you in the organization.

■ *Seeking Evaluative Feedback*

• • • • • • • • • • • • • • • • • • • •

Just as important as knowing how to give feedback is knowing when to ask for it and how to accept it. The purposes for seeking feedback are the same as those for giving it to others. The criteria for evaluating the feedback you receive are also the same (Box 3–3).

WHEN IS EVALUATIVE FEEDBACK NEEDED?

There are a number of different situations in which you need to seek feedback. For example, you could find yourself in a work situation where you receive very little feedback from any source except your own

---

Box 3–3 Situations in which you should ask for feedback

◆ When you do not know how well you are doing

◆ When you receive only positive comments

◆ When you receive only negative comments

◆ When you believe that your accomplishments have not been recognized

---

evaluation of your work. Or you may be getting only positive and no negative comments (or vice versa).

Another time when you need to look for feedback is when you feel uncertain about how well you are doing or whether you have correctly interpreted the expectations of the job. The following are examples of these situations:

> ◆ You have been told that good client care is the first consideration of your job but feel totally frustrated by never having enough staff members to give good care.
>
> ◆ You thought you were expected to do case finding and health teaching in your community but receive the most recognition for the number of home visits made and the completeness of your records.

An additional instance in which you should request feedback is when you feel that your needs for recognition and job satisfaction have not been met adequately.

Requests for feedback should be made in the form of "I" messages. If you have received only negative comments, ask, "In what ways have I done well?" If you receive only positive comments, you can ask, "In what areas do I need to improve?" Or, if you are seeking feedback from a client, you could ask, "How can I be of more help to you?"

RESPONDING TO EVALUATIVE FEEDBACK

There are times when it is appropriate to critically analyze the feedback you are getting. If the feedback seems totally negative or you feel threatened on receiving it, ask for further explanation. You may have misunderstood what the person meant to say.

It is hard to avoid responding defensively to negative feedback that is subjective or laced with threats and blame. But if you are the recipient of such a poorly done evaluation, it may help both you and your supervisor to try to guide the discussion into more constructive areas. You can ask for reasons why the evaluation was negative, on what standard it is based or what the person's expectations were, and what the person suggests as alternative behavior.

When the feedback is positive but nonspecific, you may also want to ask for some clarification so that you can find out what that person's expectations really are. Do not hesitate to seek that psychological paycheck. Tell other people about your successes—most are happy to share the satisfaction of a successful outcome or positive development in a client's care.

■ *Performance Appraisal*
• •

Performance appraisal is the term generally used to describe the formal evaluation of an employee by a superior, usually a manager or supervisor. The employee's behavior is compared with a standard describing how the employee is expected to perform. Employees need to know what has to be done, how much has to be done, and when it has to be done (Hansen, 1986). The standards that provide this information are often written in the form of objectives. Actual performance is evaluated, not good intentions.

PROCEDURE

In the ideal situation, the performance appraisal begins when the employee is hired. Based on the written job description, the employee and manager discuss the expected standard of performance and then write a set of objectives that they think the employee can reasonably accomplish within a given time. The objectives should be written as a level of performance that demonstrates that some learning, attainment, refinement of skill, or advancement toward some long-range objective has taken place. The following are examples of objectives that could be set for a new staff nurse to accomplish in the first 6 months of employment:

> ● Complete the staff nurse orientation program successfully.
>
> ● Master the basic skills necessary to function as a staff nurse on the assigned unit.
>
> ● Supervise the client care technicians assigned to his or her patients

Six months later, at the previously agreed-on time, the staff nurse and nurse manager sit down again and evaluate the staff nurse's performance in terms of the previously set goals. The evaluation should be based on both the staff nurse's self-assessment and the nurse manager's observation of specific behaviors. New objectives for the next 6 months and plans for achieving them may be agreed on at the time of the appraisal or at a separate meeting (Beer, 1981). A copy of the performance appraisal and the projected goals must be available to employees so that they can refer back to them and check on the progress toward the agreed-on goals.

It is important to set aside adequate time for feedback and goal-setting processes. Both the staff nurse and the nurse manager bring data for use at this session. These data should include a self-evaluation by the staff nurse and observations by the evaluator of the employee's activities and their outcomes. Data may also be obtained from peers and clients. Some organizations use surveys for getting this information from clients.

Most of the guidelines for providing informal evaluative feedback discussed earlier apply to the conduct of performance appraisals. Although not as frequent or immediate as informal feedback, formal evaluation should be just as objective, private, non-threatening, skillfully communicated, and growth-promoting.

STANDARDS FOR EVALUATION

Unfortunately, many organizations have employee evaluation procedures that are far from ideal. Their procedures may be inconsistent, subjective, and even unknown to the employee in some cases. The following is a list of standards for a fair and objective employee evaluation procedure that you can to use to judge your employer's procedures:

- ◆ Standards are clear, objective, and known in advance.
- ◆ Criteria for pay raises and promotions are clearly spelled out and uniformly applied.
- ◆ Conditions under which employment may be terminated are known.
- ◆ Appraisals are part of the employee's permanent record and have space for employee comments.
- ◆ Employees may inspect their own personnel file.
- ◆ Employees may request and be given a reasonable explanation of any rating and may appeal the rating if they do not agree with it.
- ◆ Employees are given a reasonable amount of time to correct any serious deficiencies before other action is taken, unless the safety of self or others is immediately threatened.

In some organizations, collective bargaining agreements are used to enforce adherence to fair and objective performance appraisals. However, collective bargaining agreements may emphasize seniority (length of service) over merit in giving raises and promotions, a situation that does not promote growth and change.

■ *Peer Review*

Peer review is the evaluation of an individual's practice by colleagues (peers) who have similar education, experience, and occupational status. Its purpose is to provide the individual with feedback from those who are best acquainted with the requirements and demands of that particular position. Peer review includes both process and outcomes of practice.

On an informal basis, professionals frequently observe and judge their colleagues' performance. But many feel uncomfortable about telling others what they think of their performance, and so their evaluations are not shared with the individual practitioner unless informal feedback is shared regularly or a formal system of peer review is established.

Whenever staff members meet to audit records or otherwise evaluate the quality of care they have given, they are actually engaging in a kind of peer review. However, formal peer review programs are often one of the last formal evaluation procedures to be implemented in a healthcare organization.

FUNDAMENTALS OF PEER REVIEW

There are a number of possible variations in the peer review process. For example, the observations may be shared only with the person being reviewed, with the person's supervisor, or with a review committee. The evaluation report may be written by the reviewer, or it may come from the review committee. The use of a committee defeats the purpose of peer review if the committee members are not truly peers of the individual being reviewed.

A COMPREHENSIVE PEER REVIEW SYSTEM

Peer review systems can simply be informal feedback regularly shared among colleagues or comprehensive systems that are fully integrated into the formal evaluation structure of a healthcare organization. When a peer review system is fully integrated, the evaluative feedback from one's peers is joined with the performance appraisals done by the nurse manager, and both are used to determine pay raises and promotions for individual staff nurses. This is a far more collegial approach than the hierarchical one generally used in which employees are evaluated only by their manager.

A comprehensive peer review system begins with the development of job descriptions (Table 3–2) and performance standards (Table 3–3) for each level within the nursing staff. If you compare Tables 3–2 and 3–3, you will note that the job description is a very general statement, whereas the standards are specific behaviors that can be observed and recorded.

In some organizations, the standards may be considered the minimal qualifications for each level. In this case, additional activities and professional development are expected before promotion to the next level. The candidate for promotion to an advanced-level position prepares a promotion portfolio for review (Schultz, 1993). The promotion port-

folio may include a self-assessment, peer reviews, patient surveys, management performance appraisal, and evidence of professional growth. Evidence of professional growth could be based on participation in the quality improvement program, evaluation of a new product or procedure, serving as a translator or disaster volunteer, making postdischarge visits to clients from the unit, or taking courses related to nursing.

In a participative environment, the standards are developed by committees having representatives from different units and from each staff level, from the new staff nurse to top-level management.

Writing useful job descriptions and measurable standards of performance is an arduous but rewarding task. It requires clarification and explication of the work nurses actually do that go beyond our usual generalizations about what nursing is and what nurses do. Under effective group leadership and with strong administrative support for this process, it can be a challenging and stimulating experience. Without their support and guidance, however, the committee work

TABLE 3–2
SAMPLE JOB DESCRIPTIONS

Clinical Nurse I (CN I)

The CN I supports the philosophy of primary nursing by planning and coordinating nursing care for a group of patients within his/her district.

It is the CN I's responsibility to direct auxiliary personnel for full implementation of the plan of care.

The CN I supports the management of the unit and uses resource persons and/or materials when the need arises. He/She has satisfactorily mastered the basic skills required to work on the assigned unit.

The CN I's scope of nursing practice is focused on his/her assigned group of patients and does not extend into the administrative aspects of the unit at large.

Clinical Nurse IV (CN IV)—Unit Clinician

The CN IV is an advanced clinical nurse who supports the practice of primary nursing on the unit, as well as hospital-wide. He/She is recognized within the specialty area, as well as throughout the hospital, as being proficient in the delivery of complicated nursing care.

The CN IV has mastered the many facets of nursing care required at the CN II and CN III levels. This qualification is validated through the acquisition of national certification in the appropriate specialty area.

The CN IV coordinates and directs emergency situations, seeks out learning opportunities for the unit staff and serves as a resource for all aspects of nursing care delivery.

The CN IV collaborates closely with physicians on the unit for the implementation of the plan of care. This may be facilitated through assessing special equipment needs, as well as planning multidisciplinary programs.

The CN IV works closely with the nurse manager in planning unit goals and objectives and unit specific orientation programs, as well as assisting with staff performance evaluations.

The CN IV acts as a liaison between his or her unit and the Departments of Nursing Education and Patient Education.

Source: Adapted from Professional Nursing Advancement Program, Baptist Hospital of Miami, Florida.

TABLE 3–3
SAMPLE PERFORMANCE STANDARDS

Responsibility	CN I	CN II	CN III	CN IV
To patient				
1. Plans care for duration of stay on clinical unit.	a. Family/social concerns are addressed in the assessment process, as evidenced by nursing care documentation.	a. through e. f. Utilizes nursing history for care planning by auditing charts for integration of problem statements.	a. through h. i. Identifies need for and/or initiates appropriate family/social referrals with documentation.	a. through k. l. Collaborates with the Department of Patient Education in designing and revising patient teaching materials.
	b. All admission documentation on assigned patients is recorded.	g. Assesses supplies/ equipment and has them readily available for patient use.	j. Assesses and documents cultural differences, patient support systems and expectations for hospitalization.	
	c. History reflects information relevant to current hospitalization.	h. Initiates discharge summary sheet prior to discharge	k. Documents patient's response to teaching as identified in nursing care documentation.	
	d. Patient problem/ outcome statement are current and/or designated as achieved.			
	e. Patient teaching, transfer and/or discharge preparation is documented.			
To peers				
1. Avails himself/ herself to co-workers at all times.	a. Notifies peers when required to leave the clinical area.	a. through c. d. Takes initiative to offer assistance to other nurses and with assigned patients.	a. through e. f. Acts as senior resource coordinator in absence of nurse manager.	a. through f. g. Coordinates/teaches two programs in conjunction with the Dept. of Nursing Education annually.
	b. Assumes responsibility for I.V.'s and orders of LPN on assigned patients.	e. Serves as preceptor to students/ orientees.		h. Conducts staff conferences to evaluate clinical competencies of personnel with documentation.
	c. Responds promptly to all emergency situations that arise in the district.			

Source: Adapted from Professional Nursing Advancement Program, Baptist Hospital of Miami, Florida.

can be frustrating when the group gets bogged down in details and disagreements.

Once the job descriptions and performance standards for each level have been developed and agreed on, a procedure for their use must also be worked out. There are several ways in which this can be done. An evaluation form listing the performance standards can be completed by one or two colleagues selected by the individual staff member. The information from these forms is then used along with the nurse manager's evaluation to determine pay raises and promotions in some organizations. In others the evaluation from one's peers is used for counseling purposes only and is not taken into consideration in determining pay raises or promotions, an approach that provides useful feedback but weakens the impact of peer review on the individual or the system as a whole.

A different approach is the use of a professional practice committee. This committee, composed of colleagues selected by the nursing staff, reviews the peer evaluation forms and makes its recommendations to the director of nursing (or vice president for client care services), who then makes the final decision regarding the appropriate rewards (raises, promotions, commendations) or punishment (demotion, transfer, termination of employment). It may surprise the reader who has not participated in such a peer review process that the recommendations of one's peers may be harsher than the recommendations made by management (Dison, 1986).

■ *Conclusion*

• • • • • • • • • • • • • • • • • •

A comprehensive evaluation system can be an effective mechanism both for increasing the quality of care by improving staff skills and morale and for reducing the costs of providing that care by increasing staff productivity. Constructive feedback demands objectivity and fairness in dealing with each other and leadership on the part of both staff members and management. Done well, it can provide many opportunities for increased professionalism and learning and ensure appropriate rewards for high performance levels and professionalism on the job.

? *Study Questions*

1. Why is feedback important? Who should give feedback to healthcare providers? Who needs to receive feedback?

2. In your own words, describe the difference between constructive and destructive feedback.

3. Describe an ideal version of a 3-month performance appraisal of a new staff nurse. Why do nurse managers sometimes fail to meet this ideal when providing formal evaluative feedback? Is there anything new staff nurses can do to improve these procedures in their place of employment?

4. What is peer review? How is it different from other types of evaluation? Why is it important?

Critical Thinking Exercise

Tyrell Jones is a new client care technician who has been assigned to your acute rehabilitation unit. Tyrell is a hard worker—he comes in early and often stays late to finish his work. But Tyrell is gruff with the clients, especially with the male clients. If a client is reluctant to get out of bed, Tyrell often challenges him saying, "C'mon, man. Don't be such a wimp. Move your big butt." Today, you overheard Tyrell telling a female client who said she didn't feel well, "You're just a phony. You like being waited on, but that's not why you're here." The woman started to cry.

1. You are the newest staff nurse on this unit. How would you handle this situation? What would happen if you ignored it?

2. If you decided that you should not ignore it, with whom should you speak? Why? What would you say?

3. Why do you think Tyrell speaks to clients this way?

REFERENCES

Beer, M. (1981, Winter). Performance appraisal: Dilemmas and possibilities. *Organizational Dynamics, 24.*

Del Bueno, D. (1977). Performance evaluation: When all is said and done, more is said than done. *J Nurs Adm, 7*(10).

Dison, C. (1986). *Professional Nursing Advancement in the Work Place.* Paper presented at the Annual Nursing

Research Conference, Sigma Theta Tau, Beta Tau Chapter, Miami, Fla.

Gabor, D. (1994). *Speaking Your Mind in 101 Difficult Situations*. New York: Stonesong Press (Simon & Schuster).

Gellerman, S.W., & Hodgson, W.G. (1988). Cyanamid's new table on performance appraisal. *Harvard Business Review, 88*(3), 36–41.

Glaser, S.R. (1994). Teamwork and Communication. *Management Communication Quarterly, 7*(3), 282–296.

Hansen, M.R. (1986). To-do lists for managers. *Supervisory Management, 31*(5), 37–39.

Kron, T. (1981). *The Management of Patient Care: Putting Leadership Skills to Work*. Philadelphia: W.B. Saunders.

Matejka, J.K., Ashworth, D.N., & Dodd-McCue, D. (1986). Discipline without guilt. *Supervisory Management, 31*(5), 34–36.

Rosen, R.H. (1996). *Leading People: Transforming Business from the Inside Out*. New York: Viking Penguin.

Schultz, A.W. (1993). Evaluation for clinical advancement system. *J Nurs Adm, 23*(2), 13–19.

U N I T II

Leading and Managing

CHAPTER 4

Managing Client Care

OBJECTIVES   *After reading this chapter, the student will be able to:*

- Describe the economic climate of the healthcare system.
- Compare and contrast the traditional and contemporary models of client care delivery.
- Discuss the role of the nurse in quality management.
- Discuss how continuous quality improvement methodology improves quality of care.
- Explain how a critical pathway can be used to measure patient outcomes.

All the results of good nursing, as detailed in these notes, may be spoiled or utterly negated by one defect, viz.: in petty management, or in other words, by not knowing how to manage.... How few men, or even women, understand, either in great or in little things, ... know how to carry out a "charge." To be "in charge" is certainly not only to carry out the proper measure yourself but to see that every one else does so too; to see that no one either willfully or ignorantly thwarts or prevents such measures. It is neither to do everything yourself nor to appoint a number of people to each duty, but to ensure that each does that duty to which he is appointed. (Nightingale, 1859, pp. 20, 24)

Although Florence Nightingale wrote these words in the 1800s, they are still true today. Major changes in our healthcare system are occurring as administrators in all types of agencies try to find the correct balance between "lean and mean" efficiency and high-quality care (Sharp, 1994, p. 32). These efforts affect the way nursing care is delivered. The search for ways to provide safe, effective health care without spending too much money has led to the creation of new models for managing nursing care.

This chapter will assist you in understanding and developing your role in the management of client care. The chapter begins by considering the economic context in which health care is provided. A review of the past, present, and future models for managing nursing care is presented next. This includes the traditional models of total care, primary care, functional, and team. The contemporary use of case management, the multidisciplinary team approach, product line management, and differentiated practice complete this section. This is followed by a discussion of the ways in which the quality of the care given is monitored and evaluated.

■ *The Economic Climate in the Healthcare System*
• • • • • • • • • • • • • • • • • • • •

In the past, the centerpiece of our healthcare system was the hospital. However, with the movement to shorten the length of hospital stay to save money, attention has turned to providing care in the home and community-based health centers. For many years, decisions about care were based primarily on providing the best-quality care, whatever the cost. As the economic support for health care is challenged, however, healthcare providers are pressured to seek methods of care delivery that achieve quality outcomes at lower cost.

More changes in the way health care is delivered and paid for are anticipated. Lean, flexible, highly productive workforces, better management of clients identified as high risk or high utilization, and satisfied consumers will be the key to healthcare success in the future. The associate degree nurse will assume a significant role in providing direct client care now and in the future (Curtin, 1994; AONE, 1994).

■ *Traditional Models of Care Delivery*
• • • • • • • • • • • • • • • • • • • •

TOTAL CARE

The total care or case method was one of the earliest models of nursing care delivery. One nurse assumes total responsibility for the planning and delivery of care to a particular client or group of clients. This method may be used today in community health nursing, in private duty, in intensive care and isolation units, and in making assignments for students in nursing school. The client may have different nurses within a 24-hour period, but each nurse provides all of the care needed for the time period assigned. The case method is considered a precursor of primary nursing. Although the method has the advantage of being extremely client-focused, it is not considered the most efficient use of staff and is not used in the majority of healthcare settings today.

FUNCTIONAL

The functional method of care delivery grew out of the 1950s emphasis on an assembly-line style of management focusing on division of labor specifics and tasks that need to be completed. The nurse manager is responsible for making work assignments. Roles such as those of the medication nurse and treatment nurse are part of the functional delivery approach. Job descriptions, procedures, policies, and lines of communication are clearly defined. The functional model is generally considered efficient, economical, and productive. The disadvantage is that this model leads to fragmentation of care because the client receives care from several different types of nursing personnel. In addition, the emotional needs of both the staff members and client are overlooked in the interest of time management and task completion (Loveridge & Cummings, 1996).

TEAM

In the later 1950s and 1960s, the emphasis moved from a task focus to group dynamics and promotion of job satisfaction. In response to the fragmentation of the functional method and the continued scarcity of registered nurses after World War II, the team method was developed. Each team consists of a mix of staff members such as a registered nurse, licensed practical nurse, and nursing assistant. The team is responsible for providing care to a group of assigned clients during the shift. The team leader, usually the registered nurse, is responsible for making assignments for the team based on the team member's abilities and the needs of the clients. Compared to the functional method, the team method emphasizes holistic care and increases client and employee satisfaction. The team method is a time-consuming, expensive delivery system and may cause undue workload stress for the team leader (Loveridge & Cummings, 1996).

PRIMARY CARE

Primary nursing became popular in the 1960s and 1970s as nurses voiced concern over the fragmentation of care provided to their clients. In this model, a registered nurse is assigned care of a client for 24 hours a day for the client's entire hospital stay, including discharge planning. This registered nurse is responsible for developing the care plan and managing the associate nurses and other staff members who provide additional care for the client. Primary nursing decreases the number of persons having contact with each client and usually increases accountability and client satisfaction. However, primary nursing severely limits the number of clients each nurse can serve and can place the client in jeopardy if the primary nurse is not capable of meeting the client's needs (Loveridge & Cummings, 1996).

■ *Contemporary Models of Care Delivery*

• •

As healthcare administrators search for the model of care delivery that will ensure quality, promote client and staff satisfaction, and contain costs, the "R-words" appear: restructuring and redesign. Among the newer (or reemerging models) are case management, client-focused care with cross-training, product line management, and differentiated practice.

CASE MANAGEMENT

The term *case management* is used to describe a variety of healthcare delivery systems in acute, long-term, and community settings. Case management is not a new concept. Public health programs have used case management to provide care since the early 1900s. When mental health services moved out of institutions into the community in the 1960s, case management programs became important to psychiatric–mental health nursing as well (Lyon, 1993).

The American Nurses Association (ANA) defines case management as "provision of quality care along a continuum, decreased fragmentation of care across many settings, enhancement of the quality of life, and cost containment" (ANA, 1988).

According to Newell (1996), the primary functions of case managers include:

● **NEGOTIATION SERVICES AND/OR TREATMENTS.** Obtaining maximum-quality services at an acceptable cost (e.g., negotiate registered nurse hourly rates for home care services, obtain prices for equipment such as a wheelchair).

◆ **COMMUNICATION.** Communicating with service providers, clients, families, and information systems.

◆ **COORDINATION OF CARE.** Overseeing services and resources to avoid duplication and breakdowns in quality.

◆ **CLINICAL EXPERTISE.** Technical knowledge of disease processes and interventions to assess, plan, and evaluate client services.

◆ **HOLISTIC APPROACH.** The ability to understand human beings' biologic, social, and behavioral needs.

◆ **ETHICS OF CARING.** A focus on advocacy, honesty, and understanding in dealing with clients.

◆ **COACHING.** An important skill that affects all of the preceding functions, allowing the case manager to be successful in working with clients, families, staff, and physicians.

Nursing care management is designed to decrease fragmentation of care, use of hospitalization, and cost through better coordination and monitoring of the client's care. Effective nursing case management can improve the quality of services, the quality of life for clients, and function of the interdisciplinary team.

> Case management systems must act like human beings that are well functioning: they are focused on the task at hand, interact without duplicity, they learn and respond to new situations and information, they are honest and forthright in communicating with all parties. Well-functioning case managers and case management systems may not always do everything right, but they should strive to do the right thing, thus affecting others in the system to also act with integrity. (Newell, 1996)

Nursing care management is a system for delivering nursing care that is based on the philosophy of case management.

The goals of nursing care management are as follows (Girard, 1994):

◆ **OUTCOMES BASED ON STANDARDS OF CARE.** Evaluation of the quality of nursing practice is based on desired measurable outcomes and accepted practices of the nursing profession.

◆ **WELL-COORDINATED CONTINUITY OF CARE THROUGH COLLABORATIVE PRACTICE.** All providers of services work together to plan services and meet client needs. Effective collaboration requires that providers also work together to meet each other's needs.

◆ **EFFICIENT USE OF RESOURCES TO REDUCE WASTED TIME, ENERGY, AND MATERIALS.** Continued monitoring of material and personnel resources can eliminate duplication of steps and services, resulting in increased efficiency and job satisfaction.

◆ **TIMELY DISCHARGE WITHIN PROSPECTIVE PAYMENT GUIDELINES.** The grouping of medical conditions into categories that have allowable lengths of stay and payment schedules designated by Medicare has been in effect since the 1980s. Enabling clients to be discharged safely within the designated length of stay is an ongoing challenge for the nursing care manager.

◆ **PROFESSIONAL DEVELOPMENT AND SATISFACTION.** Through coordination of services and collaboration with providers, family, and clients, use of the case management model can enhance clients' quality of life (Christensen & Bender, 1994).

Although many different healthcare personnel claim to have in-depth knowledge of client and family care needs, understanding of organizational and financial services, and community resources, the registered nurse is ideally suited to serve as care manager. Nursing has traditionally considered the client from a total systems perspective of person, environment, and health with a focus on the multidisciplinary efforts needed to optimize care for the individual. Nurses, accustomed to focusing on a holistic approach to nursing care, are best able to use a whole-system approach to care delivery rather than a parts-oriented approach (Newell, 1996).

The case management system of care assists clients in learning to cope with the challenges of their illness. Case management services can be delivered in a variety of settings. External case management involves activities that are external to provider organizations. For example, case managers may work with victims of catastrophic motor vehicle accidents, workers' compensation cases, major medical insurance cases, and individual clients with complex chronic conditions. Internal case managers provide services "within the walls" of institutions or provider organizations. Facilities that often use internal case managers include (Newell, 1996):

- Acute care
- Subacute care
- Rehabilitation
- Long-term care
- Home care
- Managed care organizations

The following is a case management example:

Maria is a 71-year-old Salvadoran-American woman with a history of childhood rheumatic heart disease. She has given birth to four children, the last one at the age of 41. During that pregnancy, she spent the last trimester on bed rest. She continued to complain of fatigue, shortness of breath, and swelling in her feet and ankles after her last child was born. Four years later, she had a mitral commissurotomy to open the calcified mitral valve.

Since then, she has complained of the same symptoms. She has been unable to walk up the flight of stairs in her two-story home. Maria and her husband depend on his small pension and social security for their living expenses. Their home is paid for, and the children are always "sending gifts," but money is limited. The couple joined a Medicare HMO (health maintenance organization) to cover the cost of drugs and avoid having to carry a supplemental policy to augment traditional Medicare coverage.

As Maria's condition deteriorated, she experienced liver enlargement, sleep apnea, and petechiae on her face. She was very depressed regarding her continued illness. The HMO physician tried to talk Maria into a mitral valve replacement. She stated emphatically, "I will never go through what I did when I had that surgery, so don't even mention it!" The physician asked the nurse case manager to see Maria.

The nurse case manager met with Maria and her husband in their home. She observed that, although the house appeared clean, Maria complained that she is unable to keep house like she used to and feels useless as a wife and mother. The case manager helped Maria and her husband evaluate their options for treatment of Maria's illness. She made several visits to their home and, after forming a positive relationship with them, began to discuss the potential benefits of surgery and the possibility of improving Maria's quality of life. Maria finally consented to having a cardiac catheterization, which showed that both the mitral and tricuspid valves were leaking. She agreed to surgery, which was successful. The case manager continues to call Maria on a monthly basis to monitor her progress. Maria said recently, "I owe my new life to my wonderful nurse."

CLIENT-FOCUSED CARE

In the client-focused care model, services and staff are organized around client needs rather than the other way around. Traditionally, hospitals have been organized by departments to which the client is brought for services. In the client-focused care model, the services are brought to the client (Greenberg, 1994). Clients with similar needs are placed on the same nursing units, with ancillary and support services present on the unit.

The traditional boundaries between disciplines are blurred. Although licensed members of the team retain their professional expertise and function within state and national practice acts and accrediting agency requirements, all nonregulated tasks are shared by members of the team. Members of disciplines such as nursing, physical therapy, respiratory therapy, and pharmacy are unit-based. They receive additional training so that they can provide services across disciplinary lines. Their combined functions may range from clinical to managerial responsibilities and may be of higher, lower, or parallel levels when compared to their original functions. In addition, new all-purpose "client care technicians" or "unlicensed assistive personnel" roles are usually created. These new workers perform tasks such as meal delivery, cleaning and maintenance of rooms, and assisting clients with comfort needs. Under the supervision of licensed personnel, patient care technicians may also perform skilled tasks that are not restricted by various practice acts such as insertion of indwelling urinary catheters or simple dressing changes (Flarey, 1995; Christensen & Bender, 1994).

Response to this new model of care delivery has been mixed. Some nursing administrators say that staff dissatisfaction and stress have increased, whereas others report favorable client experiences and staff satisfaction (Christensen & Bender, 1994). Since its inception in 1989, the use of the client-focused care model has increased, but the need for further research on its effectiveness continues (Clouten & Weber, 1994). The following is a client-focused care example:

Esperanza has been the nurse manager on a 50-bed medical-surgical unit for 5 years. Since the advent of the prospective payment system, the reimbursement for care has been limited. Patients come in sicker and go home more quickly. Esperanza just left a management meeting in which the CEO had informed them that nursing costs make up over half of the hospital's total budget. To cut costs and maximize effectiveness, the nurse managers must decrease the number of nurses on each shift, making sure that registered nurses do only those tasks that require a registered nurse. A consultant will be brought in to implement a new system called client-focused care.

Each unit formed a committee of management, staff nurses, and nursing assistants to meet with the consultant. In addition, representatives of other services such as rehabilitation services, respiratory care, pharmacy, and housekeeping were included. The consultant made it clear that the decisions made would be what worked for this organization, not a blueprint from another organization.

The committees met weekly. Specific indirect and direct client care activities that could be delegated to nonlicensed personnel in accordance with the state Nurse Practice Act were identified. It was decided that there would be two levels of clinical assistants. Job descriptions and work standards were developed for each level. Training workshops were developed, and a skill competency workshop was required for all new personnel. The hospital worked in conjunction with the local community college to offer certificates for the two clinical assistant levels. By the end of the program, 9.6 full-time registered nurse positions were converted into 15.6 clinical assistant positions. The hospital predicted savings in recruitment, orientation, and training costs as well as increased job satisfaction for all participants. Esperanza felt that "only time will tell if the program works for both the staff and the clients."

PRODUCT LINE MANAGEMENT

Product line management is used in business to create a center to plan, manage, and market a specific product within the larger company. In healthcare delivery, use of this system results in a new organizational structure in which components of various clinical services or departments are merged to create a distinct "product line" such as drug abuse treatment, women's health care, or pediatric care. For example, the orthopedic product line would include nursing care, therapies, technician services, orthotic and prosthetic devices, and educational programs. In this type of delivery system, a product line manager directs these operations. Unlike traditional systems in which the registered nurse was the manager, the product line manager may be a member of a discipline other than nursing. In some instances, the manager may not even have a related healthcare background (Christensen & Bender, 1994, p. 68).

The non-nurse manager may have a great deal of business and financial background and makes purely business decisions regarding client care. Unfortunately, the non-nurse manager may have difficulty focusing on client and family needs that are incongruent with business decisions.

DIFFERENTIATED PRACTICE

Differentiated practice is the structuring of nursing roles and functions based on the individual's education, experience, and competence. For example, the nurse with an associate degree would care for clients in the hospital setting under the supervision of a nurse manager, whereas the nurse with a baccalaureate degree would plan the client's care in the home. As health care continues to evolve, there is an even greater need to provide nurses with differentiated scopes of nursing practice (AONE, 1994).

Informally, differentiated practice among registered nurses exists in almost every setting. It occurs each time a nurse manager plans staff assignments according to the knowledge, competence, and licensure of the staff members involved, for example. Other members of the healthcare team and even clients develop a "sixth sense" about the abilities of the nurses with whom they interact (McClure, 1991).

The controversy over registered nurse licensure has raged within the profession since 1965, when the American Nurses Association endorsed the concept of two levels of education preparation and licensure. Thirty years later, the organization is still fighting the idea that "a nurse is a nurse is a nurse." Regardless of educational preparation or background, nurses are often used interchangeably in the workplace. The result is that they are not used in a cost-effective manner and many are not challenged to reach their full potential.

The rationale for implementing differentiated nursing practice is both professional and economic. Professionally, differentiated practice for the registered nurse may lead to increased satisfaction and improved client care. Used effectively, differentiated practice models also ensure efficient use of nursing resources (Vena & Oldaker, 1994; Koerner et al., 1995; Ray & Hardin, 1995; Allender, Egan, & Newman, 1995).

Several models of differentiated practice have been developed. The following is one such model (AONE, 1994) (Table 4–1):

◆ **ASSOCIATE DEGREE NURSE.** The associate nurse is responsible for the shift of service, with a strong emphasis on meeting the physiological and comfort needs of the client assigned by the primary nurse. The associate nurse role is to implement nursing care plans developed by the nurse clinician and primary nurse.

TABLE 4–1

A MODEL OF DIFFERENTIATED NURSING PRACTICE

Associate Degree	Bachelor's Degree	Master's Degree
Shift-oriented	Admission-to-discharge-oriented	Across-the-life span focus
Meets physiological and comfort needs	Focus on coordination of medical and nursing orders	Multiple settings
Implements nursing care plans		Decision making
Technical skill focus	Continuity of care focus	Integrated care focus
Well-defined boundaries	Fluid boundaries	Situational settings
Outcomes: Comfort Physiological well-being	Outcomes: Continuity of care Timely discharge	Outcomes: Integrated care Empowerment

Source: Adapted from American Organization of Nurse Executives (1994). Differentiated competencies for nursing practice. *Nursing Management, 25*(9), 34.

◆ **BACCALAUREATE DEGREE NURSE OR PRIMARY NURSE.** The primary nurse's responsibility extends from admission to discharge, focusing on coordination of medical and nursing orders, client education, and a well-planned, timely discharge. The primary nurse must be able to match client needs with staff abilities using an interdisciplinary team approach.

◆ **MASTER'S DEGREE NURSE.** This advanced practice role may include the advanced registered nurse practitioner (ARNP), advanced practice nurse (APN), and certified nurse midwife (CNM). The advanced practice nurse assumes the role of case manager and client advocate. The role of the advanced nurse practitioner extends beyond the acute care setting into multiple healthcare arenas.

■ *Monitoring and Evaluating the Quality of Care*

• •

CRITICAL PATHWAYS

Successful implementation of the newer models of client care delivery, especially case management, requires administrative support and development of reliable, user-friendly tools to measure client outcomes. One of the most commonly used tools is the critical pathway (CP, sometimes called clinical pathway). A critical pathway is a "multidisciplinary map" that outlines the expected course of treatment for clients with similar diagnoses. This standardized "map" is designed to describe the course of events that lead to successful client outcome within the diagnostic-related group (DRG) defined time frame. For the client with an uncomplicated myocardial infarction (MI), a proposed course of events leading to successful client outcomes within the 4-day DRG-defined time frame might be as follows (Doenges, Moorhouse, & Geissler, 1997):

◆ State that chest pain is relieved

◆ Have resolution of ST and T wave changes and pulse oximeter reading of greater than 90 percent; have clear breath sounds

◆ Ambulate in hall without experiencing extreme fatigue or chest pain

◆ Verbalize feelings about having an MI and future fears; identify effective coping strategies

◆ Ventricular dysfunction, dysrhythmia, or crackles

The critical pathway is an outgrowth of the nursing care plan. Unlike the traditional nursing care plan, however, critical pathways are developed by representatives of the many disciplines involved in the client's care.

Critical pathways are clinical protocols involving all disciplines. They are designed for tracking a planned clinical course for clients based on average and expected lengths of stay. Financial outcomes can be evaluated from critical pathways by assessing any variances from the proposed length of stay. The agency can then focus on problems within the system that extend the length of stay or drive up costs because of overutilization or repetition of services.

Mr. J. was admitted to the telemetry unit with a diagnosis of MI. He had no previous history of heart disease and no other complicating factors such as diabetes, hypertension, or elevated cholesterol levels. His DRG prescribed length of stay was 4 days. He had an uneventful hospitalization for the first 2 days. On the third day, he complained of pain in the left calf. The calf was slightly reddened and warm to the touch. This condition was diagnosed as thrombophlebitis, which increased his length of hospitalization. A review of the events leading up to the complaints of calf pain by the case manager indicated that, although compression stockings were ordered for Mr. J. by the physician, they never arrived and no one followed through on the order. The variances related to his proposed length of stay were discussed with the team providing care, and measures were instituted to make sure that this oversight did not occur again.

Critical pathways provide a framework for communication and documentation of care. They are also excellent teaching tools through which staff members from various disciplines can learn about the expected care of given client populations and an institution's practice patterns. Critical pathways can be used by an institution to evaluate the cost of care for different client populations (Capuano, 1995; Crummer & Carter, 1993; Lynam, 1994; Flarey, 1995).

Most institutions have adopted a chronologic, diagrammatic format for presenting a critical pathway. Time frames may range from daily (day 1, day 2, day 3) to hourly depending on client needs. Key elements of the critical pathway include discharge planning, patient education, consultations, activities, nutrition, medications, diagnostic tests, and treatment (Crummer & Carter, 1993). Table 4–2 is an example of a critical pathway. Although originally developed for use in acute care institutions, critical pathways can be developed for home care and long-term care settings as well.

The client's nurse is usually responsible for monitoring and recording any deviations from the critical pathway. When deviations occur, the reasons are discussed with all members of the healthcare team, and the appropriate changes in care are made. The nurse must also identify general trends in client outcomes and develop plans to improve the quality of care to reduce the number of deviations in critical pathways. Through this close monitoring, the healthcare team can avoid last-minute surprises that may delay client discharge and can more effectively predict lengths of stay.

■ *Quality Improvement*

In 1951 the Joint Commission on Accreditation of Healthcare Organizations (JCAHO) was established. The focus of its evaluation at that time was on structural measures of quality: the physical plant, number of client beds per nurse, credentialing of service providers, and other standards for each department. Since that time, this system of evaluation has given way to a more process- and outcome-focused model, continuous quality improvement (CQI). To encourage the de-

velopment of innovative methods of care delivery, teamwork, and cost control, the JCAHO incorporates the principles of quality improvement into their accreditation procedures (JCAHO, 1994) (Box 4–1). In

---

Box 4–1 Definitions of dimension of performance

I. Doing the Right Thing
  A. Efficacy
    Did the care or intervention given to the patient accomplish the desired outcome(s)?
  B. Appropriateness
    Was the test, procedure, or service given to the patient relevant to the patient's clinical needs?

II. Doing the Right Thing Well
  A. Availability
    Was the apppropriate care or intervention available to meet the patient's needs?
  B. Timeliness
    Was the care or intervention provided on time or at the most beneficial time?
  C. Effectiveness
    Were interventions provided in the correct manner to achieve the desired outcome?
  D. Continuity
    Was care coordinated among the practitioners, among all services, and over time?
  E. Safety
    Were all risks considered and reduced to minimal for the patient and healthcare providers?
  F. Efficiency
    Was efficiency exercised in use of resources and outcomes achieved?
  G. Respect and Caring
    Was the patient or designee involved in care decisions? Were services provided with respect, sensitivity, and cultural awareness?

Source: Adapted form JCAHO (1994). *Framework for Improving Performance: A Guide for Nurses.* Illinois: JCAHO.)

TABLE 4–2

SAMPLE CP: HEART FAILURE, HOSPITAL. ELOS 4 DAYS CARDIOLOGY OR MEDICAL UNIT

ND and Categories of Care	Day 1 _____	Day 2 _____	Day 3 _____	Day 4 _____
Decreased cardiac output R/T decreased myocardial contractility, altered electrical conduction, structural changes	Goals Participate in actions to reduce cardiac workload	Display VS within acceptable limits; dysrhythmias controlled; pulse oximetry within acceptable range Meet own self-care needs with assist as necessary	→ Dysrhythmias controlled or absent Free of signs of respiratory distress Demonstrate measurable increase in activity tolerance	→ → →
Fluid Volume Excess R/T compromised regulatory mechanism	Verbalize understanding of fluid/food restrictions	Verbalize understanding of general condition and healthcare needs Breath sounds clearing Urinary output adequate Wt loss (reflecting fluid loss)	Plan for lifestyle/ behavior changes Breath sounds clear Balanced I & O Edema resolving	Plan in place to meet post-discharge needs Wt stable (continued loss if edema present)
Referrals	Cardiology Dietitian	Cardiac Rehab Occupational therapist (for ADLs) Social Services Home care	Community Resources	
Diagnostic studies	ECG Echo-Doppler CXR ABGs/Pulse oximetry Cardiac enzymes BUN/Cr CBC, lytes, Mg++ PT/aPTT Liver function studies Serum glucose Albumin Uric Acid Digoxin level (as indi) UA	Echo-Doppler (if not done day 1) or MUGA Cardiac enzymes (if ↑) BUN/Cr Electrolytes PT/aPTT (if on anticoagulants)	CXR BUN/Cr Electrolytes PT/aPTT (as indi) Repeat digoxin level (if indi)	
Additional assessments	Apical pulse, heart/breath sounds q8h Cardiac rhythm (Telemetry) q4h → B/P, P, R q2h til stable, q4h → Temp q8h →	→ q8h →	→ D/C →	bid → →

TABLE 4–2

SAMPLE CP: HEART FAILURE, HOSPITAL. ELOS 4 DAYS CARDIOLOGY OR MEDICAL UNIT (*Continued*)

ND and Categories of Care	Day 1 _____	Day 2 _____	Day 3 _____	Day 4 _____
Additional assessments (*Continued*)	I & O *q8h* →		→	→ D/C
	Weight *q*AM →		→	→
	Peripheral edema *q8h* →		→ bid	→ qd
	Peripheral pulses *q8h* →		→ bid	→ D/C
	Sensorium q8h →		→ bid	→ D/C
	DVT check *qd* →		→	→
	Response to activity →		→	→
	Response to therapeutic interventions →		→	→
Medications Allergies: _____ _____	IV diuretic → po		→	→
	ACE inhibitor →		→	→
	Digoxin →		→	→
	PO/Cutaneous nitrates →		→	→
	Morphine sulfate →		→ D/C	
	Daytime/HS sedation →		→	→ D/C
	PO/low dose anticoagulant →		→ po or D/C	→
	IV/PO potassium →		→ D/C	
	Stool softener/ laxative →		→	→
Patient education	Orient to unit/room	Cardiac education per protocol	Signs/systems to report to healthcare provider	Provide written instructions for homecare
	Review advanced directives	Review medications: Dose, time, route, purpose, side effects	Plan for homecare needs	Schedule for follow-up appointments
	Discuss expected outcomes, diagnostic tests/results	Progressive activity program		
	Fluid/nutritional restrictions/needs	Skin care		
Additional nursing actions	Bed/chair rest	→ BPR/Ambulate as tol, cardiac program	→ Up ad lib/graded program	→
	Assist with physical care →		→	→
	Egg-crate mattress →		→	→ (send home)
	Dysrhythmia/ angina care per protocol →		→	→
	Supplemental O₂ →		→ D/C	
	Cardiac diet →		→	→

Source: Doenges, M.E., Moorhouse, M.F., and Geissler, A.C. (1997). *Nursing Care Plans: Guidelines for Individualizing Patient Care* (ed. 4), pp. 59–60. Philadelphia: F.A. Davis, with permission. CP = critical path; ND = nursing diagnosis; ELOS = estimated length of stay.

simple terms, the JCAHO is concerned that the correct treatment be given (doing the right thing) and that this treatment be given in the most skillful manner possible (doing the right thing well).

ASPECTS OF HEALTH CARE TO EVALUATE

Three different aspects of health care can be evaluated in a quality improvement program: the *structure* within which the care is given, the *process* of giving that care, and the *outcome* of that care. To be comprehensive, an evaluation program must include all three aspects of health care (Brook, Davis, & Kamberg, 1980; Donabedian, 1969, 1977, 1987).

Structure

Structure refers to the *setting* in which the care is given and the *resources* that are available. It is the easiest of the three aspects to measure and yet is still overlooked in some evaluation procedures. The following is a list of some of the structural aspects of a healthcare organization that can be evaluated:

◆ **FACILITIES.** Comfort, convenience of layout, accessibility of support services, safety

◆ **EQUIPMENT.** Adequate supplies, state-of-the-art equipment, staff ability to use it

◆ **STAFF.** Credentials, experience, absenteeism, turnover rate, staff-client ratios

◆ **FINANCES.** Salaries, adequacy, sources

None of these structural factors alone can guarantee that good care will be given, but they are factors that make good care more likely. High nurse-client ratios and low staff absenteeism rates, for example, are structural factors that are generally associated with quality nursing care (Chance, 1980).

A common pitfall in evaluating structural factors, however, has been to neglect the other two aspects, process and outcome. The following example illustrates the problems that occur when only structure is evaluated:

A hospital measured the quality of nursing care given in its eight-bed critical care unit by comparing its staffing ratio with the standard ratio of one nurse to two clients. The inadequacy of this structural measure became apparent during a period when the unit had six (out of a total of eight) clients who each required the care of one nurse. Under the standard that was set, there were only four nurses on duty, which created a severe staff shortage because seven nurses were actually needed to provide adequate care.

Process

Process refers to the actual activities carried out by the healthcare providers. It includes psychosocial interventions, such as teaching and counseling, as well as physical care measures.

There are several ways to collect process data. The most direct way is by observation of caregiving activities. Another is self-report of the caregiver. A third source of data is the chart or record that is kept, called an *audit*.

Whichever source of data is used, some set of objectives is needed as a standard against which to compare the activities. This set of objectives can be very specific, such as listing all the steps in a catheterization procedure, or it can be a very general list of objectives, such as "offer information on breast-feeding to all expectant parents" or "conduct weekly staff meetings."

Outcome

Outcome refers to the results of the activities in which the healthcare providers have been involved. Outcome measures evaluate the effectiveness of these nursing activities by answering such questions as the following: Did the patient recover? Is the family more independent now? Has team functioning improved?

These questions are very general and reflect overall goals of healthcare providers and the organizations in which they work. The outcome questions asked during an actual evaluation should be far more specific and should measure observable behavior, such as the following:

Client: Wound healed
            Blood pressure within nor-
            mal limits
            Infection absent
Family: Increased time between vis-
            its to the emergency de-
            partment
            Applied for food stamps

You can see that some of these outcomes, such as blood pressure or time between emergency department visits, are easier to measure than are other equally important outcomes, such as increased satisfaction or changes in attitude. Although these less tangible outcomes cannot be measured as precisely, it is still important to include them. Omitting them may imply that they are not important (Lynch, 1978).

A major problem in using and interpreting outcome measures in evaluation is that outcomes are influenced by many factors. For example:

> The outcome of client teaching done by a nurse on a home visit is affected by the client's interest and ability to learn, the quality of the teaching materials, the presence or absence of family support, the information given by other caregivers (which may conflict), and the environment in which the teaching is done. If the teaching is successful, can the nurse be given full credit for the success? If it is not successful, who has failed?

You can see that it would be necessary to evaluate the process as well as the outcome to determine why an intervention such as client teaching succeeds or fails. A comprehensive evaluation would include all three aspects: structure, process, and outcome.

CONTINUOUS QUALITY IMPROVEMENT

The purpose of CQI is to continuously improve the capability of everyone involved in providing care, including the organization itself, to provide the highest-quality healthcare.

Employees are empowered to make decisions to improve quality. Education, training, participation at all levels, and empowerment of staff members are keys to CQI success. Improvements are accomplished through the use of quality improvement teams. Their purpose is to identify processes that may be too costly or ineffective in order to change them. With this supporting data, decisions can be made regarding changes needed to improve quality. These teams are composed of representatives from every area involved in the process under study.

CQI relies on collecting information and analyzing it. You may think this is the responsibility of the "number crunchers," not the nurses. In the CQI framework, however, data collection becomes everyone's responsibility. You may be asked to "brainstorm" your ideas with other nurses or members of the interdisciplinary team, complete surveys or check sheets, or even keep a time log of your daily activities for a week or longer. Collecting comprehensive, accurate, and representative data is the first step in relooking at the process. How do you actually administer medications to a group of clients? What steps are involved? Are the medications always available at the right time and in the right dose, or do you have to wait for the pharmacy to bring them to the floor? Is the pharmacy technician delayed by emergency orders that must be processed? Looking at the entire process and actually mapping it out on paper in the form of a flowchart may be part of the CQI process for your organization (Fig. 4–1).

QUALITY IMPROVEMENT AT THE UNIT LEVEL

In this section, we consider how the process of quality improvement works at the unit level, where nursing is often the central focus. For the sake of simplicity, we focus almost exclusively on nursing's effect on client care, although it is generally recommended that quality improvement be interdisciplinary for maximum effectiveness.

Once the policies and procedures for implementing quality improvement projects are defined at the organizational level, much of the responsibility for carrying them out may be delegated to staff members of each unit. At the unit level, the first step is to assign responsibility to various staff members.

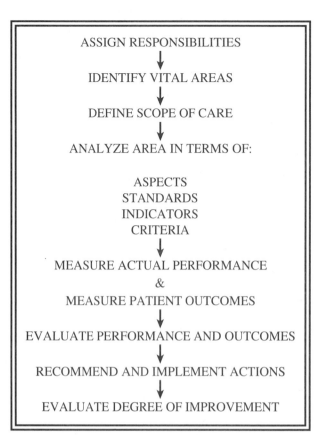

ASSIGN RESPONSIBILITIES

↓

IDENTIFY VITAL AREAS

↓

DEFINE SCOPE OF CARE

↓

ANALYZE AREA IN TERMS OF:

ASPECTS
STANDARDS
INDICATORS
CRITERIA

↓

MEASURE ACTUAL PERFORMANCE
&
MEASURE PATIENT OUTCOMES

↓

EVALUATE PERFORMANCE AND OUTCOMES

↓

RECOMMEND AND IMPLEMENT ACTIONS

↓

EVALUATE DEGREE OF IMPROVEMENT

FIGURE 4–1 Unit level quality improvement process. (Adapted from Hunt, V.D. [1992]. *Quality in America: How to Implement a Competitive Quality Program.* Homewood, IL: Business One, Irwin; and Duquette, A.M. [1991]. Approaches to monitoring practice: Getting started. In Schroeder, P. [Ed.]. *Monitoring and Evaluation in Nursing.* Gaithersburg, Md: Aspen.)

All staff members may be brought together to act as a quality circle, or a representative group may be appointed to a committee to implement quality improvement activities in consultation with the rest of the nursing staff. It is preferable to have as high a level of staff participation as possible, including representation from all three shifts in an inpatient setting.

Once staff members understand the purpose of quality improvement, they can begin to identify areas for study. Staff members may use their own judgment about which areas are in greatest need of evaluation, or they may conduct preliminary surveys to determine the most problem-prone areas. Some guidance from the nurse manager may be needed to select a priority area and to prevent avoidance of a difficult problem or one that is hard to define.

Some broad examples of areas for study might include the highest-risk clients, the most common client problems, or the source of a high number of incident reports (Elrod,

1991). Other, more selectively focused examples might be physical restraint use, dysphagia, ventilator-assisted breathing, respiratory treatments, preoperative teaching, human immunodeficiency virus (HIV)–positive clients, or urinary incontinence. Each of these defines the *scope* of the problem to be evaluated (Duquette, 1991).

Once the scope is defined, the problem itself is further analyzed in terms of its important aspects, the generally accepted standards of care for these aspects, *indicators* (evidence) that these standards have been met, and the *criteria* (threshold) for determining whether they were met (Table 4–3). For example:

Let's say that one area for study chosen by an outpatient clinic staff is patient teaching with newly diagnosed hypertensive clients. Three important aspects of this area of care would be teaching the client about the dis-

TABLE 4–3

EXAMPLE OF QUALITY IMPROVEMENT GUIDELINES

I	II	III	IV	V
SCOPE	ASPECTS OF CARE	STANDARD OF PATIENT CARE	INDICATORS	CRITERIA
Patient teaching: newly diagnosed hypertensives	1. Pharmacological therapy 2. Disease Process 3. Lifestyle Modification	Patient will receive information about: a. alcohol use b. exercise c. smoking d. stress reduction e. dietary modifications	1. Patient describes diet modifications 2. Patient modifies diet as recommended 3. Patient achieves or maintains weight within 10% of ideal weight	50% of patients' weights will be within 10% of ideal weight within six months

ease process, about lifestyle modifications, and about pharmacological treatment (Johannsen, 1993). In regard to one of these, lifestyle modification, the *standard of care* would state, "The client will receive information about exercise, dietary modifications, smoking, alcohol use, and stress reduction." *Indicators* for the dietary modification portion would be that the client can describe the recommended modifications, modifies the diet as recommended, and maintains weight within 10 percent of ideal weight. A *criterion* or *threshold* for this last indicator would be that a least 50 percent of clients would achieve this level within 6 months of the original recommendation (see Table 4–3).

A standard of nursing practice describes what nurses do for or with clients and their families, whereas a nursing standard of care describes the kind of care clients can expect and receive from nurses (JCAHO, 1994).

An *indicator* is an objective, measurable variable of care. The listed indicators are those variables on which data will be collected in a quality improvement project. If data are to be collected on a continuing basis, it is usually referred to as monitoring. The criteria, or threshold, sets a predetermined level of the indicator that will be considered an acceptable level of care (Betta, 1992). For some indicators, such as documenting patient response to a blood infusion, a 100 percent level of achievement is expected. In other cases, such as weight reduction or smoking cessation, a 75 percent level of achievement would be considered excellent.

Once these variables are well defined, a *plan for data collection* is devised. Usually, some type of worksheet is designed to facilitate data collection. For example:

A form (Fig. 4–2) could be devised listing each newly diagnosed hypertensive client, the weight at diagnosis, ideal weight, and weight at subse-

Patient Identification Number	Weight at 1st Visit	Ideal Weight	Difference Ideal vs. Actual Weight	Weight at 2nd Visit	Weight at 3rd Visit	Weight at 4th Visit	Weight at 5th Visit	Weight at Six Months
01723	135	130	5	136	137	135	133	130
01799	210	145	65	205	204	201	199	197
23045	175	165	10	173	175	176	178	180

FIGURE 4–2 Sample quality improvement worksheet for collecting data.

quent clinic visits. A final column for noting whether clients were within 10 percent of ideal weight could be added to indicate how many met the criteria after 6 months.

After data are collected, the staff review the findings and evaluate the degree to which the criteria were met. For example, if only 25 percent of the newly diagnosed hypertensive clients were within 10 percent of their ideal weight in 6 months, the clinic staff might decide to offer weight reduction classes or a support group. They might also decide to invite the clinic psychologist and nutritionist to participate in the group.

A reevaluation of client weights after another 6 months indicating that 50 percent of the clients were now within 10 percent of their ideal weights would be evidence that the group was effective in improving the quality of the client outcomes. As a result, the clinic staff might decide to continue the group but to work on making it even more effective and perhaps seeking other avenues to help the other 50 percent of the clients who had not met their weight reduction goals.

■ Conclusion

Pressure from the JCAHO, consumers of health care, healthcare payors, and healthcare providers has caused the shift in focus in the healthcare system to issues of cost and quality. Experts tell us that quality promotes decreased costs and increased satisfaction. This should be viewed as an opportunity for nursing to increase professionalism and empower nurses to organize and manage client care so that it is safe, efficient, and of the highest quality.

？ Study Questions

1. As a new graduate, how can you assist the case manager on your floor in planning care for your clients?

2. What problems have you identified during your clinical experiences that could be considered issues to be addressed using CQI?

3. How would you begin discussion of these problems with the nurse manager?

4. How would you develop your career goals based on the concepts of differentiated practice discussed in the chapter?

5. Considering today's healthcare climate, discuss the pros and cons of providing nursing care using a primary care model, team model, and client-focused care model.

Critical Thinking Exercise

The director of quality improvement has called a meeting of all the staff members on your floor. Based on last quarter's statistics, the length of stay of clients with uncontrolled diabetes is 2.6 days longer than that of clients for the first half of the year. She has requested that the staff identify members who wish to participate in looking at this problem. You have volunteered to be a member of the quality improvement team. The team will consist of the diabetes educator, a client-focused care assistant, a pharmacist, and you, the staff nurse.

1. Why were these people selected for the team?

2. What data need to be collected to evaluate this situation?

3. What are potential outcomes for clients with uncontrolled diabetes?

4. Develop a flowchart of a typical hospital stay for a client with uncontrolled diabetes.

REFERENCES

Allender, C., Egan, E., & Newman, M. (1995). An instrument for measuring differentiated nursing practice. *Nursing Management, 26*(4), 42–45.

American Nurses Association (ANA). (1988). *Nursing Case Management*. Kansas City, Mo: ANA.

American Organization of Nurse Executives (AONE). (1994). Differentiated competencies for nursing practice. *Nursing Management, 25*(9), 34.

Betta, P.A. (1992). Developing a successful ambulatory QA program. *Nursing Management, 23*(4), 31–33, 47–54.

Brook, R.H., Davis, A.R., & Kamberg, C. (1980). Selected reflections on quality of medical care evaluations in the 1980s. *Nurs Res, 29*(2), 127.

Capuano, T.A. (1995). Clinical pathways. *Nursing Management, 26*(1), 34–37.

Chance, K.S. (1980). The quest for quality: An exploration of attempts to define and measure quality nursing care. *Image, 12*(2), 41.

Christensen, P., & Bender, L. (1994). Models of nursing care in a changing environment: Current challenges and future directions. *Orthopaedic Nursing, 13*(2), 64–70.

Clouten, K., & Weber, R. (1994). Patient-focused care . . . playing to win. *Nursing Management, 25*(2), 34–36.

Crummer, M.B., & Carter, V. (1993). Critical pathways: The pivotal tool. *Cardiovasc Nurs, 7*(4), 30–37.

Curtin, L. (1994). Learning from the future. *Nursing Management, 25* (1), 7–9.

Doenges, M.E., Moorhouse, M.F., and Geissler, A.C. (1997). *Nursing Care Plans: Guidelines for Individualizing Patient Care* (4th ed.) Philadelphia: F.A. Davis.

Donabedian, A. (1969). A guide to medical care administration. In *Medical Care Appraisal: Quality and Utilization* (Vol. II). New York: American Public Health Association.

Donabedian, A. (1977). Evaluating the quality of medical care. *Milbank Memorial Fund Quarterly, 44* (Part 2), 166.

Donabedian, A. (1987). Some basic issues in evaluating the quality of health care. In Rinke, L.T. (Ed.). *Outcome Measures in Home Care.* New York: National League of Nursing.

Duquette, A.M. (1991). Approaches to monitoring practice: Getting started. In Schroeder, P. (Ed.). *Monitoring and Evaluation in Nursing.* Gaithersburg, MD: Aspen.

Elrod, M.E.B. (1991). Quality assurance: Challenges and dilemmas in acute care medical-surgical environments. In Schroeder, P. (Ed.). *Monitoring and Evaluation in Nursing.* Gaithersburg, MD: Aspen.

Flarey, D.L. (1995). *Redesigning Nursing Care Delivery.* Philadelphia: J.B. Lippincott.

Girard, N. (1994). The case management model of patient care delivery. *AORN, 60*(3), 403–415.

Greenberg, L. (1994). Work redesign: An overview. *Journal of Emergency Nursing, 20*(3), 28A–32A.

Hunt, V.D. (1992). *Quality in America: How to Implement a Competitive Quality Program.* Homewood, IL: Business One Irwin.

Johanssen, J.M. (1993). Update: Guidelines for treating hypertension. *Am Nurs, 93*(3), 42–49.

Joint Commission on Accreditation of Healthcare Organizations (JCAHO). (1994). *Framework for Improving Performance: A Guide for Nurses.* Chicago: JCAHO.

Koerner, J., Bunkers, L., Gibson, S., Jones, R., Nelson, B., & Santema, K. (1995). Differentiated practice: The evaluation of a professional practice model for integrated client care services. In Flarey, D.L. Ed. *Redesigning Nursing Care Delivery.* Philadelphia: J.B. Lippincott.

Loveridge, C., & Cummings, S. (1996). *Nursing Management in the New Paradigm.* Gaithersburg, MD: Aspen.

Lynam, L. (1994). Case management and critical pathways: Friend or foe. *Neonatal Network, 13*(8), 48–51.

Lynch, E.A. (1978). Evaluation: Principles and processes. NLN Publication, No. 123, 1721.

Lyon, J.C. (1993). Models of nursing care delivery and case management: Clarification of terms. *Nursing Economics, 11*(3), 163–69.

McClure, M. (1991). In American Academy of Nursing. *Differentiating Nursing Practice.* Kansas City, MO: AAN.

Newell, M. (1996). *Using Nursing Case Management to Improve Health Outcomes.* Gaithersburg, Md.: Aspen.

Nightingale, F., & Barnum, B.S.: *Notes on Nursing: What It Is, and What It Is Not.* Commemorative Edition (1992). Philadelphia: Lippincott-Raven.

Ray, G., & Hardin, S. (1995). Advanced practice nursing. *Nursing Management, 26*(2), 45–47.

Sharp, M. (1994). Every citizen deserves care and every patient deserves a nurse. *Nursing Management, 25*(9), 32–33.

Vena, C., & Oldaker, S. (1994). Differentiated practice: The new paradigm using a theoretical approach. *Nursing Administration Quarterly, 19*(1), 66–73.

CHAPTER 5

Time Management

OBJECTIVES   *After reading this chapter, the student will be able to:*

- Describe his or her perception of time.
- Set short-term and long-term personal career goals.
- Analyze activities at work using a time log.
- Organize work to make more effective use of available time.
- Set limits on the demands made on one's time.

Coming onto the unit, Sofia, the evening charge nurse, already knew that a hectic day was in progress. Scattered throughout the unit were clues from the past 8 hours. Two clients on emergency department stretchers were parked outside observation rooms already occupied by clients admitted yesterday in critical condition. Stationed in the middle of the hall was the code cart, drawers opened and electrocardiograph paper cascading down the sides. Approaching the nurses' station, Sofia found Daniel buried deep in paperwork. He glanced at her with a face that had exhaustion written all over it. His first words were, "Three of your RNs called in sick. I called staffing for additional help, but only one is available. Good luck!"

Sofia surveyed the unit, looked at the number of staff members available, and reviewed the client acuity level of the unit. She decided not to let the situation upset her. She would take charge of her own time and reallocate the time of her staff. She began to mentally reorganize her staff and alter the responsibilities of each member. Having taken steps to handle the problem, Sofia felt ready to begin the shift.

In today's fast-paced healthcare environment, time management skills are critical to a nurse's success. Learning to take charge of your time is the key to time management (Gonzalez, 1996).

Many nurses feel that they never seem to have enough time to accomplish the tasks that need to be completed. Like the White Rabbit in *Alice in Wonderland*, they are constantly in a rush against time.

■ *The Tyranny of Time*

How often do you look at your watch during the day? Do you divide your day into blocks of time? Do you steal a quick glance at the clock when you come home after putting in a full day's work? Do you mentally calculate the amount of time left to complete the day's tasks of grocery shopping, driving in a car pool, making dinner, and leaving again to take a class or attend a meeting? In our society, calendars, clocks, watches, newspapers, television, and radio all remind us of our position in time. Our perception of time is important because it affects our use of time and our response to time (Box 5–1).

Box 5–1 Time perception

Webber (1980) has collected a number of interesting tests of people's perception of time. You may want to try several of these:

● Do you think of time more as a galloping horseman or a vast motionless ocean?

● Which of these words best describes time to you: sharp, active, empty, soothing, tense, cold, deep, clear, young, or sad?

● Is your watch fast or slow? (You can check it with the radio.)

● Ask a friend to help you with this test. Go into a quiet room without any work, reading material, radio, food, or other distractions. Have your friend call you after 10 to 20 minutes have elapsed. Try to guess how long you were in that room.

Webber test results interpreted. A person who has a circular concept of time would compare it to a vast, still ocean. A galloping horseman would be characteristic of a linear conception of time, emphasizing speed and motion forward. A fast-tempo, achievement-oriented person would describe time as clear, young, sharp, active, or tense rather than empty, soothing, sad, cold, or deep. These same fast-tempo people are likely to have fast watches and to overestimate the amount of time that they sat in a quiet room (Webber, 1980).

Source: Adapted from Webber, R.A. (1980). *Time is Money! Tested Tactics that Conserve Time for Top Executives.* New York: Free Press.

Computers complete operations in a fraction of a second, and we can measure speeds to the nanosecond. Timeclocks that record the minute we enter and leave work are commonplace, and few excuses for being late are really considered acceptable. Time sheets and schedules are part of most healthcare givers' lives. We are expected to follow precisely set schedules and meet deadlines for virtually everything we do, from distributing medications to getting reports done on time. Many agencies produce vast quantities of computer-generated data that can be analyzed in terms of the amount of time spent on various activities. It is no wonder some of us seem obsessed with time.

Individual personality, culture, and environment all interact to influence our perceptions of time (Matejka & Dunsing, 1988). Each of us has an internal tempo (Chappel, 1970). Some internal tempos may be quicker than others. Environment also affects the way we respond to time. A fast-paced environment influences most of us to work at a faster pace despite our internal tempo. For those individuals with a slower tempo, this pace can cause discomfort. If you are a high-achievement-oriented person, you are likely to have already set some career goals for yourself and to have a mental schedule of deadlines for reaching these goals ("go on to complete my BSN in 4 years; an MSN in 6 years").

Many healthcare professionals are linear, fast-tempo, achievement-oriented people. Simply working at a fast pace, however, is not necessarily equivalent to achieving a great deal. Much energy can be wasted in rushing around, stirring things up but actually accomplishing very little. The rest of this chapter looks at ways in which you can use your time and energy wisely to accomplish your goals.

■ *How Do Nurses Spend Their Time?*

• • • • • • • • • • • • • • • • • • • •

Nurses are the largest group of healthcare professionals. Because of the number of nurses and the shift variations, attention concerning the efficiency and effectiveness of their time management is needed. The effect of rotating shifts has long been a concern in nursing. Nurses who rotate shifts are twice as likely to report medication errors than those who do not rotate. Night shift staff members and rotating shift staff members also report getting less sleep, a poorer quality of sleep, greater use of sleep medication, and a problem with nodding off at work or while driving home after work (Am J Nurs, 1993).

> A new graduate worked the 7 AM to 3 PM shift and rotated every third week to the 11 PM to 7 AM shift in a medical intensive care unit, working 7 days straight before getting 2 days off. It was not difficult to remain awake during the entire shift the first night on duty, but each night thereafter, staying awake became increasingly more difficult. After the 2 AM vital signs were taken and recorded, the new graduate inevitably fell asleep at the nurses' station. He was so tired that it was necessary to check and recheck client medications and other procedures for fear of making a fatal error. He became so anxious over the possibility of injuring someone that sleep during the day became impossible. Because of his obsession with going over his work, he had difficulty completing tasks and was always behind at the end of the shift (of course, napping didn't help his time management).

There have been a number of studies on how nurses use their time, especially nurses in acute-care settings. For example, a study by Arthur Andersen found that only 35 percent of nursing time is spent in direct client care (including care planning, assessment teaching, and technical activities). Documentation accounts for another 20 percent of nursing time. The remainder of time is spent on transporting clients, transaction processing, administrative responsibilities, and "hotel services" (in Brider, 1992) (Fig. 5–1). Categories may change from study to study, but the amount of time spent on direct client care is usually less than half of the workday. As hospitals continue to re-engineer, downsize, and cross-train personnel, nurses are finding themselves more in-

Record your activities every half hour as accurately as possible, including time spent thinking, planning, stalling, daydreaming, worrying, talking, socializing, delegating, negotiating, networking, and so forth. Continue the log until a pattern emerges. Repeat after 6 months.

Daily Time Log

Activities	Comments
6:30	
7:00	
7:30	
8:00	
8:30	
9:00	
9:30	
10:00	
10:30	
11:00	
11:30	
12:00	
12:30	
1:00	
1:30	
2:00	
2:30	
3:00	
3:30	
4:00	
4:30	
5:00	

FIGURE 5–1 Time log. (Adapted from Robichaud, A.M. [1986]. Time documentation of clinical nurse specialist activities. *J Nurs Adm, 16[1]*, 31–36.

volved with tasks that are not client-related, such as quality improvement, developing critical pathways, and so forth. These are added to their already existing client care functions. The result in some cases is that nurses are able to meet only the highest-priority client needs.

Any change in the distribution of time spent on various activities can have a considerable impact on client care and on the organization's bottom line. Prescott (1991)

offers the following example of this: If more unit management responsibilities could be shifted from nurses to non-nursing personnel, about 48 minutes per nurse shift could be redirected to client care. In a large hospital with 600 full-time nurses, the result would be an additional 307 hours of direct client care a day. Calculating the results of this timesaving strategy in another way shows an even greater impact: the changes would contribute the equivalent of the work of 48 additional full-time nurses to direct client care. Many healthcare institutions are presently looking at integrating units with similar patient populations and having them managed by a non-nurse manager, someone with business and management expertise, not necessarily nursing skills.

■ *Organizing Your Work*

SETTING YOUR OWN GOALS

How can you get somewhere if you do not know where you want to go? It is important to explore your own personal and career goals. This can help you make decisions about the future. This concept can be applied to day-to-day activities as well as help in career decisions. Ask yourself questions about what you want to accomplish over a particular time period.

Short-term goals are those that you wish to accomplish within the near future. Setting up your day in an organized fashion is a short-term goal. Scheduling a required AIDS course is a short-term goal.

Long-term goals are those you wish to complete over a long period of time. Advanced education and career goals are examples. A good question to ask yourself is, "What do I see myself doing 5 years from now?" Every choice you make requires a different allocation of time (Moshovitz, 1993).

Eleanor, a licensed practical nurse returning to school to obtain her associate degree in nursing, was faced with a multitude of responsibilities. A wife, a mother of two toddlers, and a full-time staff member at a local hospital, Eleanor suddenly found herself in a situation in which there were just not enough hours in a day. She became convinced that becoming a registered nurse was an unobtainable goal. When asked where she wanted to be in 5 years, she answered, "At this moment, I think, on an island in Tahiti!"

Several of her instructors helped Eleanor develop a time plan. First, she was asked to list what she did each day and how much time each task required. This list included basic child care, driving children to and from day care, shopping, cooking meals, cleaning, hours spent in the classroom, study hours, work hours, and time devoted to leisure. Once this was established, she was asked which tasks could be allocated to someone else (e.g., her husband), which tasks could be clustered (e.g., cooking for several days at a time), and which tasks could be shared. Eleanor's husband was willing to assist with car pools, grocery shopping, and cleaning. Eleanor had never asked him for help before. Cooking meals was clustered so that all meals for the week were made in 1 day, frozen, and labeled to be used later. This left time for other activities.

Eleanor graduated at the top of her class and has subsequently completed her BSN and become a clinical preceptor for other associate degree students on a pediatric unit in a county hospital. She never did get to Tahiti, though.

Organizing your work can eliminate extra steps or serious delays in completing your work. It can also reduce the amount of time spent doing things that are neither productive nor satisfying.

LISTS

One of the most useful organizers is the "things-to-do list." You can make this list either at the end of every day or at the beginning of each day before you do anything else. Some people say they do it at the end of the day because something always interferes at the beginning of the next day. Do not include the routine tasks because they will make the list too long and you will do them without the extra reminder. If you are a team leader, place the unique tasks of the day on the list: team conference, telephone calls to families, discussion of a new project, or an in-service demonstration on that new piece of equipment. You may also want to arrange these things to do in order of their priority, starting with those that must be done on that day.

Ask yourself the following questions regarding the tasks on the list (Moshovitz, 1993):

♦ What is the relative importance of each of these tasks?

♦ How much time will each task require?

♦ When must each task be completed?

♦ How much time and energy do you have to devote to these tasks?

If you find yourself postponing an item for several days, decide whether it should be given top priority the next day or dropped from the list as an unnecessary task.

The list itself should be in a user-friendly form: on your electronic organizer, in your pocket, or on a clipboard. Checking the list several times a day quickly becomes a good habit. Your daily things-to-do list may become your most important time manager.

TICKLER FILES

Tickler files might be called long-term lists. The basic principle of a tickler file is that you create a system to remind yourself of approaching deadlines and due dates.

> At the beginning of the semester, students are told the examination dates and when papers will be due. Many students find it helpful to enter the dates on a semester-long calendar so that they can be seen at a glance. Then the students can see when clusters of assignments are due at the same time. This allows for advance planning or perhaps requests to change dates or get extensions.

SCHEDULES AND BLOCKS OF TIME

Without some form of a schedule, you are more likely to drift through a day or bounce from one activity to another in a disorganized fashion. Assignment sheets, worksheets, flow sheets, and critical pathways are all designed to help you plan client care and schedule your time effectively. The critical pathway is a guide to recommended treatments and optimal client outcomes (see Chap. 4). Assignment sheets indicate the clients for whom each staff member is responsible. Worksheets are then created to organize the daily care that must be given to the assigned clients (see Chaps. 2 and 4 for examples of worksheets). Flow sheets are lists of items that must be recorded for each client.

Effective worksheets and flow sheets schedule and organize the day. They provide reminders of the various tasks and when they need to be done. The danger in them, however, is that the more they divide the day into discrete segments, the more they fragment the work and discourage a holistic approach. If the worksheet becomes the focus of attention, the perspective of the whole and of the individuals who are our clients may be lost.

Some activities must be done at a certain time. These structure the day or week to a great extent, and their timing may be out of your control. However, in every job there are tasks that can be done whenever you want to do them, as long as they are done on time.

In certain nursing jobs, reports and presentations are often required. For these activities, you may need to set aside blocks of time during which you can concentrate on the task. Trying to create and complete a report in 5- or 10-minute blocks of time is unrealistic. By the time you reorient yourself to the project, the time allotted is over and nothing has been accomplished. Setting aside large blocks of time to do complex tasks is much more efficient.

Consider your energy levels when beginning a big task. Start when levels are high, not at 4:00 in the afternoon if that is when you find yourself winding down.

Some people go to work early to have a block of uninterrupted time. Others take work home with them for the same reason. This extends the workday and cuts into leisure time. The higher your stress level, the less effective you will be on the job—so don't bring your work home with you. You need some time off to recharge your batteries (Turkington, 1996).

FILING SYSTEMS

Filing systems are helpful to keep track of important papers. Every professional needs to maintain copies of licenses, certification, continuing education credits, and current information about their specialty area. Keeping these organized in an easily retrievable system saves time and energy when you need to refer to them. Using color-coded folders is often helpful. Each color holds documents that are related to one another. For example, all continuing education credits would be placed in a blue folder, anything pertaining to licensure in a yellow folder, and so on.

■ *Setting Limits*
• • • • • • • • • • • • • • • • • • • •

To set limits, it is necessary first to identify your objectives and arrange the actions needed to meet them in order of their priority (Haynes, 1991). It is also important to stick to these objectives, which can require considerable determination.

SAYING NO

Saying no to low-priority demands on your time is an important but difficult part of setting limits. Assertiveness and determination are necessary for effective time management. Learn to tactfully say no at least once a day (Hammerschmidt & Meador, 1993).

Is it possible to say no to your supervisor or manager? It may not seem so at first, but actually many requests are negotiable. Sometimes requests are in conflict with career goals. Rather than sit on a committee in which you have no interest, respectfully decline and volunteer for one that holds promise for you as well as meeting the needs of your particular unit.

Can you refuse an assignment? Your manager may ask you to work overtime or to come in on your scheduled day off, but you can refuse. You may not refuse to care for a group of clients or take a report because you feel the assignment is too difficult or unsafe. You may, however, discuss the situation with your supervisor and together work out alternatives. You can also confront the issue of understaffing by filing an unsafe staffing complaint (see Appendix 4). Failure to accept an assignment may result in accusations of abandonment.

Some people have difficulty saying no.

Ambition keeps some people from declining any opportunity, no matter how overloaded they are. Others are afraid of displeasing others and therefore feel obligated to continuously take on all forms of additional assignments. Still others have such a great need to be needed that they continually give of themselves, not only to clients but also to their coworkers and supervisors, without replenishing themselves, until they are exhausted.

Remember, no one can be all things to all people at all times without creating serious guilt, anger, bitterness, and disillusionment. "Anyone who says it's possible has never tried it" (Turkington, 1996, p. 9).

ELIMINATING UNNECESSARY WORK

Some work has become so deeply embedded in our routines that it appears essential, although it is really unnecessary. Some nursing routines fall into this category. Taking vital signs, baths, linen changes, dressing changes, irrigations, and similar basic tasks are more often done according to schedule rather than according to client need, which may be much more or much less often than the routine specifies.

- ◆ If clients are ambulatory, bed linens may not need to be changed daily. Incontinent and diaphoretic clients need to have fresh linens more frequently. Not all clients need a complete bed bath every day. Elderly clients have dry, fragile skin; giving them good mouth, facial, and perineal care may be all that is required on certain days. This should be included in the client's plan of care.

- ◆ Much paperwork is duplicative; some is altogether unnecessary. Is it necessary to chart nursing interventions in two or three places on the client record? The use of charting by exception, flow sheets, and computerized records are attempts to eliminate some of these problems.

- ◆ Socialization in the workplace is an important aspect in maintaining interpersonal relationships. When there is a social component to interactions in a group, the result is usually positive.

However, too much socialization can reduce productivity in the workplace, so judgment must be used in deciding when socializing is interfering with work.

You may create additional work for yourself without realizing it. How often do you walk back down the hall to obtain equipment when it all could have been gathered at one time? How many times do you walk to a client's room instead of using the intercom, only to find out you need to go back to where you were to get what the client needs? Is the staff providing personal care to clients who are well enough to meet some of these needs themselves?

■ *Streamlining Your Work*

• • • • • • • • • • • • • • • • • • •

Many tasks can be neither eliminated nor delegated, but they can be done more efficiently. There are many sayings in time management that reflect the principle of streamlining work. "Work smarter, not harder" is a favorite one that should appeal to nurses facing increasing demands on time. "Never handle a piece of paper more than once" is a more specific one reflecting the need to avoid procrastination in your work. "A stitch in time saves nine" reflects the degree to which preventive action saves time in the long run.

Several methods of working smarter and not harder are:

◆ Gathering materials, such as bed linens, for all of your clients at one time. As you go to each room, leave the linen so that it will be there when you need it.

◆ While giving a bed bath or personal care, perform some of the aspects of the physical assessment, such as taking vital signs, skin assessment, and parts of the neurological and musculoskeletal assessment. Prevention is always a good idea.

◆ If a client does not "look right," do not ignore your instincts. The client is probably having a problem.

◆ If you are not sure about a treatment or medication, ask before you proceed. It is usually less time-consuming to prevent a problem than it is to resolve one.

◆ When you set aside time to do a specific task that has a high priority, stick to your schedule and complete it.

◆ Do not allow yourself to be interrupted while completing paperwork such as transcribing orders.

How else can you streamline your work? A few general suggestions follow, but the first one, a time log, can assist you in developing others unique to your particular job. If you complete the log correctly, a few surprises about how you really spend your time are almost guaranteed.

KEEPING A TIME LOG

Our perception of time is elastic. People do not accurately estimate the time they spend on any particular task, so we cannot rely on our memories for accurate information about how we have been spending our time. The time log is an objective source of information. Most people spend a much smaller amount of their time on productive activities than they estimate. Once you see how large amounts of your time are spent, you will be able to eliminate or reduce the time spent on nonproductive or minimally productive activities (Drucker, 1967; Robichaud, 1986). For example, many nurses spend a great deal of time searching for or waiting for missing medications, equipment, or supplies. Before beginning client care, assemble all of the equipment and supplies you will need, and check the client's medication drawer against the medication administration record so that you can order anything that is missing before you begin.

Figure 5–1 (see p. 70) is an example of a time log in which you enter your activities every half hour. This means that you will have to pay careful attention to what you are doing so that you can record it accurately. Do not postpone the recording; do it every 30 minutes. A 3-day sample may be enough for you to see a pattern emerging. It is suggested that you repeat the process again in 6 months, both because work situations change and to see if you have made any long-lasting changes in your use of time.

REDUCING INTERRUPTIONS

Everyone experiences interruptions. Some of these are welcome and necessary, but too many interfere with your work. Interruptions must be kept to a minimum or eliminated if possible. Closing the door to a client's room may reduce interruptions. You may have to ask visitors to wait a few minutes before you can answer their questions, although you must remain sensitive to their needs and return to them as soon as possible.

There is nothing wrong with asking a colleague who wants your assistance to wait a few minutes if you are engaged in another activity. Interruptions that occur when you are trying to pour medications or make calculations can cause errors. Often physicians and other professionals request nursing attention when nurses are involved with client care tasks. Find out if a nonlicensed person may be of assistance. If not, ask the physician to wait, stating that you will be more than glad to help as soon as you complete what you are doing. Be courteous, but be firm; you are busy also.

CATEGORIZING ACTIVITIES

Clustering certain activities helps eliminate the feeling of bouncing from one unrelated task to another. It also makes your caregiving more holistic. You may, for example, find that documentation takes less time if you do it while you are still with the client or immediately after seeing a client. The information is still fresh in your mind, and you do not have to rely on notes or recall. Try to follow a task through to completion before beginning another.

FINDING THE FASTEST WAY

Many time-consuming tasks may be made more efficient by the use of automation. Narcotic delivery systems that deliver the correct dose and electronically record the dose, the name of the client, and the name of the healthcare personnel removing the medication are being used in many institutions. This system saves staff time in documentation and in performing a narcotic count at the end of each shift (Meyer, 1992).

Efficient systems do not have to be complex. Using a preprinted color-coded sticker system helps in identifying clients who must be without food or fluids (NPO) for tests or surgery, those having 24-hour urine collections, or those having special cultures done. The information need not be written or entered repeatedly if stickers are used.

AUTOMATING REPETITIVE TASKS

Developing techniques for repetitive tasks is similar to finding the fastest method, but it focuses on specific tasks that are repeated again and again, such as client teaching.

Many clients come to the hospital or ambulatory center for surgery or invasive diagnostic tests for same-day treatment. This does not give nurses much teaching time. Using videotapes and pamphlets as teaching aids can reduce the time needed to share the information, allowing the nurse to be available to answer individual questions and create individual adaptations. Many facilities are using these techniques for cardiac rehabilitation, preoperative teaching, and infant-care instruction.

■ *Conclusion*

Time can be our best friend or our worst enemy, depending on our perspective and how we manage it. It is important to identify how you feel about time and to assess your own time management skills. Nursing requires us to perform numerous activities within what often seems to be a very short period of time. Knowing this can create stress. Learn to delegate. Learn to say, "I would really like to help you; can it wait until I finish this?" Learn to say no. Most of all, learn how to make the most of your day. Finally, remember that 8 hours should be designated as sleep time and several more as personal or leisure ("time off") time.

? *Study Questions*

1. Create your own client care worksheet. How does this worksheet help you organize your clinical day?

2. Keep a log of your clinical day. Which activities took the most amount of time and why? Which activities took the least amount of time? What situations interfered with your work? What could you do to reduce the interference?

3. Identify a task that is done again and again in your clinical area. Invent a new, more efficient way to do that task. How could you implement this new routine? How could you evaluate its efficiency?

Critical Thinking Exercise

Antonio was recently hired as a team leader for a busy cardiac step-down unit. Nursing responsibilities of the team leader in addition to client care include meeting daily with team members, reviewing all admissions and discharges for acuity and length of stay, and documentation of all clients who exceeded length of stay and the reasons. At the end of each month, the team leaders are required to meet with unit managers to review the client care load and team member performance. This is the last week of the month, and Antonio has a meeting with the unit manager at the end of the week. He is 2 weeks behind on staff evaluations and documentation of clients who exceeded length of stay. He is becoming very stressed over his team leader responsibilities.

1. Why do you think Antonio is feeling stressed?

2. Make a "things-to-do list" for Antonio.

3. Develop a time log for Antonio to use to analyze his activities.

4. How can Antonio organize and streamline his work?

REFERENCES

Brider, P. (1992). The move to patient-focused care. *Am J Nurs, 92*(9), 27–33.

Chappel, E.D. (1970). *Culture and Biological Man: Exploration in Behavioral Anthropology.* New York: Holt, Rhinehart, & Winston. (Reprinted as *The Biological Foundations of Individuality and Culture.* Huntingdon, NY: Robert Krieger, 1979.)

Drucker, P.F. (1967). *The Effective Executive.* New York: Harper & Row.

Gonzalez, S.I. (1996). "Time management." *The Nursing Spectrum in Florida, 6*(17), 5.

Hammerschmidt, R., & Meador, C.K. (1993). *A Little Book of Nurses' Rules.* Philadelphia: Hanley & Belfus.

Haynes, M.E. (1991). *Practical Time Management.* Los Altos, CA: Crisp Publications.

Matejka, J.K., & Dunsing, R.J. (1988). Time management: Changing some traditions. *Management World, 17*(2), 6–7.

Meyer, C. (1992). Equipment nurses like. *Am J Nurs, 92*(8), 32–38.

Moshovitz, R. (1993). *How to Organize Your Work and Your Life.* New York: Doubleday.

Prescott, P.A. (1991). Changing how nurses spend their time. *Image, 23*(1), 23–28.

Robichaud, A.M. (1986). Time documentation of clinical nurse specialist activities. *J Nurs Adm, 16*(1), 31–36.

Sleeping on the job. (1993). *Am J Nurs, 93*(2), 10.

Turkington, C.A. (1996). *Reflections for Working Women: Common Sense, Sage Advice, and Unconventional Wisdom.* New York: McGraw-Hill.

Webber, R.A. (1980). *Time Is Money! Tested Tactics that Conserve Time for Top Executives.* New York: Free Press.

CHAPTER 6

Organizations, Power, and Empowerment

OBJECTIVES   *After reading this chapter, the student will be able to:*

◆ Recognize the major identifying characteristics of a given healthcare organization.

◆ Define power and empowerment.

◆ Identify sources of power in a healthcare organization.

◆ Describe several ways in which nurses can be empowered.

The subjects of this chapter, organizations, power, and empowerment, are not as remote from everyday experience as you may first think. Consider the following scenarios, which are discussed later in the chapter:

Scenario 1

In school, Hazel Rivera had always received high praise for the quality of her nursing care plans. "Thorough, comprehensive, systematic, holistic —beautiful!" was the comment she received on the last one she wrote before graduation.

Now Hazel is a staff nurse on a busy orthopedic surgery unit. Although her time to write comprehensive care plans during the day is limited, Hazel often stays after work to complete them. Her friend Carla refuses to stay late with her. "If I can't complete my work during the shift, then they have given me too much to do," she explains.

At the end of their 3-month probationary period, Hazel and Carla received written evaluations of their progress and comments about their value to the organization. To Hazel's surprise, her friend Carla received a higher rating than she did. What happened?

Scenario 2

The nursing staff of the critical care department of a large urban hospital had formed a research utilization group about a year ago. They had made a number of changes in their practice based on reviews of the research on several different procedures and were quite pleased with the results.

"Let's look at the bigger picture next month," their nurse manager suggested at one of their meetings. "This time, let's look at the research on different models of client care. We might get some good ideas for our unit." The staff nurses agreed. It would be a nice change to look at the way they organized client care in their department. The nurse manager found a wealth of information on different models for organizing nursing care. One research study about a model for caring for the chronically critically ill (Rudy et al., 1995) particularly interested them because they had many clients in that category.

Several nurses volunteered to form an ad hoc committee to design a similar unit for the chronically critically ill within their critical care department. When the plan was presented, both the nurse manager and the staff thought it was excellent. The nurse manager offered to present the plan to the vice president for nursing. The staff eagerly awaited the vice president's response.

The nurse manager returned with discouraging news. The vice president did not support their concept and said that, although they were free to continue developing the idea, they should not assume that it would ever be implemented. What happened?

Were the disappointments experienced by Hazel Rivera and the staff of the critical care department predictable? Could they have been avoided? Without a basic understanding of the organizations within which we work and of the part that power plays in the decision-making processes that occur within healthcare institutions, we are doomed to be continually surprised by the responses to our well-intentioned efforts. As you read this chapter, you will find out why Hazel Rivera and the staff of the critical care department were disappointed.

We begin by looking at some of the characteristics of the organizations in which nurses work and how they operate. Then we zero in on the subject of power within organizations: what it is, how one obtains it, and how nurses can be empowered.

■ *Understanding Organizations*

• • • • • • • • • • • • • • • • •

One of the attractive features of nursing as a career is the wide variety of settings in which nurses work. From rural migrant health clinics to organ transplant units, nurses' skills are needed wherever there are concerns about people's health. Relationships with clients may extend for months or years, as they do in school health or in nursing homes, or they may be brief and never repeated, as often happens in doctors' offices, clinics, and emergency department.

TYPES OF HEALTHCARE ORGANIZATIONS

Although some nurses work as consultants, as independent practitioners, or in the corporate world, the majority are employed by healthcare organizations. These organizations can be classified into three types on the basis of their origin and financial structure:

◆ **PRIVATE NOT-FOR-PROFIT.** Many healthcare organizations were founded by charitable or religious groups and have been in existence for generations. These include many of our hospitals, nursing homes, and home care services.

◆ **PUBLICLY SUPPORTED.** Government-operated service organizations range from county public health departments to complex medical centers such as those operated by the Veterans Administration, a federal agency.

◆ **PRIVATE FOR-PROFIT.** Increasing numbers of healthcare organizations are operated for profit like any other business. These include large hospital and nursing home chains, HMOs (health maintenance organizations), and many free-standing centers providing special services such as surgical, nutritional counseling, or biofeedback centers.

The differences between these categories have become blurred in recent years for a number of reasons:

◆ All compete for clients, especially those with health care insurance or the ability to pay their own health care bills.

◆ All are feeling the effect of cost constraints.

◆ All may be eligible for government funds, particularly Medicaid and Medicare funding, if they meet government standards and provide eligible services.

ORGANIZATIONAL CLIMATE

Because of their size and complexity, healthcare organizations are often difficult to understand. One way to begin to understand them is to find a colorful image or metaphor that sums up their characteristics in a few well-chosen words. Morgan (1993) suggests using animals or other familiar images to describe an organization. For example, an aggressive organization that crushes its competitors could be likened to a bull elephant, whereas a timid organization in danger of being crushed by that bull elephant could be described as a mouse. In the same way, an organization adrift without a clear idea of its future could be described as a rudderless boat on a becalmed sea, whereas an organization with its sights set clearly on exterminating its competition could be described as a guided missile.

Organizations differ a great deal. Some are very traditional, preserving their customary ways of doing things even when they no longer work well. Others are very progressive, eternally chasing the newest management fad or buying the very latest imaging equipment. Some seem to be warm, friendly, and open to new people and new ideas. Others are cold, defensive, and indifferent or even hostile to the outside world (Tappen, 1995). These very different organizational climates have a considerable effect on the employees and the people served by the organization. The climate shapes people's behavior, especially their responses to each other, a very important factor in health care.

To find out what the climate of an organization is when you are seeking a new position or trying to familiarize yourself with your new workplace, you can ask people who work there or have considerable acquaintance with the organization to describe it in just a few words.

Once you have grasped the totality of an organization in terms of its overall climate, you are ready to analyze it in a little more detail. This involves identification of the organization's structure, processes, and goals.

STRUCTURE

Virtually all healthcare organizations have a hierarchical structure of some kind. In a *traditional hierarchical structure*, employees are ranked from the top to the bottom as if they were on the various steps of a ladder (Fig. 6–1). The number of people on the bottom rungs of the ladder is usually much greater than the number at the top. The president or chief executive officer (CEO) is usually at the top of this ladder; the maintenance crew is usually at the bottom. Nurses fall somewhere in the middle of most healthcare organizations, higher than the cleaning people, aides, and technicians but lower than physicians and administrators.

The people at the top of the ladder have authority to issue orders, spend the organization's money, and hire and fire people. Much of this authority is delegated to people below them, but they retain the right to reverse a decision or regain control of these activities.

The people at the bottom have little authority but are responsible for carrying out the directions from people above them on the ladder. The people at the bottom are not entirely without power or the ability to influence people higher up on the ladder, however. Without the people at the bottom of the ladder, the organization could not function. If there was no one at the bottom, the work of the organization would not get done.

There is much interest in restructuring organizations, not only to save money but also to make the best use of an organization's most valuable resource, its people. This begins with hiring the right people and providing them with the resources they need to function. In addition, it requires the kind of leadership that can inspire the staff and unleash their creativity (Rosen, 1996).

More *innovative* organizations have adapted a more *organic structure* that is looser, more flexible, and less centralized than the traditional hierarchical structure. In these organically structured organizations, decisions are made by the people who will implement them, not by their bosses or by their bosses' boss. More and more people recognize that organizations need to be not only efficient but also adaptable and innovative. Organizations need to be prepared for uncertainty, for rapid changes in their environment, and for rapid, creative responses to these challenges. In addition, they need to provide an internal climate that not only allows but also motivates employees to work to the best of their ability.

The organic network emphasizes increased flexibility of the organizational structure, decentralized decision making, and autonomy for working groups or teams. Rigid department or unit structures are reorganized into autonomous teams composed of professionals from different departments

CEO

Administrators

Managers

Staff nurses

Technicians
(including LPNs)

Aides
Housekeeping
Maintenance

FIGURE 6–1 The organizational ladder.

and disciplines. Each team is given a specific task or function to carry out (common examples would be a hospital infection control team or a child protection team in a community agency). These teams themselves are responsible for their own self-correction and self-control, although they may also have a designated leader. Together, team members make decisions about work assignments and how to deal with any problems that arise. In other words, the teams supervise and manage themselves.

Supervisors, administrators, and support staff have different functions in an organic network. Instead of spending their time observing and controlling other people's work, they become planners and resource people. They are responsible for providing the conditions required for the optimal functioning of the teams and are expected to ensure that the support, information, materials, and budgeted funds needed to do the job well are available to the teams. They also provide more coordination between the teams so that the teams are cooperating rather than blocking each other, working toward congruent goals, and not duplicating effort.

Very large organizations can be separated into functional divisions that operate as if they were smaller, independent organizations. This reduces complexity and allows each division to be better integrated when the integration of the entire organization as a whole becomes virtually impossible because of its great size, complexity, and diversity. However, communication among divisions can become more difficult.

Organic networks have been compared to spider plants with their central cluster and offshoots (Morgan, 1993) (Fig. 6–2). Each cluster could represent a discipline (e.g., nursing, social work, occupational therapy) or a service (e.g., psychiatry, orthopedics). Staff members may move from one cluster to another or the entire configuration of interconnected clusters may be reorganized as the organization shapes and is shaped by the environment. People with a great need for control are often uncomfortable with the organic network design.

GOALS

Try answering this true-or-false question: the goal of any healthcare organization is to keep people healthy, restore them to health, or assist them in dying as comfortably as possible. Answer: the previous statement is only partially correct. Most healthcare organizations have several goals, some more immediately apparent than others.

What other goals could a healthcare organization possibly have? The following are some examples:

◆ **SURVIVAL.** Organizations have to maintain their own existence, a goal that is threatened when, for example, the or-

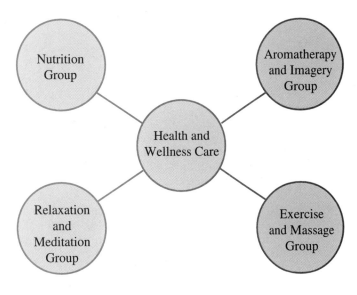

FIGURE 6–2 An organic organizational structure for a nontraditional healthcare center. (Based on Morgan, A. [1993]. *Imaginization: The Art of Creative Management*. Newbury Park, Calif: Sage.)

ganization fails to meet the Joint Commission on Accreditation of Healthcare Organization's standards or is unable to collect money owed by its clients.

- **GROWTH.** The CEOs of many organizations also want to help their organizations grow by expanding into new territories, adding new services, and bringing in new clients.

- **PROFIT.** For-profit organizations are expected to return some profit to their owners. Not-for-profit organizations at least have to pay their bills and avoid getting into too much debt. Even this is sometimes difficult for an organization.

- **STATUS.** The leaders or owners of many healthcare organizations also want to be known as the best in their field, for example, having the most active obstetric service, having "top-notch" doctors, or providing the best nursing care in town.

- **DOMINANCE.** Some organizations also want to drive others out of the healthcare business or to gobble them up, surpassing the goal of survival and achieving rapid growth by driving out the competition.

These additional goals are not as often discussed in public as the first, more lofty statement of goals in our true-or-false test. However, they still drive the organization, especially the way the organization handles its finances and treats its employees. These goals may have profound effects on every one of the organization's employees, nurses included.

Let's return now to the story of Hazel Rivera. Why did she receive a less favorable rating than her friend Carla?

After comparing ratings with her friend Carla, Hazel scheduled another meeting with her nurse manager to discuss her evaluation. The nurse manager explained the rating: Hazel's care plans were very well done, and she appreciated Hazel's efforts. The problem was that Hazel had to be paid overtime for this work according to the union contract, and this had re-

duced the amount of overtime pay the nurse manager had available when the patient care load was especially high. "The corporation is very strict about staying within the budget," she said. "In fact, my rating is higher when I don't use up all of the budgeted overtime hours."

When Hazel asked what she could do to improve her rating, the nurse manager offered to help her streamline the care plans and manage her time better so that the care plans could be done without going into overtime.

PROCESSES

In much the same way that organizations have some publicly announced goals as well as less publicized ones, they also have *formal* written processes for getting things done and unwritten, unannounced ways to get around the formal processes, the *informal* process (Perrow, 1969). Often the informal process is much simpler and faster than the formal one. Because the informal ways of getting things done are seldom discussed (and certainly not a part of your new employee orientation), it may take some time for you to figure out what they are and how to use them. Once you are aware of the existence of these informal processes, they may be easier to find. The following is an example:

Jocylene noticed that Harold seemed to get stat laboratory results back on his patients faster than she did. The results she requested came back quickly, but the turnaround time for Harold's clients seemed almost instantaneous.

At lunch one day, Jocylene asked Harold how that happened. "That's easy," he said. "The people in our lab feel unappreciated. I always tell them how helpful they are. Also, if you call and let them know that the specimens are coming, they will get to them faster. I found out that they don't watch the computer screen constantly."

Harold has just explained an informal process to Jocylene.

Sometimes the informal processes are more hidden or people are unwilling to discuss how they use them. However, careful observation of the most experienced, "system-wise" individuals will eventually reveal them to you. This will help you get things done as efficiently as they do.

■ *Power*

• •

Although the use of the leadership and management techniques discussed so far will usually help you to achieve your goals, there are times when these attempts to influence others are overpowered by other forces or individuals. Where does this power come from? Who has it? Who does not?

In the earlier section on hierarchy, it was noted that, although people at the top of the hierarchy have most of the *authority* in the organization, they do not have all of the *power*. In fact, the people at the bottom of the hierarchy also have some sources of power. In this section, we explain how this can be true.

DEFINITION

Power is the ability to influence other people or other things despite resistance on the part of the other person or object. Power may be actual or potential, intended or unintended (Lukes, 1986). It may also be used for good or for evil, for serious purposes or for selfish purposes.

SOURCES

There are many sources of power, some of which are readily available to nurses and some of which are not. Box 6–1 is a list derived primarily from the work of French & Raven and of Etzioni (Barraclough & Stewart, 1992).

Let's look at various groups of people in a healthcare organization in terms of the types of power that may be available to them:

Managers are able to reward people with salary increases, promotions, and recogni-

---

Box 6–1 Sources of power

◆ Authority: The power granted to an individual or group by virtue of position (within the organizational hierarchy, for example)

◆ Reward: The promise of money, goods, services, recognition, or other benefits

◆ Expertise: The special knowledge an individual is believed to possess

◆ Coercion: The threat of pain or of harm, which may be physical, economic, or psychological

Source: Barraclough, R.A., & Stewart, R.A. (1992). Power and control: Social science perspectives. In Richmond, V.P. & McCroskey, J.C. (Eds). *Power in the Classroom: Communication, Control and Concern.* Hillsdale, NJ: Lawrence Erlbaum, with permission.

---

tion. They can also cause economic or psychological pain for the people who work for them. They can do this through their authority to fire people.

Patients at first appear to be relatively powerless in a healthcare organization. However, if patients refused to use the services of a particular organization, that organization would eventually cease to exist. Patients reward healthcare workers by praising them to their supervisors. They can also potentially cause discomfort by complaining about them.

Nurses have expert power and some authority over licensed practical nurses, aides, and other personnel by virtue of their position in the hierarchy. They are critical to the operation of most healthcare organizations and could cause difficulties if they refused to work.

Assistants and technicians would appear to be relatively powerless because of their low position in the hierarchy. Imagine, however, how the work of the organization (e.g., hospital or nursing home) would be impeded if all of the nursing aides failed to appear one morning.

■ *Empowering Nurses*
• •

In this last section, we look at several ways in which nurses, either individually or collectively, can maximize their power and increase their feelings of empowerment.

First, however, we should distinguish between the concepts of power and empowerment. Power is the actual or potential ability to *"recognize one's will even against the resistance of others,"* according to Max Weber (quoted in Mondros & Wilson, 1994, p. 5). Empowerment refers to a psychological state, a feeling of *competence, control*, and *entitlement*. Given these definitions, it is possible to be powerful and yet not feel empowered. The reverse is also true: people can feel empowered and yet not have maximized their power (Mondros & Wilson, 1994). So, although the terms "power" and "empowerment" are closely related, power refers to *action*, and empowerment refers to *feelings*. Both are of interest to nursing leaders and managers.

Nurses, like most people, want to have some power and to feel empowered (Mondros & Wilson, 1994). They want to be heard, to be recognized, to be valued, and to be respected. They do not want to feel unimportant or insignificant to society or to the organization in which they work.

PROFESSIONAL ORGANIZATIONS

Although we will talk about the purpose of the American Nurses Association and other professional organizations in a later chapter, here we look at them specifically in terms of how they can empower nurses. Our collective voice, expressed through these organizations, is often stronger and more easily heard than is one individual's voice. By joining together in professional organizations, nurses can be heard and their value recognized.

The power base of our professional organizations is derived from the number of nurses who are members and from their expertise in health matters. The reason why there is power in numbers may need some further explanation. Large numbers of active, adult, informed members of an organization represent large numbers of potential voters to state and national legislators, most of whom wish to be remembered favorably in forthcoming elections. Large groups of people also have a louder voice: they can write more letters, speak to more friends and family members, make more telephone calls, and generally attract more attention than small groups can. Large numbers of people also have the potential to cause more psychological or economic pain (coercive power). For example, the resignation of one nursing assistant or even one nurse may cause a temporary problem but is usually resolved fairly quickly by hiring another individual. If 50 or 100 aides or nurses resign, however, the organization can be virtually paralyzed and will have much more difficulty replacing these essential workers.

There are a number of ways in which professional organizations can empower nurses. The first is *collegiality*—an opportunity to work with one's peers on issues of importance to the profession. The second is commitment to *improving the health and wellbeing* of the people served by the profession. The third is *representation* in state legislatures and in Congress when issues of importance to nursing arise. The fourth is *collective bargaining*, the protection of nurses' rights and privileges as employed professionals. The fifth is *enhancement of competence* through publications and continuing education. The sixth is *recognition* through certification programs, awards, and use of the media.

COLLECTIVE BARGAINING

Collective bargaining also uses the power of numbers, in this case for the purpose of equalizing the power of employees and employer and improving working conditions (Tappen, 1995). As indicated earlier, when people join together for a common cause, they are often more powerful than when they attempt to bring about change individually. Collective bargaining takes advantage of this power in numbers.

An effective collective bargaining contract can provide considerable protection to employees. However, the downside of collective bargaining (as with most uses of coercive power) is the tendency to encourage conflict rather than cooperation between employees and managers in contract enforcement. Many nurses are also concerned about the effect that going out on strike might have on their clients' welfare and on their own economic security.

PARTICIPATION IN DECISION MAKING

There are also actions that can be taken within an organization to increase the empowerment of the nursing staff. The amount of power available to or exercised by a given group (e.g., nurses) within an organization can vary considerably from one organization to the next. There are three sources of power that are particularly important in healthcare organizations: resources (the money, materials, and human help needed to accomplish the work), support (authority to take action without having to get permission), and information (e.g., the organization's goals, activities of other departments). In addition, nurses also need access to opportunities: opportunities to be involved in decision making, to be involved in vital functions of the organization, and opportunities to grow professionally and to move up the organizational ladder (Sabiston & Laschinger, 1995).

SHARED GOVERNANCE

Shared governance is a term used to describe various ways in which access to these sources of power and opportunity is made available to staff nurses. Under shared governance, staff nurses are included in the highest levels of decision making within the nursing department through representation on various councils that govern practice and management issues. These councils set the standard for staffing, promotion, and so forth. At the department level, staff nurses are involved in decisions that affect their particular unit (Westrope et al., 1995).

Genuine sharing of decision making is difficult to accomplish, partly because managers are reluctant to relinquish control and to trust their staff members to make wise decisions. Genuine empowerment of the nursing staff cannot occur without this sharing. For example, if the staff members cannot control the budget for their unit, they really cannot implement a decision to replace registered nurses with aides or aides with reg-

istered nurses without approval from management. If they want to increase autonomy in decision making about care of individual clients, they cannot do this if opposition by another group, such as the physicians, is given greater credence by the organization's administration.

Let's return to the example of the staff of the critical care department (Scenario 2). Why did the vice president for nursing tell the nurse manager that the plan would not be implemented?

Actually, the vice president for nursing thought that the plan had some merit. He believed that the proposal to implement a nurse-managed model of care for the chronically critically ill could save a little money, provide a high quality of client care, and result in increased nursing staff satisfaction. However, the critical care department was the centerpiece of the hospital's agreement with a nearby medical school. Under this agreement, the medical school provided the services of highly skilled critical care specialists in return for the learning opportunities afforded their students. As currently stated, the nurses' plan would not allow sufficient autonomy for the medical students, a situation that would not be acceptable to the medical school. The vice president knew that the administration of the hospital believed their affiliation with the medical school brought a great deal of prestige to the organization and that they would not allow anything to interfere with this relationship.

"If shared governance were in place here, I think that we could implement this or a similar model of care," he told the nurse manager. "How would that work?" she asked. "If we had shared governance, the nursing practice council would review the plan and, if they approved it, forward it to a similar medical council. Then committees from both councils would get together and work out a way for this to benefit everyone. It wouldn't necessarily be easy to do, but it could be done if we had real collegiality between the professions. I have been working toward this model but haven't convinced the rest of the administration to put it into practice as yet. Perhaps we could bring this up at the next nursing executive council meeting. I think it is time that I shared my ideas with the rest of the nursing staff."

In this case, the goals and processes existing at the time the nurses developed their proposal did not support their idea. However, they could see a way for it to be accomplished in the future. Implementation of real shared governance would make it possible for the critical care nurses to accomplish their goal.

ENHANCING EXPERTISE

Most healthcare professionals, including nurses, are empowered to some degree by their own professional knowledge and competence. There are a number of ways in which this competence can be enhanced, thereby increasing your sense of empowerment (Fig. 6–3):

◆ Active participation in interdisciplinary team conferences and patient-centered conferences on your unit

◆ Attendance at continuing education offerings selected to enhance your expertise

◆ Attendance at local, regional, and national conferences sponsored by relevant nursing and specialty organizations

◆ Reading journals and books in your specialty area

◆ Participating in nursing research projects related to your clinical specialty area

◆ Inquiring how colleagues in nursing and in other disciplines would handle a difficult clinical situation

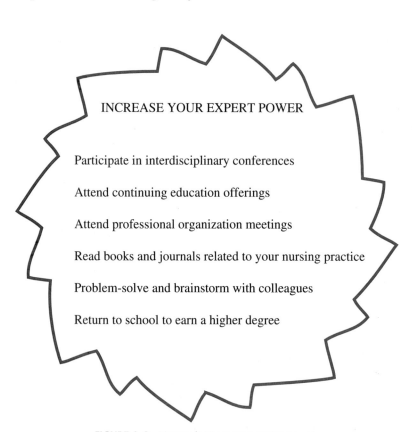

INCREASE YOUR EXPERT POWER

Participate in interdisciplinary conferences

Attend continuing education offerings

Attend professional organization meetings

Read books and journals related to your nursing practice

Problem-solve and brainstorm with colleagues

Return to school to earn a higher degree

FIGURE 6–3 How to increase your expert power.

◆ Observing the practice of experienced nurses

◆ Returning to school to earn a bachelor's and higher degrees in nursing

You can probably think of more, but this list at least gives you an idea of what you can do to enhance your expertise. The second part of the effort to increase your feeling of empowerment through enhancing expertise is to share the knowledge and experience gained with other people. This means not only using your knowledge to improve your own practice but communicating what you have learned to your colleagues in nursing and in other health care professions as well. It also means letting your supervisors know that you have enhanced your professional competence. You can share your knowledge with your clients, empowering them as well. You may even reach the point at which you have learned more about a particular subject than most nurses have and want to write about it for publication.

■ *Conclusion*

• • • • • • • • • • • • • • • • • •

Although most nurses are employed by healthcare organizations, too few have taken the time to analyze the operation of their employing organizations and the effect it has on their practice. Understanding organizations and the power relationships within them will increase the effectiveness of your leadership.

? *Study Questions*

1. Describe the organizational characteristics of a facility in which you presently have a clinical assignment. Be sure to include the following:
   a. The type of organization it is.
   b. The overall climate.
   c. How the organization is structured.
   d. The formal and informal goals and processes.

2. Define power, and describe how power affects the relationships between people of different disciplines (e.g., nursing, medicine, microbiology, administration,

finance, social work) in a healthcare organization.

3. Discuss ways in which nurses can become more empowered. How can you use your leadership skills to do this?

Critical Thinking Exercise

Tanya Washington will finish her associate degree nursing program in 6 weeks. Her preferred clinical area is parent-child nursing, and she hopes to become a pediatric nurse practitioner one day.

Tanya has received two job offers, both from urban hospitals with large pediatric populations. Several of her friends are already employed by these facilities, so she asked them for their impressions.

"Central Hospital is a good place to work," said one friend. "It is a dynamic, growing institution always on the cutting edge of change. Any new idea that seems promising, Central is the first to try it. It's an exciting place to work."

"City Hospital is also a good place to work," said her other friend. "It is a strong, stable institution where traditions are valued. Any new idea must be carefully evaluated before it is adapted. It's been a pleasure to work there."

1. Which organizational climate do you think would be best for a new graduate, Central's or City's?

2. How would each one affect a new graduate?

3. What else do you need to know about Tanya before deciding which hospital would be best for her?

4. What else would you like to know about the hospitals?

5. Would your answers differ if Tanya were an experienced nurse?

REFERENCES

Barraclough, R.A., & Stewart, R.A. (1992). Power and control: Social science perspectives. In Richmond, V.P., & McCroskey, J.C. (Eds.). *Power in the Classroom:*

Communication, Control and Concern. Hillsdale, NJ: Lawrence Erlbaum.

Lukes, S. (1986). *Power*. New York: New York University Press.

Mondros, J.B., & Wilson, S.M. (1994). *Organizing for Power and Empowerment*. New York: Columbia University Press.

Morgan, A. (1993). *Imaginization: The Art of Creative Management*. Newbury Park, Calif: Sage.

Perrow, C. (1969). The analysis of goals in complex organizations. In Etzioni, A. (Ed). *Readings on Modern Organizations*. Englewood Cliffs, N.J.: Prentice-Hall.

Rosen, R.H. (1996). *Leading People: Transforming Business from the Inside Out*. New York: Viking Penguin.

Rudy, E.B., Daly, B.J., Douglas, S., Montenegro, H.D., Song, R., & Dyer, M.A. (1995). Patient outcomes for the chronically critically ill: Special care unit versus intensive care unit. *Nurs Res, 44*(6), 324–331.

Sabiston, J.A., & Laschinger, H.K.S. (1995). Staff nurse work empowerment and perceived autonomy. *J Nurs Adm, 25*(9), 42–49.

Tappen, R.M. (1995). *Nursing Leadership and Management: Concepts and Practice*. Philadelphia: F.A. Davis.

Westrope, R.A., Vaughn, L., Bott, M., & Taunton, R.L. (1995). Shared governance: From vision to reality. *J Nurs Adm, 25*(2), 45–54.

CHAPTER 7

. . . .

Dealing with Problems and Conflicts

OBJECTIVES   *After reading this chapter, the student will be able to:*

◆ Identify the sources of various conflicts.

◆ Guide an individual or small group through the process of problem
    resolution.

◆ Participate in an informal negotiation.

◆ Discuss the purposes of collective bargaining.

E ach of us brings different experiences, beliefs, values, and habits to work with us. These differences are a natural part of our being members of different segments of our society, but they can interfere with our ability to work together. In addition, various pressures and demands of the workplace can also generate problems and conflicts among people. Consider the following example, which is the first of three used to illustrate how to deal with problems and conflicts.

Case 1 – Team A and Team B

Team A has stopped talking to Team B. If several members of Team A are out sick, no one on Team B will offer to help Team A with their work. Likewise, Team A members will not take telephone messages for anyone on Team B. Instead, they ask the person to call back later. When members of the two teams pass each other in the hall, they either glare at each other or turn away to avoid eye contact. Arguments erupt when members of the two teams need a computer or other piece of equipment at the same time. When a Team A nurse reached for the pulse oximeter at the same moment as a Team B nurse did, the second nurse said, "You've been using that all morning."

"I've got a lot of clients to monitor," was the response.

"Oh, you think you're the only one with work to do?"

"We take good care of our clients."

"Are you saying we don't?"

The nurses fell silent when the nurse manager entered the room. "Is something the matter?" she asked. Both nurses shook their heads and left quickly. "I'm not sure what's going on here," the nurse manager thought to herself, "but something's wrong and I need to find out what it is."

We will return to this case later as we discuss workplace problems and conflicts, their sources, and how to resolve them.

■ *Conflict*

Conflicts can develop whenever two or more people disagree on an issue (Vayrynen, 1991). Small or large, they seem to be a daily occurrence in the life of a nurse manager (McElhaney, 1996), and they can interfere with getting the work done, as you saw in Case 1.

The potentially harmful effects of unresolved conflict should not be underestimated. Serious conflicts can be very stressful for the people involved. Stress symptoms such as difficulty concentrating, anxiety, sleep disorders, withdrawal, or other interpersonal relationship problems can occur (Ehrlich, 1995). Anger, even violence, can erupt in the workplace if conflicts are not resolved satisfactorily.

There is also a positive side to conflict. In the process of learning how to manage conflict, people can develop more open, cooperative ways of working together (Tjosvold & Tjosvold, 1995). They can begin to see each other as people with similar needs, concerns, and dreams instead of as competitors or blocks in the way of progress. The goal, then, is to create an environment in which conflicts are dealt with in a cooperative and constructive rather than competitive and destructive manner.

■ *Sources of Conflict*

Why do conflicts occur? Health care brings people of different ages, genders, income levels, statuses, ethnic groups, educational levels, lifestyles, and professions together for the purpose of restoring or maintaining people's health. Differences of opinion over how to best accomplish this goal are a normal part of working with people of various skill levels and backgrounds (Wenckus, 1995). The workplace itself can also be a generator of conflict (Box 7-1).

Let's look at some of the reasons why conflict occurs:

Box 7–1 Potential conflict generators

- Tensions between groups
- Increased workload
- Multiple role demands
- Threats to professional identity and territory
- Threats to safety and security
- Scarce resources
- Cultural differences
- Invasion of personal space

Source: Adapted from McElhaney, R. (1996). Conflict management in nursing administration. *Nursing Management, 27*(3):49–50.

TENSIONS BETWEEN GROUPS

An increase in tension between or among various groups of people within the workplace has been the subject of much interest in the media. Union-management conflicts are a perennial problem in some workplaces. Gender-based conflicts, including equal pay for women and sexual harassment issues, are another example (Ehrlich, 1995).

INCREASED WORKLOAD

Emphasis on cost containment has resulted in increased pressure to get as much work as possible out of each employee. This leaves many healthcare workers feeling that their employers are taking advantage of them (Ketter, 1994) and causes conflict if they believe others are not working as hard.

MULTIPLE ROLE DEMANDS

Sheer overload or inappropriate task assignments (e.g., asking nurses to clean floors as well as care for their clients) can lead to disagreements about who does what task and who is responsible for the outcome.

THREATS TO PROFESSIONAL IDENTITY AND TERRITORY

When role boundaries are blurred (sometimes even erased), professional identities are threatened, and people may react in defense of them. Who, for example, is supposed to teach the discharged client about taking medication at home—the pharmacist, physician, nurse, or all three? If all three do this, who does what part of the teaching?

THREATS TO SAFETY AND SECURITY

When roles are blurred, cost constraints are emphasized, and staff members face layoffs, individuals' economic security is threatened. This can be a source of considerable stress and tension (Qureshi, 1996).

SCARCE RESOURCES

Inadequate money for pay raises, equipment, supplies, or additional help can increase competition between or among departments and individuals as they scramble to get their share of the little there is to distribute.

CULTURAL DIFFERENCES

Different beliefs about work, progress, productivity, and even what it means to arrive at work "on time" can lead to problems if not clarified.

INVASION OF PERSONAL SPACE

Crowded conditions and the constant interactions that occur at a busy nurses station can increase tension and lead to battles over precious work space (McElhaney, 1996).

■ *Conflict Levels*

Conflicts can occur at any level and involve any number of people. On the individual level, they can occur between two people working together on a team, between two people in different departments, or even between a staff member and a client or family member. On the group level, conflict can occur between two teams (as in Case 1), two departments, or two different professional groups (e.g., nurses and social workers over who is responsible for discharge planning). On the organizational level, conflicts can occur between two organizations (e.g., when two home health agencies compete for a contract with a large hospital). Our focus in this chapter is primarily on the first two levels, between or among individuals or groups of people within a healthcare organization.

■ *Resolving Problems and Conflicts*

• • • • • • • • • • • • • • • • • • • •

WIN, LOSE, OR DRAW?

Some people think about the problems and conflicts that occur at work in the same way that they think about a football game or tennis match: unless the score is tied at the end of the game, someone has to win and some-

one has to lose. There are some problems with this comparison to a sports competition. First, our aim is to work together more effectively, not to defeat the other party. Second, the people who lose are likely to feel bad about losing (Gottlieb & Healy, 1990). As a result, they may spend their time and energy preparing to win the next round rather than on their work. Third, a tie (neither side wins or loses) may be just a stalemate; no one has won or lost, but the problem is also still there.

So the answer to the question "Win, lose or draw?" is "none of the above." Instead, try to resolve the problem or conflict whenever possible. When differences and disagreements arise, *problem solving* may be sufficient. If the situation has already developed into a full-blown conflict, however, *negotiation* of a settlement may be necessary.

RESOLVING A PROBLEM

The use of the problem-solving process in client care should be familiar to you by now.

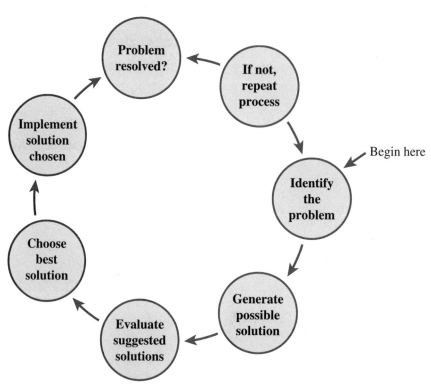

FIGURE 7–1 The process for resolving a problem.

The same approach can be used when staff problems occur. The goal in problem solving is to be as creative as possible in finding a solution to a given problem (Gottlieb & Healy, 1990). The process itself (illustrated in Fig. 7–1) includes identifying the issue or problem, generating possible solutions, evaluating the suggested solutions, choosing what appears to be the best solution, implementing that solution, evaluating the degree to which the problem has been resolved, and finally, either concluding that the problem is resolved or that it will be necessary to repeat the process to find a better solution.

Identify the Problem or Issue

Sometimes it is a simple task to identify the real issue or problem. Other times, however, it requires some discussion and exploration of the issues involved before the real problem emerges. "It would be nice," say Browne and Kelley, "if what other people were really saying was always obvious, if all their essential thoughts were clearly labeled for us . . . and if all knowledgeable people agreed about answers to important questions" (1994, p. 5). Of course, this is not what usually happens when a problem arises. People are often vague about what their real concern is. Sometimes they are genuinely uncertain what the real problem is. Emotional involvement may further cloud the issue. All of this needs to be sorted out so that the problem is clearly identified and a solution can be sought.

Generate Possible Solutions

Here creativity is especially important. If you are guiding people through this process, try to discourage them from using old solutions for new problems. It is natural for people to try to repeat something that worked well for them in the past, but solutions that were previously successful may not work in the future (Walsh, 1996).

Evaluate Suggested Solutions

An open-minded, objective evaluation of each suggestion is needed but not always easy to accomplish. When problem solving is done by a group, it is sometimes difficult to separate the suggestion from its source. For example, on an interdisciplinary team, the status of the person who made the suggestion may influence whether the suggestion is judged to be useful. Whose solution is most likely to be the best one—the physician's or the client care assistants? That depends. The suggestion should be judged on its merits, not its source.

Choose the Best Solution

Which of the suggested solutions is most likely to work? Often a combination of suggestions may be the best solution.

Implement the Solution Chosen

The true test of any suggested solution is how well it actually works. Once a solution has been implemented, it is important to give it time to work. Sometimes impatience leads to premature abandonment of a good solution.

Is the Problem Resolved?

Or is it necessary to repeat the process? Not every problem is resolved successfully on the first attempt. If the problem has not been resolved, the process needs to be resumed with even greater attention to what the real problem is and how it can be successfully resolved.

Let's consider a situation in which problem solving would be helpful:

Case 2—The Vacation

Francine Deloit has been a unit secretary for 10 years. She is prompt, efficient, accurate, courteous, flexible, and productive—everything a nurse manager could ask for in a unit secretary. When nursing staff members are very busy, she distributes afternoon snacks or sits with a family for a few minutes until a nurse is available. There is only one issue on which Ms. Deloit is insistent and stubborn: taking her 2-week vacation over the Christmas and New Year holidays. This is forbidden by hospital policy, but every nurse manager has allowed her to do this because it is the only special request she ever makes and because it is the only time she visits her family during the year.

A reorganization of the administrative structure eliminated several layers of nursing managers and supervisors. Each remaining nurse manager was given responsibility for two or three units. The new nurse manager for Ms. Deloit's unit refused to grant her request for vacation time at the end of December. "I can't show favoritism," she explained. "No one else is allowed to take vacation time at the end of December." Assuming that she could have the time off as usual, Francine had already purchased a nonrefundable ticket for her visit home. When her request was denied, she threatened to quit. On hearing this, one of the nurses on Francine's unit remarked to the new nurse manager, "We are going to lose the best unit secretary we ever had."

The nurse manager asked Ms. Deloit to meet with her to discuss the problem. The following is a summary of the problem solving they did:

◆ **THE ISSUE.** Ms. Deloit wanted to take her vacation at the end of December through early January. Assuming this was OK, she had purchased nonrefundable tickets. The policy forbids vacations from December 20 to January 5. The former nurse manager had not enforced this policy with Ms. Deloit, but the new nurse manager wanted to enforce the policy with everyone, including Ms. Deloit.

◆ **POSSIBLE SOLUTIONS:**
1. Let Ms. Deloit resign.
2. Fire Ms. Deloit.
3. Allow Ms. Deloit to take her vacation as planned.
4. Allow everyone to take vacations between December 20 and January 5 if requested.
5. Allow no one to take a vacation between December 20 and January 5.

◆ **EVALUATE SUGGESTED SOLUTIONS.** Ms. Deloit preferred solutions 3 and 4. The new nurse manager preferred 5. Neither

wanted 1 or 2. They could agree only that none of the solutions satisfied both of them, so they agreed to try again.

◆ **SECOND LIST OF POSSIBLE SOLUTIONS:**
1. Reimburse Ms. Deloit for the cost of the tickets.
2. Allow Ms. Deloit one last vacation between December 20 and January 5.
3. Allow Ms. Deloit to take her vacation over Thanksgiving instead.
4. Allow Ms. Deloit to begin her vacation on December 26 so that she would work on Christmas Day but not on New Year's Day.
5. Allow Ms. Deloit to begin her vacation earlier in December so that she can return in time to work on New Year's Day.

◆ **CHOOSE THE BEST SOLUTION.** As they discussed the alternatives, Ms. Deloit said that she could change the days of her flight without a penalty. The nurse manager said that she would allow solution 5 if Ms. Deloit understood that she could not take vacation time between December 20 and January 5 in the future. Ms. Deloit agreed to this.

◆ **IMPLEMENT THE SOLUTION.** Ms. Deloit returned on December 30 and worked both New Year's Eve and New Year's Day.

◆ **EVALUATE THE SOLUTION.** The rest of the staff members had been watching the situation very carefully. Most felt that the solution finally agreed on had been fair to them as well as to Ms. Deloit. Ms. Deloit felt she had been treated honestly and fairly. The nurse manager believed they had found a solution that was fair to Ms. Deloit but still reinforced her determination to enforce the vacation policy.

◆ **RESOLVED OR RESUME PROBLEM SOLVING?** Ms. Deloit, the staff members, and the nurse manager all felt that the problem had been solved.

NEGOTIATING AN AGREEMENT INFORMALLY

When a problem has grown too big, too complex, or too heated (emotion-laden), it may

Box 7–2 The informal negotiation process

● SCOPE THE SITUATION. ASK YOURSELF . . .
  —What am I trying to achieve?
  —What is the environment in which I am operating?
  —What problems am I likely to encounter?
  —What does the other side want?
● SET THE STAGE
● CONDUCT THE NEGOTIATION
  —Set the ground rules.
  —Clarify the problem.
  —Make your opening move.
  —Continue with offers and counteroffers.
● AGREE UPON A RESOLUTION OF THE CONFLICT

be necessary to work through a more elaborate process to resolve it. In Case 1, the tensions between Team A and Team B had become so great that the nurse manager decided this would be necessary.

The process of negotiation is a complex one that requires much thought beforehand and an equal amount of skill in its implementation (Box 7–2). The following is an outline of the most essential aspects of negotiation using Case 1 about Teams A and B to illustrate how it can be done.

Scope the Situation

To be successful, it is important to thoroughly understand the entire situation. Walker and Harris (1995, p. 42) suggest asking yourself the following three questions:

1. **What am I trying to achieve?** The nurse manager in Case 1 is concerned about the tensions between Team A and Team B. She wants the members of these two teams to be able to work together in a cooperative manner, which they are not doing at the present time.
2. **What is the environment in which I am operating?** The members of Teams A and B were openly hostile to each

other. The overall climate of the organization, however, was a benign one. The nurse manager knew that teamwork was encouraged and that her actions to resolve the conflict would be supported by administration.

3. **What problems am I likely to encounter?** The nurse manager knew that she had allowed the problem to go on too long. Even physicians, social workers, and visitors to the unit were getting caught up in the conflict. Team members were actively trying to get other staff to take sides, making it clear they felt that "if you are not with us, you are against us." This made people from other departments very uncomfortable because they had to work with both teams. The nurse manager knew that resolution of the conflict would be a relief to many people.

There is one additional question that it is important to ask in preparation for negotiations:

4. **What does the other side want?** In this situation, the nurse manager was not certain what either team really wanted. She realized that she needed this information before she could begin to negotiate.

Set the Stage

When a conflict such as the one between Teams A and B has gone on for some time, the opposing sides are often unwilling to meet to discuss the problem. If this occurs, it may be necessary to confront them with direct statements designed to open communication between them and challenge them to seek resolution of the situation. At the same time, it is important to avoid any implication of blame because this provokes defensiveness rather than willingness to change.

To confront Teams A and B with their behavior toward one another, the nurse manager called them together at the end of the day shift. "I am very concerned about what I have been observing lately," she told them. "It appears to me that instead of working together, our two teams are competing with each other." She continued with some examples of what she had observed, taking care not to mention individual names and avoiding blaming anyone for the problem. She was also prepared to take responsibility for having allowed the situation to deteriorate before taking this much needed action.

Conduct the Negotiation

As indicated earlier, conducting a negotiation requires a great deal of skill. Many conflict situations become very emotional. Without effective leadership to prevent personal attacks, confrontation and negotiation could actually worsen the situation.

1. **Set ground rules.** Members of Teams A and B began flinging accusations at each other as soon as the nurse manager made her statement. The nurse manager stopped this quickly and said, "First, we need to set some ground rules for this discussion. Everyone will get a chance to speak, but not all at once. Please speak for yourself, not for others. And please do not make personal remarks or criticize your coworkers. We are here to resolve this problem, not to make it worse." She had to remind the group of these ground rules several times during the meeting.
2. **Clarification of the problem.** The nurse manager wrote a list of problems mentioned by team members on the board in the conference room. As the list grew longer, she asked the group, "What do you see here? What is the real problem?" Finally, someone in the back of the room said, "We don't have enough people, equipment, or supplies to get the work done." The rest of the group nodded in agreement.
3. **Opening move.** Once the problem is clarified, it is time to seek everyone's agreement to discuss the matter and then seek a way to resolve the conflict. In more formal negotiations, you may make a statement about what you wish to achieve. For example, if you are negotiating a salary increase, you might begin by saying, "I am requesting a 10 percent increase for the following reasons. . . ." Of course, your employer will probably make a counteroffer such as "The best I can do is 3 percent."

These are the opening moves of a negotiation.
4. **Continue the negotiations.** The discussion should continue in an open, nonhostile manner. Further explanation and elaboration of each side's concerns may be made. Additional offers and counteroffers are common. As the discussion continues, it is usually helpful to emphasize areas of agreement as well as disagreement so that both parties are encouraged to continue the negotiations (Tappen, 1995).

Agree on a Resolution of the Conflict

After much testing for agreement, elaboration of each side's positions and concerns, and making of offers and counteroffers, the people involved should finally reach an agreement.

The nurse manager of Teams A and B led them through a discussion of their concerns related to working with severely limited resources. The teams soon realized that they had a common concern and that they might be able to help each other rather than compete with each other. The nurse manager agreed to become more proactive in seeking more resources for the unit. "We can simultaneously seek new resources and creative ways to use the resources we already have," she told the teams. Relationships between members of Team A and Team B improved remarkably after this meeting. They learned that they could accomplish more by working together then they had ever achieved separately.

FORMAL NEGOTIATION: COLLECTIVE BARGAINING

There are many varieties of formal negotiations, from real estate transactions to international peace treaty negotiations. One of the more formal negotiation processes that is of special interest to nurses is collective bargaining. Collective bargaining is a formal negotiation, a process that is governed by law and contracts (called collective bargaining agreements).

Collective bargaining involves a formal procedure governed by labor laws such as the National Labor Relations Act. Nonprofit healthcare organizations were added to the organizations covered by these laws in 1974. Once a union or professional organization has been designated as the official bargaining agent for a group of nurses, a contract defining such important matters as salary increases, benefits, time off, unfair treatment, and promotion of professional practice is drawn up. This contract then governs employee-management relations within the organization.

Case 3 is an example of how collective bargaining agreements can influence the outcome of a conflict between management and staff in a healthcare organization.

Case 3 — Collective Bargaining

The chief executive officer (CEO) of a large home health agency in a southwestern resort area called a general staff meeting. She reported that the agency had grown rapidly and was now the largest in the area. "Much of our success is due to the professionalism and commitment of our staff members," she said. "With growth come some problems, however. The most serious problem is the fluctuation in patient census. This peaks in the winter months when seasonal visitors are here and troughs in the summer. In the past, when we were a small agency, we all took our vacations during the slow season. This made it possible to continue to pay everyone their full salary all year. However, with the pressures to reduce costs and the large number of staff members we now have, we cannot continue to do this. We are very concerned about maintaining the high quality of patient care currently provided, but financially we have calculated that we need to reduce staff by 30 percent over the summer."

The CEO then invited comments from the staff members. The majority of the nurses said they wanted and needed to work full-time all year. Most supported families and had to have a steady income all year. "My rent does not go down in the sum-

mer," said one. "Neither does my mortgage or the grocery bill," said another. A small number said that they would be happy to work part-time in the summer if they could be guaranteed full-time employment from October through May. "We have friends who would love this work schedule," they added.

"That's not fair," protested the nurses who needed to work full-time all year. "You can't replace us with part-time staff." The discussion grew louder and the participants more agitated. The meeting ended without a solution to the problem. Although the CEO promised to consider all points of view before making a decision, the nurses left the meeting feeling very confused and concerned about the security of their future income. Some grumbled that they probably should begin looking for new positions "before the ax falls."

The next day, the CEO received a telephone call from the nurses' union representatives. "If what I heard about the meeting yesterday is correct," said the representative, "your plan is in violation of our collective bargaining contract." The CEO reviewed the contract and found that the representative was correct. A new solution to the financial problems caused by seasonal fluctuations in patient census would have to be found.

A collective bargaining contract is a legal document that governs the relationship between management and staff represented by the union (which, for nurses, may be the nurses' association or another healthcare workers' union). The contract may cover some or all of the following:

◆ Economic issues: salaries, shift differentials, length of the workday, overtime, holidays, sick leave, breaks, health insurance, pensions, severance pay.

◆ Management issues: promotions, layoffs, transfers, reprimands, hiring and firing procedures.

◆ Practice issues: adequate staffing, standards of care, code of ethics, other quality-of-care issues, staff development opportunities.

THE PROS AND CONS OF COLLECTIVE BARGAINING

Some nurses feel that it is unprofessional to belong to a union. Others point out that physicians and teachers are also union members and that the protection of a union outweighs the downside. There is no simple answer to this question.

Probably the greatest advantage of collective bargaining is protection of the right to fair treatment and the availability of a grievance procedure that specifies both the employee's and employer's rights and responsibilities if a disagreement arises that cannot be settled informally. The greatest disadvantage of using collective bargaining as a way to deal with conflict is that it clearly separates management-level people from staff-level people, treating them as opposing parties rather than people who are trying to work together to provide an essential service to their clients, which is our ultimate goal in dealing with problems and conflicts in the workplace.

■ *Conclusion*

• • • • • • • • • • • • • • • • • • •

Conflict is inevitable within any large, diverse group of people who are trying to work together over an extended period of time. However, it does not have to be destructive. It does not have to be a negative experience at all if it is handled skillfully by everyone involved. In fact, conflict can stimulate people to learn more about each other and its resolution can lead to improved working relationships, more creative methods of operation, and higher productivity when it is resolved to everyone's satisfaction.

? *Study Questions*

1. Debate the question of whether conflict is constructive or destructive. How can good leadership affect the outcome of a conflict?

2. Give an example of how each of the eight sources listed in this chapter could lead to a conflict. Then discuss ways to prevent conflict from each of the eight sources.

3. What is the difference between problem resolution and negotiation? Under what circumstances would you use one or the other?

4. Identify a conflict (or potential conflict) in your clinical area and explain how either problem resolution or negotiation could be used to resolve it.

Critical Thinking Exercise

A not-for-profit hospice center in a small community received a generous gift from the grateful family of a client who had died recently. The family asked only that the money be "put to the best use possible."

Everyone in this small facility had an opinion about the best use for this money. The administrator wanted to renovate their old, run-down headquarters. The financial officer wanted to put the money in the bank "for a rainy day." The chaplain wanted to add a small chapel to the building. The nurses wanted to create a food bank to help the poorest of their clients. The social workers wanted to buy a van to transport clients for healthcare needs. The staff agreed that all of the ideas had merit, that all of the needs identified were important ones, but there was only enough money to meet one of them.

The more the staff members discussed how to use this gift, the more insistent all individuals or groups became that their idea was best. At their last meeting, it was evident that some were becoming frustrated and others were becoming angry. It was rumored that a shouting match between the administration and financial officer had occurred.

1. Which idea do you think has the most merit?

2. Why did you select the one you did?

3. In your analysis of this situation, identify the sources of the conflict that is developing within this facility.

4. What kind of leadership actions are needed to prevent the escalation of this conflict?

5. If the conflict does escalate, how could it be resolved?

6. Try role-playing a negotiation between the administrator, the financial officer, the chaplain, a representative of the nursing staff, and a representative of the social work staff. Can you suggest a creative solution?

REFERENCES

Browne, M.M., & Kelley, S.M. (1994). *Asking the Right Questions: A Guide to Critical Thinking.* Englewood Cliffs, N.J.: Prentice-Hall.

Ehrlich, H.J. (1995). Prejudice and ethnoviolence on campus. *Higher Education Extension Service Review*, *6*(2), 1–3.

Gottlieb, M., & Healy, W.J. (1990). *Making Deals: The Business of Negotiating.* New York: New York Institute of Finance.

Ketter, J. (1994). Protecting RN's with the Fair Labor Standards Act. *The American Nurse*, *26*(9), 1–2.

McElhaney, R. (1996). Conflict management in nursing administration. *Nursing Management*, *27*(3), 49–50.

Qureshi, P. (1996). The effects of threat appraisal. *Nursing Management*, *27*(3), 31–32.

Tappen, R.M. (1995). *Nursing Leadership and Management: Concept and Practice.* Philadelphia: F.A. Davis.

Tjosvold, D., & Tjosvold, M.M. (1995). *Psychology for Leader: Using Motivation, Conflict and Power to Manage More Effectively.* New York: John Wiley & Sons.

Vayrynen, R. (1991). *New Directions in Conflict Theory: Conflict Resolution and Conflict Transformation.* London: Sage.

Walker, M.A., & Harris, G.L. (1995). *Negotiations: Six Steps to Success.* Upper Saddle River, N.J.: Prentice-Hall, PTR.

Walsh, B. (1996, June 3). When past perfect isn't. *Forbes ASAP*, p. 18.

Wenckus, E. (1995, February 21). Working with an interdisciplinary team. *The Nursing Spectrum*, pp. 12–14.

CHAPTER 8

People and the Process of Change

OBJECTIVES   *After reading this chapter, the student will be able to:*

◆ Describe the process of change.

◆ Recognize resistance to change and identify possible sources of the resistance.

◆ Suggest strategies to reduce resistance to change.

◆ Assume a leadership role in implementing change.

When asked what the theme of a recent nursing management conference was, a top nursing executive thought a moment and then replied, "Change, change, and more change." Changes seem to be occurring more often and at a more rapid pace than ever before in the workplace. People working today can expect to make as many as 7 to 10 major job changes in their lifetime. This compares to their parents who, on average, made only one or two major job changes in their lives (Dent, 1995).

In this chapter, we discuss the process of change, how people respond to change, and how leaders and managers can influence the outcomes of this process.

■ *Change*

• • • • • • • • • • • • • • • • • • •

A NATURAL PHENOMENON

Change is a naturally occurring phenomenon, simply a part of living. Every day we have new experiences, meet new people, learn something new. We grow up, leave home, graduate from college, begin a new career, perhaps begin a new family. Some of these changes are milestones in our lives, ones we have prepared for and anticipated for some time. Others are entirely unexpected, sometimes welcome, and sometimes not. Many are exciting, leading us to new opportunities and challenges. But when these changes occur too rapidly or demand too much of us, they can make us very uncomfortable.

MACRO AND MICRO CHANGE

The "ever-whirling wheel of change" (Dent, 1995, p. 287) in health care seems to spin faster every year. Cost containment, managed care, Medicare and Medicaid reform, work redesign, restructuring, and downsizing are major concerns (Aiken, 1995). The changes sweeping through our healthcare system affect clients and caregivers alike. These changes in the healthcare system are *macro*-level (large-scale) changes that have affected virtually every healthcare facility: changes in the way client care is delivered, reduction in the number of staff members employed, restrictions on spending, and so forth. The macro-level changes are discussed in more detail in other chapters of this book.

Every change that occurs at this macro level filters down to the *micro* (small-scale) level, to our employing organizations, units, and teams and to us as individuals. For better or worse, nurses, their colleagues in other disciplines, and their clients are participants in these changes. This micro level of change is the primary focus of this chapter.

■ *The Process of Change*

• • • • • • • • • • • • • • • • • • •

Lewin's (1951) model of change is one of the most frequently used and easily understood approaches to planning and implementing change in organizations. Many people have added their own elaborations to this model, but its basic ideas remain the same. The basic elements of Lewin's change model are *unfreezing, change, and refreezing*. Let's assume that a work situation is basically stable before change is introduced. Although some changes occur naturally, people are generally accustomed to each other, have a routine for doing their work, and are pretty confident that they know what to expect and how to deal with whatever problems may arise in the course of a day. Farrell and Broude (1987) call this the "comfort zone." A change of any magnitude is likely to move people out of this comfort zone into discomfort. Lewin calls this movement *unfreezing* (Fig. 8–1).

Many healthcare institutions have offered nurses the choice of weekday or weekend work on day, evening, or night shifts. Given these choices, nurses with young children are likely to find their "comfort zone" on weekday evening or night shifts. Imagine the discomfort that they would experience if confronted with a change to alternate weekends or day shifts on call.

Announcement of such a change would rapidly unfreeze their usual routine and

FIGURE 8–1 The change process. (Based on Farrell, K. & Broude, C. [1987]. *Winning the Change Game: How to Implement Information Systems with Fewer Headaches and Bigger Paybacks.* Los Angeles: Breakthroughs Enterprises, Inc.; and Levin, K.: [1951]. *Field Theory in Social Science: Selected Theoretical Papers.* New York: Harper & Row.)

move them into the discomfort zone, the *change* phase.

> They might have to find a new babysitter or begin a search for a new child care center that is open on weekends. An alternative would be the establishment of a child care center where they work. Another alternative would be to find a new position that allows greater choice of working hours.

Whatever alternative they chose, the nurses would be challenged to find a solution that allows them to move into a new comfort zone. To do this, they would have to find a consistent, dependable source of child care suited to their new schedule and to the needs of their children—in other words, a way to *refreeze* their situation and move into a new comfort zone. If the nurses do not find a satisfactory alternative, they could remain in an unsettled state, in the discomfort zone, caught in a conflict between their professional and personal responsibilities.

As this example illustrates, even a small change can be disruptive to the people involved in it. In the next section, we will consider why change can be unsettling, leading people to resist it.

■ *Resistance to Change*

People resist change for a variety of reasons, which vary from person to person and from situation to situation. For example, you may find one client care technician happy about an increase in responsibility while another one is upset about being given the same in-

crease in responsibility. You might also find that one change in routine provokes a storm of protest while another change is hardly noticed at all. Let's see why this is so.

SOURCES OF RESISTANCE

Resistance to change comes from three major sources: technical concerns, psychosocial needs, and threats to a person's position and power (Araujo Group, no date).

Technical Concerns

Some resistance to change is based on concerns about whether the proposed change itself is a good idea. In some cases, these concerns are justified.

> The Professional Practice Committee of a small hospital suggested replacing a commercial mouthwash with a mixture of hydrogen peroxide and water to save money. A staff nurse objected to this proposed change, saying that she had read a research study several years ago that found peroxide solutions to be an irritant to the oral mucosa (Tombes & Gallucci, 1993).
>
> Fortunately, the chairperson of the Professional Practice Committee recognized that this objection was based on technical concerns and requested that a more thorough study of the research literature be done before instituting the change. "From now on," she told the staff nurse, "we will investigate the implications of a proposed change more thoroughly before recommending it. Thank you."

Psychosocial Needs

According to Maslow (1970), human beings have a hierarchy of needs, from the basic physiological needs for oxygen, fluids, and nutrients to the higher-order needs for belonging, self-esteem, and self-actualization (Fig. 8–2). Maslow observed that the more basic needs (those lower on the hierarchy) must be at least partially met before a person is motivated to seek fulfillment of the higher-order needs.

Change can make it more difficult for a person to meet any or all of these physiological and psychosocial needs. For example, if a massive downsizing occurs and a person's job is eliminated, fulfillment of virtually all of these levels of needs may be threatened, from having enough money to pay for food and shelter to opportunities to fulfill one's career potential.

In other cases, the threat is more subtle and may be harder for the leader or manager to anticipate. For example, an institution-wide evaluation of the effectiveness of the advanced practice role would be a great threat to a staff nurse who was working toward accomplishment of a lifelong dream of becoming an advanced practice nurse in oncology. In contrast, it would have little impact on nursing aides unless further action was taken. A staff reorganization that involved reassigning aides to different units, however, would threaten the belonging needs of an aide who had very close friends on his or her unit but few friends outside of work.

Position and Power

Once gained, status, power, and influence within an organization are hard to give up. This applies to people anywhere in the organization, not just those at the top.

A clerk in the surgical suite had been preparing the operating room schedule for many years. Although his supervisor really had the authority to revise the schedule, she rarely did so because the clerk was quite skillful in preparing realistic schedules that balanced the needs and desires of various parties, including some very demanding surgeons.

When the operating room supervisor was transferred to another facility, her replacement decided that she had to review the schedules before they were posted because they were ultimately her responsibility. The clerk became defensive. He tried to avoid the supervisor and posted the sched-

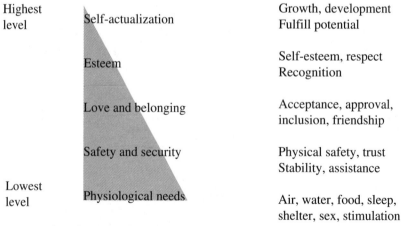

		EXAMPLES
Highest level	Self-actualization	Growth, development Fulfill potential
	Esteem	Self-esteem, respect Recognition
	Love and belonging	Acceptance, approval, inclusion, friendship
	Safety and security	Physical safety, trust Stability, assistance
Lowest level	Physiological needs	Air, water, food, sleep, shelter, sex, stimulation

FIGURE 8–2 Maslow's hierarchy of needs. (Based on Maslow, A.H. [1970]. *Motivation and Personality.* New York: Harper & Row.)

ules without her approval whenever he could. This surprised the new supervisor. She had heard how skillful the clerk was and did not think that her review of the schedules would be threatening. She had not realized the importance of this task to the clerk. The opportunity to tell others when and where they could operate had given him a feeling of power and importance. Her insistence on reviewing his work had reduced the importance of his position.

TABLE 8–1
RESISTANCE TO CHANGE

Active	Passive
Direct attacks	Avoiding discussion
Refusal to change	Ignoring the change
Killer memos attacking the change	Refusing to commit to the change
Organizing resistance of other people	Agreeing but not acting

What seemed to the new supervisor to be a very small change in routine had provoked surprisingly strong resistance because it threatened the clerk's position and power within the organization.

As you learned in Chapter 6 on power and organizations, empowerment is a source of motivation and satisfaction for most people. Although change can empower people, it can also threaten their empowerment, especially when they feel that the change was imposed on them, that they had no choice in the matter.

RECOGNIZING RESISTANCE

It is easy to recognize resistance to a change when it is direct. When a person says to you, "That's not a very good idea," "I'll quit if you reassign me to the night shift," or "There's no way I'm going to do that," there is no doubt that you are encountering resistance. When resistance is less direct, however, it can be difficult to recognize unless you know what to look for.

Resistance may be *active* or *passive* (Del-Bueno, 1995; Farrell & Broude, 1987). Active resistance can take the form of direct attacks or refusals, such as the statements in the previous paragraph, writing "killer" memos that destroy the idea or the person who suggested it, quoting existing rules that make the change difficult or impossible to implement, or organizing resistance to the change (encouraging others to resist). Passive approaches use avoidance: canceling appointments to discuss implementation of the change, being "too busy" to make the change, refusing to commit to changing or

agreeing to it but doing nothing to change, and simply ignoring the entire process as much as possible (Table 8–1). Once resistance has been recognized, action can be taken to lower or even eliminate it.

LOWERING RESISTANCE

A great deal can be done to lower people's resistance to change. Strategies fall into four categories: information dissemination, disconfirmation of currently held beliefs, provision of psychological safety, and by command (Tappen, 1995).

Information Dissemination

Much resistance is simply the result of misunderstandings about a proposed change. Sharing information about the proposed change can be done on a one-to-one basis, in group meetings, or through written materials distributed to everyone involved using print or electronic means.

Disconfirmation of Currently Held Beliefs

Often leaders can take action that provides a catalyst for change (Lichiello & Madden, 1996). For example, simply providing information is often persuasive enough to lower resistance to change when people are reluctant to give up their current beliefs, opinions, or comfortable routines. When this happens, providing evidence that what people are doing or believing is inadequate, incorrect, or inefficient can increase their willingness to change.

Jolene was a little nervous when it was her turn to present information on a new enteral feeding procedure to the Clinical Practice Committee. Committee members were very demanding: they wanted clear, research-based information presented in a concise manner. Opinions, generalities, and vague references ("Somebody told me . . . ") were not acceptable. She had prepared thoroughly and even practiced her presentation at home until she could speak without referring to her notes.

The presentation went well. Committee members commented on the thoroughness of her presentation and the quality of the information presented. To her disappointment, however, no action was taken on her proposal to adopt the new procedure. Returning to her unit, she shared her disappointment with the nurse manager. Together, they reviewed the presentation and Lewin's approach to bringing about change. The nurse manager agreed that the information on enteral feeding had been thoroughly reviewed by Jolene.

The problem, she explained, was that Jolene had not attended to the need to unfreeze a situation to lower resistance to change. As they talked, Jolene realized that she had not put any emphasis on the high risk of contamination and resulting gastrointestinal disturbances of the procedure currently in use. In other words, members of the committee were still feeling comfortable with the current procedure because she had not emphasized the risk involved in failing to take action.

At the next meeting, Jolene presented additional information on the risks presented by the current enteral feeding procedures. This *disconfirming evidence* was persuasive. The committee accepted her proposal to adapt the new, lower-risk procedure.

Without the addition of the disconfirming evidence that Jolene presented at the second meeting, it is likely that her proposed change in procedure would never have been implemented. The inertia (tendency to remain in the same state rather than to move toward change) exhibited by the Clinical Practice Committee is not unusual (Pearcey & Draper, 1996).

Psychological Safety

When a proposed change threatens the basic human needs of individuals or groups of individuals in some way, resistance can be lowered by reducing that threat, leaving people feeling more comfortable about the proposed change. Although each situation poses different kinds of threats and requires different actions to reduce these threats, the following is a list of common strategies that help increase psychological safety and reduce resistance to change:

◆ Point out the similarities between the old and new procedures.

◆ Express approval of people's concern for providing the best care possible.

◆ Recognize the competence and skill of the people involved.

◆ Provide assurance (if possible) that no one will lose his or her position because of the change.

◆ Suggest ways in which the change can provide new opportunities and challenges (that is, new ways to increase self-esteem and self-actualization).

◆ Express your valuing of each individual's and group's contributions in general and to the proposed change.

◆ Ensure involvement of as many people as possible in both the design of the change and the implementation (Hastings & Waltz, 1995).

◆ Provide opportunities for people to express their feelings and ask questions about the proposed change.

◆ Allow time for practice and learning of any new procedures, if possible, before a change is implemented.

◆ Provide a climate of acceptance in which some mistakes can be made without negative consequences for the person.

When all of the preceding are done within a climate of trust and acceptance of each other's differences, changes are far easier to implement.

Command

An entirely different approach to change can be used. People in authority within an organization can simply *require* people to make a change in what they are doing or can reassign people to new positions (Porter-O'Grady, 1996). This is effective in many situations but may not work well if there are ways for people to resist:

◆ When passive resistance can undermine the change

◆ When high motivational levels are necessary to make the change successful

◆ If people can refuse to obey the order without negative consequences

The following is an example of an unsuccessful attempt to bring about change by command:

A new and still somewhat insecure nurse manager believed that her staff members were taking advantage of her inexperience by taking more than the two 15-minute coffee breaks allowed during an 8-hour shift. She decided that staff members would have to sign in and out for their coffee breaks as well as for their 30-minute meal break.

The staff members were outraged by this change. Most had been taking less than two 15-minute coffee breaks and 30 minutes for meals because of the heavy client care demands of the unit.

Staff members refused to sign the "coffee break sheet." When asked why they hadn't signed it, they replied "I forgot," "I couldn't find it," or "I was called away before I had a chance." This organized passive resistance was sufficient to overcome the nurse manager's authority. The nurse manager decided that the "coffee break sheet" had been a mistake, removed it from the bulletin board, and never spoke of it again.

Had administration stepped in to back up the manager, the outcome of this example could have been quite different.

For people in authority, acting by command often seems to be the easiest way to bring about change: just tell people what to do and don't listen to any arguments about it. There is risk in this approach, however. Even when staff members do not resist authority-based change, overuse of commands can lead to staff members who are passive, dependent, unmotivated, and disempowered. Providing high-quality patient care requires staff members who are active, motivated, and highly committed to their work, just the opposite of the results of authority-based change.

■ *Leading the Implementation of Change*

Given the current climate of "change, change, and more change," even new graduates find themselves given responsibility for bringing about change. Some examples of the kinds of changes that you might be asked to assist in implementing are the following:

◆ Revising old procedures or adding new technical procedures

◆ Devising new ways to record, store, and retrieve patient data

◆ Developing new policies on staff evaluation and promotion

◆ Participating in quality improvement projects

◆ Preparing for accreditation visits

Now that you understand how change can affect people and have learned some ways to lower their resistance to change, we can discuss taking a leadership role in successful implementation of change.

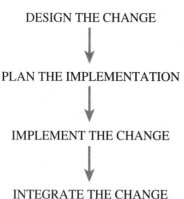

DESIGN THE CHANGE

↓

PLAN THE IMPLEMENTATION

↓

IMPLEMENT THE CHANGE

↓

INTEGRATE THE CHANGE

FIGURE 8–3 Four phases of planned change.

The entire process of bringing about change can be divided into four phases: designing the change itself, deciding how to implement the change, the actual implementation of the change, and following through to make sure that the change has been integrated into the regular operation of the facility (Fig. 8–3).

DESIGNING THE CHANGE

The first step in bringing about change is to carefully craft the change itself. It cannot be assumed that every change is for the better. Some changes fail because they are poorly conceived in the first place.

> **Ask yourself:**
> ◆ What is the purpose of this change? What are we trying to accomplish?
> ◆ Is the change necessary?
> ◆ Is the change technically correct?
> ◆ Will this work?
> ◆ Is there a better way to do this?

PLANNING THE IMPLEMENTATION

The next step is to prepare a careful plan for implementing the change. All of the information presented previously about sources of resistance and ways to overcome that resistance should be taken into consideration when deciding how to implement a change.

> **Ask yourself:**
> ◆ Why might people resist this change?
> ◆ Would their resistance be justified?
> ◆ What can be done to prevent or overcome this resistance?

The context in which the change will take place is another factor to consider when assessing resistance to change (Lichiello & Madden, 1996). This includes the amount of change occurring at the same time, the organizational climate, and the environment in which the organization exists. For example, in some situations there may be external pressure to change because of the competitive nature of the healthcare market in a particular community. In other situations, government regulations may make it difficult to bring about a desired change.

Almost everything that you have learned about effective leadership is useful in planning the implementation of change: motivating people, involving people in decisions that affect them, dealing with conflict, eliciting cooperation, providing coordination, and fostering teamwork. All of these should be taken into consideration in formulating a plan for implementation of a proposed change and then acted on in the next step, implementing the change.

IMPLEMENTING THE CHANGE

Now, finally, you are ready to make the change that has been so carefully planned. In addition to the strategies to lower resistance and the leadership skills needed to increase motivation and help people work well together, it may also be helpful to consider the following factors related to change:

> **Ask yourself:**
> ◆ What is the magnitude of this change? Is this a major change that affects almost everything people do or is it a minor one with little impact on what people do every day?
> ◆ What is the complexity of this change?

Is this a difficult change to make? Does it require much new knowledge or skill or both? How long will it take for people to acquire the necessary knowledge and skill?

- What is the pace of the change? How urgent is this change? Can it be done gradually or must it be implemented all at once?
- What is the current stress level of the people involved in this change? Is this the only change that is taking place? Or is it just one of many changes taking place? How stressful are these changes? How can you help people keep their stress levels within tolerable bounds?

As indicated earlier, some discomfort is likely to occur with almost any change, but it is important to keep it within tolerable limits.

INTEGRATING THE CHANGE

Don't forget this last step. After the change has been made, it is important to make sure that everyone has moved into a new "comfort zone."

Ask yourself:
- Is the change well integrated into everyday operations?
- Are people comfortable with it now?
- Is it well accepted? If not, why not? What can be done to increase acceptance?
- Is there any residual resistance that could still undermine full integration of the change? If there is, how can this resistance be overcome?

■ Conclusion

Change is an inevitable part of living and working. How people respond to change, the amount of stress it causes, and the amount of resistance it provokes can be influenced

by your leadership. Handled well, most changes can become opportunities for professional growth and development rather than just more stressors for nurses and their clients to cope with.

❓ Study Questions

1. Why is change inevitable? What would happen if no change at all occurred in health care?

2. Why do people resist change?

3. How can leaders overcome resistance to change?

4. Describe the process of implementing a change from beginning to end. Use an example from your own clinical experience to illustrate this process.

Critical Thinking Exercise

A small (50-bed) rural nursing home was recently purchased by a large healthcare corporation. A new director of nursing was brought in to replace the former one, who had retired after 30 years at this facility.

The new director addressed the staff members at the reception held to welcome him. "My philosophy is that you cannot manage anything that you haven't measured. Everyone tells me that you have all been doing an excellent job here. With my measurement approach, we will be able to analyze everything you do and become more efficient than ever."

The nursing staff members soon found out what the new director meant by his "measurement" approach. Every bath, episode of incontinence care, feeding of a resident, or trip off the unit had to be counted and the amount of time each activity required had to be recorded. Nurse managers were required to review these data with staff members every week, questioning any time that was not accounted for. Time spent talking with families or consulting with other staff members was considered time wasted unless the staff member could justify the "interruption" in his or her work.

No one complained publicly about the change, but absenteeism rates increased rapidly. Personal day and vacation time requests soared. Staff members nearing retirement crowded the tiny personnel office, overwhelming the single staff member with their requests to "tell me how soon I can retire on full benefits." The director of nursing found that shortage of staff was becoming a serious problem and that few new applications were coming in despite the fact that this rural area offered few good job opportunities.

1. What evidence of resistance to change can you find in this case study?

2. What kind of resistance to change did the staff members of this nursing home exhibit?

3. If you were a staff nurse at this facility, how do you think you would have reacted to this change in administration?

4. Why did staff members resist this change?

5. What could the director of nursing do to increase acceptance of this change? What could the nurse managers and staff nurses do?

REFERENCES

Aiken, L.H. (1995). Transformation of the nursing workforce. *Nurs Outlook, 43*, 201–209.

Araujo Group (no date). A compilation of opinions of experts in the field of the management of change. Unpublished report.

DelBueno, D. (1995). Ready, willing, able? Staff competence in workplace redesign. *J Nurs Adm, 25*(9), 14–16.

Dent, H.S. (1995). *Job Shock: Four New Principles Transforming Our Work and Business.* New York: St. Martin's Press.

Farrell, K., & Broude, C. (1987). *Winning the Change Game: How to Implement Information Systems with Fewer Headaches and Bigger Paybacks.* Los Angeles: Breakthrough Enterprises.

Hastings, C., & Waltz, C. (1995). Assessing the outcomes of professional practice redesign: Impact on staff nurse perceptions. *J Nurs Adm, 25*(3), 34–42.

Lewin, K. (1951). *Field Theory in Social Science: Selected Theoretical Papers.* New York: Harper & Row.

Lichiello, P., & Madden, C.W. (1996). Context and catalysts for change in health care markets. *Health Aff, 15*(2), 121–129.

Maslow, A.H. (1970). *Motivation and Personality.* New York: Harper & Row.

Pearcey, P., & Draper, P. (1996). Using the diffusion of innovation model to influence practice: A case study. *J Adv Nurs, 23*, 724–726.

Porter-O'Grady, T. (1996). The seven basic rules for successful redesign. *J Nurs Adm, 26*(1), 46–53.

Tappen, R.M. (1995). *Nursing Leadership and Management: Concept and Practice.* Philadelphia: F.A. Davis.

Tombes, M.B., & Gallucci, B. (1993). The effects of hydrogen peroxide rinses on the normal oral mucosa. *Nurs Res, 42*(6), 332–337.

CHAPTER 9

Work-Related Stress and Burnout

OUTLINE

Consider the Statistics

Stress
Effects of Stress
Responses to Stress

Reality Shock
Differences in Expectations
Additional Pressures on the New
  Graduate

Burnout
Definition

Aspects
Stressors Leading to Burnout
Consequences
A Buffer against Burnout

Stress Management
ABCs of Stress Management
Physical Health Management
Mental Health Management

Conclusion

OBJECTIVES *After reading this chapter, the student will be able to:*

◆ Identify signs and symptoms of stress, reality shock, and burnout.

◆ Describe the impact of stress, reality shock, and burnout on the individual and the healthcare team.

◆ Evaluate his or her own and colleagues' stress levels.

◆ Develop strategies to manage personal and professional stresses.

TABLE 9–1
HOW OFTEN ARE YOU STRESSED OUT AT WORK?

	Total	Men	Women	Professionals
Daily	25%	25%	25%	28%
Almost every day	12%	12%	12%	14%
Several days a week	9%	10%	9%	13%
Once or twice a week	29%	28%	30%	26%
Less than once a week	14%	13%	15%	10%
Never	10%	12%	8%	9%

Source: Wall Street Journal, October 2, 1996. New York: Schelhardt, with permission.

■ *Consider the Statistics*

Many people are concerned about the amount of stress that they face in our fast-paced world and its effect on health and well-being. Consider the following:

- More people have heart attacks on Monday morning as they prepare to go to work than on any other day.

- Two-thirds of all office visits to physicians are the result of stress.

- Stress plays a role in the two major killers of adults: heart disease and cancer.

- Job stress is so prevalent that Objective 6.11 of Healthy People 2000 is to "increase to at least 40% the proportion of worksites employing 50 or more people that provide programs to reduce employee stress" (Wolinski, 1993, p. 721; USDHHS, 1991).

Stress in the workplace is increasing. The October 2, 1996 *Wall Street Journal* (Schelhardt, 1996) provided the workplace statistics illustrated in Tables 9–1 and 9–2.

■ *Stress*

EFFECTS OF STRESS

Hans Selye (1956) first explored the concept of stress in the 1930s. His description of the general adaptation syndrome (GAS) has had an enormous influence on our present-day notions about stress and its effect on humans. Currently, stress is assessed on three levels: environmental, psychological, and biologic. External factors, (e.g., high unemployment rates) that make people more or less susceptible to disease are viewed as environmental stressors. On the psychological level, the individual's perception and evalu-

TABLE 9–2
MEASURING STRESS

	1988	1991	1995
Think workload is excessive	37%	41%	44%
Often bothered by excessive job pressure	41%	41%	43%
Frequently worry about being laid off	22%	25%	46%
Worry a lot about company's future	36%	40%	55%
Feel sure job is secure if performed well	73%	66%	50%

Source: Wall Street Journal, October 2, 1996. New York: Schelhardt, with permission.

their program. Compare this with your "next clinical rotation," your first real job as a nurse. You may work 7 to 10 days in a row on 8- to- 12-hour shifts, caring for 10 or more clients. You may also have to supervise several technicians or licensed practical nurses. These drastic changes from school to employment cause many to experience what is called *reality shock* (Kramer, 1981; Kraeger & Walker, 1993).

Most agencies expect new graduates to come to the work setting able to organize their work, set priorities, and provide leadership to ancillary personnel. New graduates often say, "I had no idea that nursing would be this demanding." Even though your program of study is designed to help you prepare for the demands of the work setting, you will still need to continue to learn on the job. In fact, experienced nurses will tell you that what you learned in school is only the beginning: it provides you with the fundamental knowledge and skills needed to continue to grow and develop as you practice nursing in various capacities and work settings. Graduation signals not the end of learning but the beginning of your journey toward becoming an expert nurse (Benner, 1984).

Well-supervised orientation programs are very helpful for newly licensed nurses. Many facilities provide an 8- to 12-week preceptor program. Unfortunately, this program is sometimes at the graduate's expense. Although the new graduate works side by side with an experienced nurse, employers sometimes consider this a pre-employment period for which they provide opportunities for further learning but no salary. The advantage of orientation programs is that they assist the new nurse in the transition from school to work environment, thus buffering the stressors that can lead to reality shock.

The first few weeks on a new job are the "honeymoon" phase. The new employee is excited and enthusiastic about the new position. Coworkers usually go out of their way to make the new person feel welcome and overlook any problems that arise. Everything seems rosy. Unfortunately, honeymoons do not last forever.

The new graduate is soon expected to behave just like everyone else and discovers that expectations for a professional employed in an organization are quite different from expectations for a student in school. Those behaviors that brought rewards in school are not necessarily valued by the organization. In fact, some of them are criticized. The new graduate who is not prepared for this change feels confused, shocked, angry, and disillusioned. The tension of the situation can become almost unbearable if it is not resolved.

DIFFERENCES IN EXPECTATIONS

The enthusiasm and eagerness of the first new job quickly disappear as reality sets in. Regardless of the career one chooses, there is no perfect job. The problem begins when reality and expectations collide. To cope with reality, we must recognize several facts of work life (Goliszek, 1992, pp. 36, 46):

1. Expectations are usually distortions of reality. Unless we accept this and react positively, we will go through life experiencing disappointment.
2. To some extent, you need to fit yourself into your work, not fit the work to suit your needs or demands. Having a positive attitude helps to maintain flexibility and a sense of humor.
3. Regardless of the job, the way you perceive events on the job will influence how you feel about your work. Your mental attitude will affect whether work is a pleasant or unpleasant experience.
4. Feelings of helplessness and powerlessness at work cause frustration and unrelieved job stress.

What are these differences in expectations? Kramer (1981), who studied reality shock for many years, found a number of them, which are listed in Table 9–4.

Ideally, health care should be comprehensive. Not only should it meet all of a client's needs, but also it should be delivered in a way that considers the client as a whole person, a member of a particular family that has certain unique characteristics and needs, and a member of a particular community. Most healthcare professionals, however, are not employed to provide comprehensive, holistic care. Instead, they are asked to give medications, provide counseling, make home visits, or prepare someone for surgery,

TABLE 9–4
PROFESSIONAL IDEALS AND WORK REALITIES

Professional Ideals	Work Realities
Comprehensive, holistic care	Mechanistic, fragmented care
Emphasis on quality of care	Emphasis on efficiency
Explicit expectations	Implicit (unstated) expectations
Balanced, frequent feedback	Intermittent, often negative feedback

but rarely to do all these things. These tasks are divided among different people, each a specialist, for the sake of efficiency rather than continuity or effectiveness.

When efficiency is the goal, the speed and amount of work done are rewarded rather than the quality of the work. This also creates a conflict for the new graduate, who was allowed to take as much time as needed to provide good care while in school.

Expectations are also communicated in different ways. In school, an effort is made to provide explicit directions so that students know what they are expected to accomplish. In many work settings, however, instructions are brief, and many expectations are left unspoken. New graduates who are not aware of these expectations may find that they have unknowingly left tasks undone or are considered inept by coworkers. The following is an example:

Brenda, a new graduate, was assigned to give medications to all the clients cared for by the team. Because this was a fairly light assignment, the graduate spent some time looking up the medications and explaining their actions to the clients receiving them. Brenda also straightened up the medicine room and filled out the order forms, which she thought would please the task-oriented team leader.

At the end of the day, Brenda reported these activities with some satisfaction to the team leader. She expected the team leader to be pleased with the way the time had been used. Instead, the team leader looked annoyed and told her that whoever passes out medications always does the blood pressures too and that the other nurse on the team, who had a

heavier assignment, had to do them. Also, because supplies were always ordered on Fridays for the weekend, it would have to be done again tomorrow, so Brenda had in fact wasted her time.

ADDITIONAL PRESSURES ON THE NEW GRADUATE

The first job a person takes after finishing school is often thought of as a proving ground where newly gained knowledge and skills are tested. Many set up mental tests for themselves that they feel must be passed before they can be confident of their ability to function. Passing these self-tests also confirms achievement of identity as a practitioner rather than a student.

At the same time, new graduates are undergoing testing by their coworkers, who are also interested in finding out whether the new graduate can handle the job. The new graduate is entering a new group, and the group will decide whether to accept this new member. This testing is somewhat like hazing of freshmen entering high school or college. It is usually reasonable, but sometimes new graduates are given tasks that they are not ready to handle. If this happens, Kramer (1981) recommends that new graduates refuse to take the test rather than fail it. Another opportunity for proving themselves will soon come along.

The discrepancies in role expectations and the need for a feeling of competency are the top two concerns of new graduates, according to most surveys. Next in order of concern are the system that must be dealt with, one's self-concept, and the type of feedback that is given (or not given). Additional problems, such as dealing with resistant staff members, cultural differences, and age differences, may also occur. Before considering ways to revolve these problems, we look at some less successful ways of coping with these problems.

◆ **ABANDON PROFESSIONAL GOALS.** When faced with reality shock, some new graduates abandon their professional goals and adopt the organization's operative goals as their own. This eliminates their conflict but leaves them less effective caregivers. It also puts the needs of the organization before their needs or the needs of the client and reinforces operative goals that might better be challenged and changed.

◆ **GIVE UP PROFESSIONAL IDEALS.** Others give up their professional ideals but do not adopt the organization's goals or any others to replace them. This has a deadening effect: they become automatons, believing in nothing related to their work except doing what is necessary to earn a day's pay.

◆ **LEAVE THE PROFESSION.** Those who do not give up their professional ideals try to find an organization that will support them. Unfortunately, a significant proportion of those who do not want to give up their professional ideals escape these conflicts by leaving their jobs and abandoning their profession. Kramer and Schmalenberg (1993) believe that there would be fewer shortages of nurses if more healthcare organizations met these ideals.

◆ **DEVELOP A PROFESSIONAL IDENTITY.** Opportunities to challenge one's competence and develop an identity as a professional can begin in school. Success in meeting these challenges can immunize the new graduate against the loss of confidence that accompanies reality shock.

◆ **LEARN ABOUT THE ORGANIZATION.** The new graduate who understands how organizations operate will not be as shocked as the naive individual. When you begin a new job, it is important to learn as much as you can about the organization and how it really operates. This not only saves you some nasty surprises but also gives you some ideas about how to work within the system and how to make the system work for you.

◆ **USE YOUR ENERGY WISELY.** Keep in mind that much energy goes into learning a new job. You may see many things that you think need to be changed, but you need to recognize that to implement change also takes time and energy on your part. It is a good idea to make a list of these things so that you do not forget them later when you have become socialized into the system and have some time and energy to invest in change.

◆ **COMMUNICATE EFFECTIVELY.** Deal with the problems that can arise with coworkers. The same interpersonal skills you use in communicating with patients can be effective in dealing with your coworkers.

◆ **SEEK FEEDBACK OFTEN AND PERSISTENTLY.** Seeking feedback not only provides you with needed information but also pushes the people you work with to be more specific about their expectations of you.

◆ **DEVELOP A SUPPORT NETWORK.** Identifying colleagues who have also held onto their professional ideals and sharing not only your problems but also the work of improving the organization with them are a helpful cushion against reality shock. Their recognition of your work can keep you going when rewards from the organization are meager. A support network is a source of strength when resisting pressure to give up professional ideals and a source of power when attempting to bring about change. Developing your skills can help to prevent the problems of reality shock. Begin early in your career to protect yourself against reality shock.

■ *Burnout*

• • • • • • • • • • • • • • • • • • • •

DEFINITION

The ultimate result of unmediated job stress is burnout. The term "burnout" became a favorite buzzword of the 1980s and continues to be part of today's vocabulary. It was formally identified as a leadership concern in 1974 by Herbert Freudenberger. The literature on job stress and burnout continues to grow as new books, articles, workshops, and videotapes appear regularly.

A useful definition of burnout is the "progressive deterioration in work and other performance resulting from increasing difficulties in coping with high and continuing levels of job-related stress and professional frustration" (Paine, 1984, p. 1).

Much of the burnout experienced by nurses has been attributed to the frustration that care cannot be delivered in the ideal manner they learned in school. For those whose greatest satisfaction comes from caring for clients, anything that interferes with providing the highest-quality care causes work stress. The often unrealistic and sometimes sexist image of nurses in the media, to which we all are exposed, adds to this frustration. Neither the school ideal nor the media image is realistic, but either may make nurses feel dissatisfied with themselves and their jobs, keeping stress levels high (Corley, Farley, Geddes, Goodloe, & Green, 1994; Fielding & Weaver, 1994; Grant, 1993; Kovner, Hendrickson, Knickman, & Finkler, 1994; Malkin, 1993; Nakata & Saylor, 1994; & Skubak, Earls, & Botos, 1994).

> Sharon had wanted to be a nurse for as long as she could remember. She married early, had three children, and put her dreams of being a nurse on hold. Now her children are grown, and she finally realized her dream by graduating last year from the local community college with a nursing degree. However, she has been feeling overwhelmed at work, critical of coworkers and patients, and argumentative with supervisors. She is having difficulty adapting to the restructuring changes at her hospital and goes home angry and frustrated every day. She cannot stop working for financial reasons but is seriously thinking of quitting nursing and taking some computer classes. "I'm tired of dealing with people. Maybe machines will be more friendly and predictable." Sharon is experiencing burnout.

ASPECTS

Goliszek (1992) has identified four stages of the burnout syndrome:

1. **High expectations and idealism.** At the first stage, the individual is enthusiastic, dedicated, and committed to the job and exhibits a high energy level and positive attitude.
2. **Pessimism and early job dissatisfaction.** In the second stage, frustration, disillusionment, or boredom with the job develops and the individual begins to exhibit the physical and psychological symptoms of stress.
3. **Withdrawal and isolation.** As the individual moves into the third stage, anger, hostility, and negativism are exhibited. The physical and psychological stress symptoms worsen. Through stage three, simple changes in job goals, attitudes, and behaviors may reverse the burnout process.
4. **Irreversible detachment and loss of interest.** As the physical and emotional stress symptoms become severe, the individual exhibits low self-esteem, chronic absenteeism, cynicism, and total negativism. Once the individual has moved into this stage and remained there for any length of time, burnout is inevitable. Regardless of the cause, experiencing burnout leaves an individual emotionally and physically exhausted.

STRESSORS LEADING TO BURNOUT

Job Stress

Researchers have identified five sources of job stress that can lead to burnout (Crawford, 1993; Duquette, Sandhu, & Beaudet, 1994; Carr & Kazanowski, 1994).

◆ **INTRINSIC FACTORS.** Characteristics of the job itself, such as the multiple aspects of complex client care that many nurses provide.

◆ **ORGANIZATIONAL STRUCTURE.** Characteristics of the organization in which you work, such as limited financial resources.

◆ **REWARD SYSTEM.** The way in which employees are rewarded or punished, particularly if these are obviously unfair.

◆ **HUMAN RESOURCES SYSTEM.** In particular, the amount and availability of opportunities for staff development.

◆ **LEADERSHIP.** The way in which managers relate to their staff, particularly if they are unrealistic, uncaring, or unfair.

Personal Factors

Some of the personal factors influencing job stress and burnout are age, sex, number of children, education, experience, and favored coping style. For example, the fact that many nurses are single parents raising families alone adds to the demands of already difficult days at work. Competitive, impatient, and hostile personality traits have also been associated with emotional exhaustion and subsequent burnout (Borman, 1993).

Work Environments

Recent studies indicate that different demands are placed on nurses in different work environments. For example, the strict boundaries and bureaucratic organization of acute-care and inpatient long-term care facilities can be stressful for those who have difficulty with a great deal of structure. On the other hand, the ambiguity, autonomy, and flexibility of community-based practice can be uncomfortable for those who need structure and clearly defined work expectations (Borman, 1993).

Human Service Occupations

People who work in human service organizations consistently report lower levels of job satisfaction than do people working in other types of organizations. Much of the stress experienced by nurses is related to the nature of their work: continued intensive, intimate contact with people who often have serious, sometimes fatal physical, mental, emotional, and/or social problems. Efforts to save clients or help them achieve a peaceful ending to their lives are not always successful. Despite our best efforts, many of our clients get worse, not better. Some return to

their destructive behaviors; others do not recover but die. The continued loss of clients alone can lead to burnout (Tappen, 1995). Even exposure to medicinal and antiseptic substances, unpleasant sights, and high noise levels can cause stress for some people. Healthcare providers experiencing burnout may become cynical and even hostile toward their coworkers and colleagues (Carr & Kazanowski, 1994; Dionne-Proulx & Pepin, 1993; Goodell & Van Ess Coeling, 1994; Stechmiller & Yarandi, 1993; Tumulty, Jernigan, & Kohut, 1994).

In some instances, human service professionals also experience lower pay, longer hours, and more extensive regulation than do professionals in other fields. Inadequate advancement opportunities for women and minorities in lower-status, lower-paid positions are apparent in many healthcare areas.

Conflicting Demands

Meeting work-related responsibilities and maintaining a family and personal life can increase stress when there is insufficient time or energy for all of these. The perception of balance in one's life is a personal one. There appear to be some differences in the way that men and women find a comfortable balance. Men often define themselves in terms of their separateness and their career progress; women are more likely to define themselves through attachment and connections with other people. Women who try to focus on occupational achievement and pursue personal attachments at the same time are likely to experience conflict in both their work and personal lives. In addition, society evaluates the behaviors of working adult men and women differently. "When a man disrupts work for his family, he is considered a good family man, while a woman disrupting work for family risks having her professional commitment questioned" (Borman, 1993, p. 1).

Lack of Balance in Life

When your interests and satisfactions are limited to your work, you are more susceptible to burnout; trouble at work becomes trouble with your whole life. Your job can become the center of your world, and your world can become very small. Two ways out of this are to set limits on your commitment to work and to expand the number of satisfying activities and relationships outside of work. Many people in the helping professions have difficulty setting limits on their commitment. This is fine if they enjoy working extra hours and taking calls at night and on weekends, but if it exhausts them, then they need to stop doing it or risk serious burnout. For example, when you are asked to work another double shift or the third weekend in a row, you can say no (see Appendix B). At the same time as you are setting limits at work, you can expand your outside activities so that you live in a large world in which a blow to one part can be cushioned by support from other parts. If you are the team leader or nurse manager, you also need to recognize and accept staff members' need to do this as well.

CONSEQUENCES

You can see that certain combinations of personal and organizational factors can increase the likelihood of burnout. Finding the right fit between your own preferences and the characteristics of the organization you work for can be keys to preventing burnout. Health care demands adaptable, innovative, competent employees who care about their clients, desire to continue learning, and try to remain productive despite the constant challenges. Unfortunately, these are the same individuals who are prone to burnout if preventive action is not taken (Lickman, Simms, & Greene, 1993; McGee-Cooper, 1993).

Burnout has financial, physical, emotional, and social implications for the professional, the clients, and the organization. Burnout can happen to anyone, not just to people with a history of emotional problems. In fact, it is not considered an emotional disturbance in the sense that depression is, but a reaction to sustained organizational stressors (Duquette, Sandhu, & Beaudet, 1994).

A BUFFER AGAINST BURNOUT

The idea that personal hardiness provides a buffer against burnout has been explored in recent years. Hardiness includes the following:

- A sense of personal control rather than powerlessness
- Commitment to work and life's activities rather than alienation
- Seeing both life's demands and change as challenges rather than threats

The hardiness that comes from having this perspective leads to the use of adaptive coping responses such as optimism, effective use of support systems, and healthy lifestyle habits (Duquette, Sandhu, & Beaudet, 1994; Nowak & Pentkowski, 1994).

■ *Stress Management*

Although we cannot always control the demands placed on us, we can learn to manage our reactions to them and to make healthy lifestyle choices that better prepare us to meet demands.

ABCs OF STRESS MANAGEMENT

Frances Johnston (1994, pp. 5–6) suggests using the ABCs of stress management (awareness, belief, and commitment) to have as constructive a response to stress as possible (Box 9–1). Let's look at these ABCs in a little more detail.

Box 9–1 ABCs of stress management

- **Acquire** awareness of your own responses to stress and the consequences of too much stress.
- **Believe** that you can change your perspective and your behavior.
- **Commit** yourself to taking action in preventing conflicts that cause stress, to learning techniques that help you cope in situations over which you have no control, and to understanding that you can choose how to react in stressful situations.

AWARENESS. How do you know that you are under stress and may be beginning to burn out? The key is being honest with yourself. Asking yourself the questions in Box 9–2 and answering them honestly are one way to assess your personal risk. To further analyze your responses to stress, you may also want to answer the questions in Box 9–3. The answers to these questions require some thought. You should not have to share your answers with others unless you want to, but you do need to be completely honest with yourself when you answer them or the exercise will not be worth the time spent on it. Try to determine the sources of your stress (Goliszek, 1992, p. 13):

- Is it the *time of day* when you are doing the activity?
- Is it the *reason* why you are doing the activity?
- Is it the *way* in which you are doing the activity?
- Is it the *amount of time* you need to do the activity?

BELIEF. Now that you have done the "A" part of stress management, you are ready to move on to "B," which is belief in yourself. Your relationship with your inner self may be the most important relationship of all. Building your own self-image and self-esteem will enable you to block out negativism (Davidhizar, 1994). You must also believe that your destiny is not inevitable but that change is possible. Be honest with yourself. Truly value your life. Ask yourself, "If I could live one more month, what would

---

Box 9–2 Assessing your risk for burnout

- Are you feeling more fatigued than energetic?
- Are you working harder but accomplishing less?
- Are you feeling cynical or disenchanted most of the time?

- Do you often feel sad or cry for no apparent reason?
- Are you feeling hostile, negative, or angry at work?
- Are you short-tempered? Withdrawing from friends or coworkers?
- Are you forgetting appointments or deadlines? Frequently misplacing personal items?
- Are you becoming insensitive, irritable, and short-tempered?
- Are you experiencing more physical symptoms such as headaches, stomachaches?
- Do you feel like avoiding people?
- Are you laughing less? Feeling joy less?
- Are you interested in sex?
- Do you crave junk food more often?
- Are you skipping meals?
- Have your sleep patterns changed?
- Are you taking more medication than usual? Using alcohol or other substances to alter your mood?
- Do you feel guilty when your work isn't perfect?
- Are you questioning whether the job is right for you?
- Do you feel as if no one cares what kind of work you do?
- Are you constantly pushing yourself to do better, yet feel frustrated that there isn't time to do what you want to do?
- Do you feel as if you were on a treadmill all day?
- Are you using holidays, weekends, or vacation time to catch up?
- Do you feel as if you were "burning the candle at both ends"?

Source: Adapted from Golin, M., Buchlin, M., & Diamond, D. (1991). *Secrets of Executive Success.* Emmaus, Pa: Rodale Press, Inc.; and Goliszek, A.: (1992): *Sixty-Six Second Stress Management: The Quickest Way to Relax and Ease Anxiety.* Far Hills, N.J.: New Horizon NJ.

ation of a situation influence the stress response, whereas the activation of the body on a physiological level is the biologic perspective on stress. Working together, these three factors influence our responses to stress (Cohn, Kessler, & Gordon, 1995).

TABLE 9–3
SIGNS AND SYMPTOMS OF STRESS

Physical Signs and Symptoms

Rapid heart rate and respirations

Dry mouth and throat

Increased body temperature

Weakness, dizziness

Trembling hands, fingers, body

Nervous tics

Menstrual problems

Loss of appetite

Frequent urination

Diarrhea

Psychological/Behavioral Signs & Symptoms

Absenteeism

Alcoholism

Apathy

Irritability/Anger

Boredom

Callousness

Conflicts with workers

Cynicism

Defensiveness

Depersonalization

Depression

Feelings of helplessness and hopelessness

Decreased interest in sexual activity

Depression

Drug dependence

Nightmares

Inability to concentrate

Impaired judgment

Isolation

Withdrawal

Procrastination

Excessive worry, anxiety

Source: Adapted from Martin, K. (1993). To cope with stress. *Nursing 93*, May, pp 39–41, with permission; and Goliszek, A.: (1992) *Sixty-Six Second Stress Management: The Quickest Way to Relax and Ease Anxiety.* Far Hills, N.J.: New Horizon NJ.

Epidemiological research has shown that long-term stress contributes to cardiovascular disease, hypertension, ulcers, substance abuse, immune system disorders, emotional disturbances, and job-related injuries (Crawford, 1993; Lusk, 1993). Table 9–3 lists the most common physical and psychological signs of stress (Martin, 1993; Goliszek, 1992).

RESPONSES TO STRESS

Some people manage potentially stressful events more effectively than others (Crawford, 1993; Teague, 1992). Perceptions of events and the subsequent stress response vary considerably from one person to another. A patient crisis that you consider stressful, for example, may not seem stressful at all to a coworker. The following is an example:

> A new graduate was employed on a busy telemetry floor. Often, when clients were admitted, they were in acute distress with shortness of breath, diaphoresis, and chest pain. Family members were distraught and anxious. Each time the new graduate had to admit a client, she experienced a "sick-to-her-stomach" feeling, tightness in the chest and throat, and difficulty concentrating. She was afraid that she would miss something important and that the client would die during the admission. The more experienced nurses seemed to handle each admission with ease, even if the client's physical condition was severely compromised.

■ *Reality Shock*

• • • • • • • • • • • • • • • • • • •

You have probably thought, "Nothing can be more stressful than going to school. I can't wait to go to work and not have to study for tests, go to the clinical agency for my assignment, do client care plans, and so forth." In most associate degree programs, students are assigned to care for one to three clients a day, working up to six or seven clients under a preceptor's supervision by the end of

I do?"—and start doing it (Johnston, 1994)!

- **COMMITMENT.** As you move forward to step "C," you will need to make a commitment to continuing to work on stress recognition and reduction. Once you have recognized the warning signs of stress and impending burnout and gained some insight into your personal needs and reactions to stress, it is time to find the stress management techniques that are right for you.

The stress management techniques in the next section are divided into physical and mental health management for ease in reading and remembering them. However, we would like to remind you that this is really an artificial division and that mind and body interact continuously. Stress affects both mind and body, and we need to care for both if we are to be successful in managing stress and preventing burnout.

PHYSICAL HEALTH MANAGEMENT

Nurses spend much of their time teaching their clients the basics of keeping themselves healthy. However, many fail to apply these principles in their own lives. We will review some of the most important aspects of health promotion and stress reduction in this section: deep breathing, good posture, rest, relaxation, proper nutrition, and exercise.

Deep Breathing

Most of the time people use only 45 percent of their lung capacity when they breathe. Remember all the times that you have instructed your clients to "take a few deep breaths"? Practice taking a few slow, deep, "belly" breaths. When faced with a stressful situation, people often hold their breath for a few seconds. This reduces the amount of oxygen delivered to the brain and causes them to feel more anxious. Anxiety can lead to faulty reasoning and a feeling of losing control. Often you can calm yourself by taking a few deep breaths. Try it right now. Don't you feel better already?

Good Posture

A common response to pressure is to slump down into your chair, tensing your upper torso and abdominal muscles. Again, this restricts blood flow and the amount of oxygen reaching your brain. Instead of slumping, imagine a hook on top of your head pulling up your spine, relax your abdomen, and look up. Now, shrug your shoulders a few times to loosen the muscles, and picture a sunny day at the beach or a walk in the woods. Do you feel more relaxed?

Rest

Sleep needs are different for each one of us. Find out how much sleep you need and work on arranging your activities so that you get enough sleep. If it is impossible to get enough sleep on a given day, perhaps a short nap or just closing your eyes for a few minutes will help. Irregular sleep cycles over the long term can be unhealthy and increase stress.

Relaxation

Many people have found that relaxation with guided imagery or other forms of meditation decrease both the physiological and psychological impact of chronic stress. Guided imagery has been used in competitions for many years. Research studies have shown that creation of a mental image of the desired results enhances our ability to reach the goal. Positive behavior or goal attainment is even more enhanced if you imagine the details of the process of achieving your desired outcome (Vines, 1994). Box 9–4 lists useful relaxation techniques.

Imagine taking the NCLEX examination. You sit down at the computer, take a few deep breaths, and begin. Visualize yourself reading the questions, smiling as you identify the correct answer, and hitting the enter key after recording your answer. You complete the examination, feeling confident that you were successful. A week later, you go to your mailbox and find a letter waiting for you. Congratulations, you have passed the test and are now a licensed registered nurse. You imagine telling your family and friends. What an exciting moment!

Proper Nutrition

New research results endorsing the benefits of healthful eating habits seem to appear almost daily. Although specific authorities may prescribe somewhat different regimens, the bottom line appears to be that too little or too much of any nutrient can be harmful. Some general guidelines for good nutrition are included in Box 9–5.

Exercise

Regular aerobic exercise for 20 minutes 3 times a week is recommended for most peo-

---

Box 9–4 Useful relaxation techniques

- Guided imagery
- Yoga
- Transcendental meditation
- Relaxation tapes or music
- Favorite sports or hobbies
- Quiet corners or favorite places

Box 9–5 Guidelines for good nutrition

- Eat smaller, more frequent meals for energy. Six small meals are more beneficial than three large ones.
- Eat foods that are high in complex carbohydrates, contain adequate protein and are low in fat content.
- Eat at least five servings of fruits and vegetables daily.
- Avoid highly processed foods.
- Use salt and sugar sparingly.
- Drink plenty of water.
- Make sure you take enough vitamins including C, B, E, and beta carotene; calcium; and minerals including copper, manganese, zinc, magnesium, and potassium.

Source: Adapted from Bowers, R. (1993). Stress and your health. *National Women's Health Report,* 15(3):6.

ple. The exercise may be walking, swimming, jogging, bicycling, stair-stepping, or low-impact aerobics. Whichever you choose, work at a pace that is comfortable for you and increase it gradually as you become conditioned. Don't overdo it. The experience should leave you feeling invigorated, not exhausted.

The physiological benefits of exercise are well-known. Exercise may not eliminate the stressors in our lives, but it has been shown to be an important element in a healthy lifestyle. Exercise has been shown to improve people's mood and to induce a state of relaxation through the reduction of physiological tension.

Exercise can also be a useful distraction, allowing time to regroup before entering a stressful situation again (Long & Flood, 1993). It is important to choose an exercise that you enjoy doing and that fits into your lifestyle. Perhaps you could walk to work every day or pedal an exercise bicycle during your favorite television program. It is not necessary to join an expensive club or to buy elaborate equipment or clothing to begin an exercise program. It is necessary to get up and get moving, however.

Some people recommend an organized exercise program to obtain the most benefit. For some, however, the cost or time required may actually contribute to their stress. For others, the organized program is an excellent motivator. Find out what works for you.

Keep your exercise plan reasonable. Plan for the long haul, not just until you get past your next performance evaluation or lose that extra 5 pounds. Box 9–6 lists keys to physical health management.

Box 9–6 Keys to physical health management

- Deep breathing
- Posture
- Rest
- Relaxation
- Nutrition
- Exercise

MENTAL HEALTH MANAGEMENT

Mental health management begins with *taking responsibility for your own thoughts and attitudes*. Do not allow self-defeating thoughts to dominate your thinking. You may have to remind yourself to stop thinking that you have to be perfect all the time. You may also have to adjust your expectations and become more realistic. Do you always have to be in control? Does everything have to be perfect? Do you have a difficult time delegating? Are you constantly frustrated because of the way you perceive situations? If you are answering yes to many of these questions, you may be setting yourself up for failure, resentment, low self-esteem, and burnout. Give yourself positive strokes even if no one else does (Davidhizar, 1994; Wolinski, 1993).

Much research has been done to show that the presence of *social support* and the *quality of relationships* can significantly influence how quickly we become ill and how quickly we recover. A sense of belonging and community, an environment in which we can share our feelings without fear of condemnation or ridicule, helps us maintain our well-being. Having friends with whom to share hopes, dreams, fears, and concerns, to laugh and cry with, is paramount to our mental health and stress management. In the work environment, coworkers who are trusted and respected become part of our social support systems (Wolinski, 1993). Box 9–7 lists some additional coping tips for dealing with work stress.

Nurses are professional caregivers. Many years ago, Carl Rogers (1977) said that you cannot care for others until you have taken care of yourself. The word *selfish* may bring to mind someone who is greedy, self-centered, and egotistical, but to take care of yourself, you have to be *creatively selfish*. Learn to nurture yourself so you will be better able to nurture others.

Stress reduction, relaxation techniques, exercise, and good nutrition are all helpful in keeping energy levels high. However, although they can prepare people to cope with the stresses of a job, they are not solutions to the conflicts that lead to reality shock and burnout. It is more effective to resolve the problem than to treat the symptoms (Lee & Ashforth, 1993).

Box 9–7 Coping with daily work stress

- Spending time on outside interests
- Increasing professional knowledge
- Identifying problem-solving resources
- Identifying realistic expectations for your position
- Assessing the rewards your work can realistically deliver
- Developing good communication skills
- Joining rap sessions with coworkers
- Not exceeding your limits—you do not always have to say "yes"!
- Dealing with other people's anger by asking, "Whose problem is this?"
- Recognizing that you can teach other people how to treat you

Source: Adapted from Light, J. (1994). How to steer clear of burnout. *Emergency,* January, 1994, 40–43; McAbee, R. (1994). Job stress and coping strategies among nurses. *AAOHN Journal, 42*(10), 483–487; and Wolinksi, K. (1993). Self-awareness, self-renewal, self-management. *AORN Journal, 58*(4), 721–730.

Box 9–8 Ten daily de-stress reminders

- Express yourself! Communicate your feelings and emotions to friends and colleagues in order to avoid isolation and share perspectives. Sometimes another opinion helps you see the situation in a different light.
- Take time off. Taking breaks, doing something unrelated to work, will help you feel refreshed as you begin work again.
- Understand your individual energy patterns. Are you a morning or afternoon person? Schedule stressful duties during those times when you are most energetic.
- Do one stressful activity at a time. Although this may take advanced planning, avoiding more than one stressful situation at a time will make you feel more in control and satisfied with your accomplishments.
- Exercise! Physical exercise builds physical and emotional resilience. Don't put physical activities on the back burner as you get busy.
- Tackle big projects one piece at a time. Having control of one part of a project at a time will help you to avoid feeling overwhelmed and out of control.
- Delegate if possible. If you can delegate and share in problem solving—do it! Not only will your load be lighter, but others will be able to participate in decision making.
- It's okay to say no! Don't take on every extra assignment or special project.
- Be work-smart. Improve your work skills with new technologies and ideas. Take advantage of additional job training.
- Relax. Find time each day to consciously relax and reflect on the positive energies you need to cope with stressful situations more readily.

Source: Adapted from Bowers, R. (1993). Stress and your health. *National Women's Health Report,* May–June, *15*(3).

■ *Conclusion*

• • • • • • • • • • • • • • • • • • • •

You already know that the work of nursing is not easy and may sometimes be quite stressful. Yet nursing is also a profession filled with much personal and professional satisfaction. We suggest that you periodically ask yourself the questions designed to help you assess your stress level and risk for burnout and review the stress management techniques described in this chapter.

There is no one right way to manage stress and avoid burnout. Rather, by managing small segments of each day, you will learn to identify and manage your stress. This chapter contains many reminders to help you destress during the day (Box 9–8). You can also help your colleagues do the same. If you find yourself in danger of job burnout during your career, you will have learned how to bring yourself back to a healthy, balanced position.

Unfortunately, we can't live in a problem-free world, but we can learn how to handle stress. Using the suggestions in this chapter, you will be able to adopt a healthier personal and professional lifestyle. Good luck, and happy stress management.

❓ *Study Questions*

1. Discuss the characteristics of healthcare organizations that may lead to burnout among nurses. Which of these have you observed in your clinical rotations? How could they be eliminated?

2. How can the new graduate adequately prepare for reality shock? Whose responsibility is it to prevent reality shock?

3. What are the signs of stress, reality shock, and burnout? How are they related?

4. How can you help colleagues deal with their stress?

5. Identify the physical and psychological signs and symptoms you exhibit during stress. What sources of stress are most likely to affect you? How do you deal with these signs and symptoms?

6. Develop a plan to manage stress on a long-term basis.

Critical Thinking Exercise

Shawna, the "new kid on the block," has been working from 7 A.M. to 3 P.M. on an infectious disease floor since obtaining her registered nurse (RN) license 4 months ago. Most of the staff she works with have been there since the unit opened 5 years ago. On a typical day, the staffing consists of a nurse manager, two RNs, a licensed practical nurse (LPN), and one technician for approximately 40 clients. The majority of the clients are HIV-positive with multisystem failure. Many are severely debilitated and need help with their activities of daily living. Although the staff members encourage family members and loved ones to help, most of them are unavailable because they work during the day. Several days a week, the nursing students from Shawna's community college program are assigned to the floor.

Tina, the nurse manager, does not participate in any direct client care, saying that she is "too busy at the desk." Laverne, the other RN, says the unit depresses her and that she has requested a transfer to pediatrics. Lynn, the LPN, wants to "give meds" because she is "sick of the clients' constant whining," and Sheila, the technician, is "just plain exhausted." Lately Shawna has noticed that the other staff members seem to avoid the nursing students and reply to their questions with terse, short answers. Shawna is feeling alone and overwhelmed and goes home at night worrying about the clients, who need more care and attention. She is afraid to ask Tina for more help because she doesn't want to be seen as incompetent or a complainer. When she confided in Lynn about her concerns, Lynn replied, "Get real—no one here cares about us or the clients. All they care about is the bottom line! Why did a smart girl like you choose nursing in the first place?"

1. What is happening on this unit in leadership terms?

2. Identify the major problems and the factors that contributed to these problems.

3. What factors might have contributed to the behaviors exhibited by Tina, Lynn, and Sheila?

4. How would you feel if you were Shawna?

5. Is there anything Shawna can do for herself, for the clients, and for the staff members?

6. What do you think Tina (the nurse manager) should do?

7. How is the nurse manager reacting to the changes in her staff members?

8. What is the responsibility of administration?

9. How are the clients affected by the behaviors exhibited by all staff members?

REFERENCES

Benner, P. (1984). *From Novice to Expert*. Menlo Park, California: Addison Wesley.

Borman, J. (1993). Chief nurse executives balance their work and personal lives. *Nursing Administration Quarterly*, *18*(1), 30–39.

Bowers, R. (1993). Stress and your health. *National Women's Health Report*, *15*(3).

Carr, K., & Kazanowski, M. (1994). Factors affecting job satisfaction of nurses who work in long-term care. *J Adv Nur*, *19*, 878–883.

Cohn, S., Kessler, R., & Gordon, L. (1995). *Measuring Stress*. New York: Oxford University Press.

Corley, M., Farley, B., Geddes, N., Goodloe, L., & Green, P. (1994). The clinical ladder: Impact on nurse satisfaction and turnover. *J Nurs Adm*, *24*(2), 42–48.

Crawford, S. (1993). Job stress and occupational health nursing. *American Association of Occupational Health Nurses Journal*, *41*(11), 522–529.

Davidhizar, R. (1994). Stress can make you or break you. *Advance Practice Nurse*, *10*(1), 17.

Dionne-Proulx, J., & Pepin, R. (1993). Stress management in the nursing profession. *Journal of Nursing Management*, *1*, 75–81.

Duquette, A., Sandhu, B., & Beaudet, L. (1994). Factors related to nursing burnout: A review of empirical knowledge. *Issues in Mental Health Nursing*, *15*, 337–358.

Fielding, J., & Weaver, S. (1994). A comparison of hospital and community-based mental health nurses: Perceptions of their work environment and psychological health. *J Adv Nurs*, *19*, 1196–1204.

Freudenberger, H.J. (1974). Staff burn-out. *Journal of Social Issues*, *30*(1), 159.

Golin, M., Buchlin, M., & Diamond, D. (1991). *Secrets of Executive Success*. Emmaus, Pa.: Rodale Press.

Goliszek, A. (1992). *Sixty-six Second Stress Management. The Quickest Way to Relax and Ease Anxiety*. Far Hills, N.J.: New Horizon NJ.

Goodell, T., & Van Ess Coeling, H. (1994). Outcomes of nurses' job satisfaction. *J Nurs Adm*, *24*(11), 36–41.

Grant, P. (1993). Manage nurse stress and increase potential at the bedside. *Nursing Administration Quarterly*, *18*(1), 16–22.

Johnston, F. (1994, May–June). Stress can kill. *Today's OR Nurse*, pp. 5–6.

Kovner, C., Hendrickson, G., Knickman, J., & Finkler, S. (1994). Nurse care delivery models and nurse satisfaction. *Nursing Administration Quarterly*, *19*(1), 74–85.

Kraeger, M., & Walker, K. (1993). Attrition, burnout, job dissatisfaction and occupational therapy manager. *Occupational Therapy in Health Care*, *8*(4), 47–61.

Kramer, M. (1981, January 27–28). *Coping with Reality Shock*. Workshop presented at Jackson Memorial Hospital, Miami, FL.

Kramer, M., & Schmalenberg, C. (1993). Learning from success: Autonomy and empowerment. *Nursing Management*, *24*(5), 58–64.

Lee, R.T., & Ashforth, B.E. (1993). A further examination of managerial burnout: Toward an integrated model. *Journal of Organizational Behavior*, *14*(1), 3–20.

Lickman, P., Simms, L., & Greene, C. (1993). Learning environment: The catalyst for work excitement. *Journal of Continuing Education in Nursing*, *24*(5), 211–216.

Light, J. (1994, January). How to steer clear of burnout. *Emergency*, pp. 40–43.

Long, B., & Flood, K. (1993). Coping with work stress: Psychological benefits of exercise. *Work and Stress*, *7*(2), 109–119.

Lusk, S. (1993). Job stress. *American Association of Occupational Health Nurses Journal*, *41*(12), 601–606.

Malkin, K.F. (1993). Primary nursing: Job satisfaction and staff retention. *Journal of Nursing Management*, *1*, 119–124.

Martin, K. (1993, May). To cope with stress. *Nursing 93*, pp. 39–41.

McAbee, R. (1994). Job stress and coping strategies among nurses. *American Association of Occupational Health Nurses Journal*, *42*(10), 483–487.

McGee-Cooper, A. (1993, September–October). Shifting from high stress to high energy. *Imprint*.

Nakata, J., & Saylor, C. (1994). Management style and staff nurse satisfaction in a changing environment. *Nursing Administration Quarterly*, *18*(3), 51–57.

Nowack, K., & Pentkowski, A. (1994). Lifestyle habits, substance use, and predictors of job burnout in professional women. *Work and Stress*, *8*(1), 19–35.

Paine, W.S. (1984). Professional burnout: Some major costs. *Family and Community Health*, *6*(4), 1–11.

Rogers, C. (1977). *Carl Rogers on Personal Power*. New York: Dell.

Schelhardt, T.D. (1996, October 2). Company memo to stressed-out employees: "Deal with it." New York: *Wall Street Journal*.

Selye, H. (1956). *The Stress of Life*. New York: McGraw-Hill.

Skubak, K., Earls, N., & Botos, M. (1994). Shared governance: Getting it started. *Nursing Management*, *25*(5), 80I–J, 80N, 80P.

Stechmiller, J., & Yarandi, H. (1993). Predictors of burnout in critical care nurses. *Heart Lung*, *22*(6), 534–540.

Tappen, R.M. (1995). *Nursing Leadership and Management: Concepts and Practice, ed. 3*. Philadelphia: F. A. Davis.

Teague, J.B. (1992). The relationship between various coping styles and burnout among nurses. *Dissertation Abstracts International*, 1994,198402.

Tumulty, G., Jernigan, E., & Kohut, G. (1994). The impact of perceived work environment on job satisfaction of hospital staff nurses. *Applied Nursing Research*, *7*(2), 84–90.

U.S. Department of Health and Human Services (USDHHS). (1991). *Healthy People 2000* (DHHS Publication No. [PHS] 91–50212). Washington, DC: Department of Health and Human Services.

Vines, S. (1994). Relaxation with guided imagery. *American Association of Occupational Health Nurses Journal*, *42*(5), 206–213.

Wolinski, K. (1993). Self-awareness, self-renewal, self-management. *AORN Journal*, *58*(4), 721–730.

Woodhouse, D. (1993). The aspects of humor in dealing with stress. *Nursing Administration Quarterly*, *18*(1), 80–89.

CHAPTER 10

The Workplace

OBJECTIVES   *After reading this chapter, the student will be able to:*

- Recognize threats to safety in the workplace.
- Identify agencies responsible for overseeing workplace safety.
- Describe methods of dealing with violence in the workplace.
- Recognize situations that may reflect sexual harassment.
- Make suggestions for improving the physical and social environment.

Almost half of our waking hours are spent in the workplace. For this reason alone, the quality of the workplace environment is a major concern. Yet it is neglected to a surprising extent in many healthcare organizations. It is neglected by administrators who would never allow peeling paint or poorly maintained equipment but leave their staff, their most costly and valuable resource, unmaintained and unrefreshed. The "do more with less" thinking that has predominated in many organizations places considerable pressure on staff and management alike (Chisholm, 1992). Improvement of the workplace environment is more difficult to accomplish under these circumstances but is more important than ever.

Much of the responsibility for enhancing the workplace environment rests with upper-level management people who have the authority and resources to encourage organization-wide growth and change. However, nurses can contribute to the identification of problems and support efforts to foster a positive work environment. Issues of workplace safety, violence, sexual harassment, impaired workers, and enhancement of the quality of work life, including managing diversity, are the focus of this chapter.

■ *Workplace Safety*

Safety is not a new concept in the workplace. Although guidelines for safe working conditions have existed since the early Egyptians, the major movement began during the Industrial Revolution. In 1913, the National Council for Industrial Safety (now the National Safety Council) was formed. Through the National Safety Council, national standards for occupational safety issues are developed and statistics on accident and injury rates collected. The National Safety Council believes that safety in the workplace is the responsibility of both the employer and employee. The employer must ensure a safe, healthful work environment, and employees are accountable for knowing and following safety guidelines and standards (National Safety Council, 1992).

THREATS TO SAFETY

Threats to safety in the workplace can range from exposure to potentially lethal chemical, infectious, and radioactive agents to violence from clients or other staff members.

In 1993, 300 of Brigham Young Hospital's 1000 staff nurses reported the following symptoms: hives; rashes; headache; dizziness; nausea; eye, nose, and throat irritation; menstrual irregularities; urticaria; cardiac and respiratory distress; hair loss; joint pain; and memory loss. The mysterious illness began with the operating room staff and soon spread to all areas of the hospital. The hospital, undergoing reconstruction, was soon given a diagnosis of "sick building syndrome." Several nurses became so sensitized to the chemicals floating in the hospital air that they have been on permanent leave since 1994 and may never be able to return to nursing (Himali, 1995).

A survey of 1540 Milwaukee nurses found that many of them had experienced physical or verbal abuse. Fifty-three percent of the nurses responding to the survey said that they had been hit, pushed, or had something thrown at them by clients. Another 6 percent said that they had had the same experience with physicians. Verbal abuse was even more common: 58 percent said that they had been verbally abused by clients, 51 percent by physicians, and 22 percent by their supervisors ("RNs Cite," 1993).

Exposure to the human immunodeficiency virus (HIV) is another concern. Between 1985 and 1992 there were 32 clearly documented cases of healthcare workers acquiring an HIV infection in the workplace in the United States; 12 were in nurses. Laboratory technicians were the second highest group, with 11 documented cases (CDC, 1992).

Threats to safety in the workplace vary from one setting to another and from one individual to another. The pregnant staff member may be more vulnerable to risks from radiation; staff members working in the emergency room of a large urban public hospital would be at more risk for HIV and tuberculosis than the staff members working in the newborn nursery. All staff members have the right to be made aware of potential risks. No worker should feel intimidated or uncomfortable in the workplace.

REDUCING RISK

Occupational Safety and Health Administration

The Occupational Safety and Health Act of 1970 and the Mine Safety and Health Act of 1977 were the first federal guidelines and standards related to safe and healthful working conditions. Through these acts, the National Institute for Occupational Safety and Health (NIOSH) and the Occupational Safety and Health Administration (OSHA) were formed. OSHA regulations apply to most U.S. employers who have one or more employees and who engage in businesses affecting commerce. Under OSHA regulations, the employer must comply with standards for providing a safe, healthful work environment. Employers are also required to keep records of all occupational (job-related) illnesses and accidents. Examples of occupational accidents and injuries include burns, chemical exposures, lacerations, hearing loss, respiratory exposure, musculoskeletal injuries, and exposure to infectious diseases.

OSHA regulations provide for workplace inspections that may be conducted with or without prior notification to the employer. However, catastrophic or fatal accidents and employee complaints may also trigger an OSHA inspection. OSHA encourages employers and employees to work together to identify and remove any workplace hazards before contacting the nearest OSHA area office. If the employee has not been able to resolve the safety or health issue, the employee may file a formal complaint, and an inspection will be ordered by the area OSHA director (United States Department of Labor, 1995). Any violations found are posted where all employees can view them. The employer has the right to contest the OSHA decision. The law also states that the employer cannot punish or discriminate against employees for exercising their rights related to job safety and health hazards or participating in OSHA inspections (United States Department of Labor, 1995).

OSHA inspections focus especially on blood-borne pathogens, lifting and ergonomic (proper body alignment) guidelines, confined-space regulations, and respiratory guidelines (National Safety Council, 1992). More recently, OSHA has also been committed to preventing workplace violence (United States Department of Labor, 1996). The U.S. Department of Labor publishes fact sheets related to various OSHA guidelines and activities. They can be obtained from your employer, at the local public library, or via the Internet.

On December 6, 1992, OSHA published regulations regarding worker risk of infection from blood-borne pathogens. Violation of the blood-borne pathogen standard (or any other OSHA safety standard) may result in penalties up to $70,000 as well as criminal charges for willful violations resulting in worker death (Strader & Decker, 1995).

Centers for Disease Control and Prevention

Although not directly involved in workplace safety, the Centers for Disease Control and Prevention (CDC) are another good resource for the nurse. The CDC publishes continuous updates on recommendations for prevention of HIV transmission in the workplace and universal precautions related to blood-borne pathogens, as well as the most recent information on other infectious diseases in the workplace such as tuberculosis and hepatitis. Information can be obtained by consulting the *Mortality and Morbidity Weekly Report (MMWR)* in the library, via the Internet, or through the toll-free phone number: 1-800-232-1311. Interested healthcare workers can also be placed on the mailing list of the CDC to receive any free publications.

Box 10–1 lists the most important federal laws enacted to protect the individual in the workplace.

Box 10–1 Federal laws enacted to protect the worker in the workplace

● Equal Pay Act of 1963: Employers must provide equal pay for equal work regardless of sex.

● Title VII of Civil Rights Act of 1964: Employees may not be discriminated against in employment on the basis of race, color, religion, sex, or national origin.

● Age Discrimination in Employment Act of 1967: Private and public employers may not discriminate against persons 40 years of age or older except when a certain age group is a bona fide occupational qualification.

● Pregnancy Discrimination Act of 1968: Pregnant women cannot be discriminated against in employment benefits if they are able to discharge job responsibilities.

● Fair Credit Reporting Act of 1970: Job applicants and employees have the right to know of the existence and content of any credit files maintained on them.

● Vocational Rehabilitation Act of 1973: An employer receiving financial assistance from the federal government may not discriminate against individuals with disabilities and must develop affirmative action plans to hire and promote individuals with disabilities.

● Family Education Rights and Privacy Act—The Buckley Amendment of 1974: Educational institutions may not supply information about students without their consent.

● Immigration Reform and Control Act of 1986: Employers must screen employees for the right to work in the US without discriminating on the basis of national origin.

● Americans with Disabilities Act of 1990: Persons with physical or mental disabilities and who are chronically ill cannot be discriminated against in the workplace. Employers must make "reasonable accommodations" to meet the needs of the disabled employee. These include such things as installing foot or hand controls; readjusting light switches, telephones, desks, table and computer equipment; providing access ramps and elevators; offering flexible work hours; and providing readers for blind employees.

● Family and Medical Leave Act of 1993: Requires employers with 50 or more employees to provide up to 12 weeks of unpaid leave for family medical emergencies, childbirth, or adoption.

Source: Adapted from Strader, M. & Decker, P. (1995). *Role Transition to Patient Care Management.* Conn: Appleton and Lange.

Programs

The primary objective of any workplace safety program is to prevent staff members from harm and to protect the organization from liability related to that harm. The first step in development of a workplace safety program is to *recognize* a *potential hazard* and then take steps to control it. Based on OSHA regulations (United States Department of Labor, 1995), the employer must inform staff members of any potential health hazards and provide as much protection from these hazards as possible. In many cases, initial warnings come from the CDC, NIOSH, and other federal, state, and local agencies. For example, employers must provide tuberculosis testing and hepatitis B vaccine; protective equipment such as gloves, gowns, and masks; and immediate treatment after exposure for all staff members who may have contact with blood-borne pathogens. They are expected to remove hazards, educate employees, and establish institution-wide policies and procedures to protect their employees (Herring, 1994; Roche, 1993). For example, nurses who are not provided with latex gloves may refuse to participate in any activities involving blood or blood products.

The employee cannot be discriminated against in the workplace, and reasonable accommodations for safety against blood-borne pathogens must be provided. This may mean that the nurse with latex allergies is placed in an area where exposure to blood-borne pathogens is not an issue (Strader & Decker, 1995; United States Department of Labor, 1995).

The second step in a workplace safety program is a *thorough assessment of the degree of risk* entailed. Staff members, for example, may become very fearful in situations that do not warrant such fear.

> Nancy Wu is the nurse manager on a busy geriatric unit. The majority of the clients require total care: bathing, feeding, positioning. She has observed that several of the staff members working on the unit use poor body mechanics in lifting and moving the clients. In the last month, several of the staff members have been referred to employee health for back pain.
>
> This week, she noticed that the clients seem to remain in the same position for long periods of time and frequently are never out of bed or in the chair for an entire day. When she confronted the staff, the response was the same from all of them: "I have to work for a living. I can't afford to risk a back injury for someone who may not live past the end of the week." Nancy Wu was concerned about the care of the clients as well as the apparent lack of information her staff had about prevention of back injuries. She decided to seek assistance from the nurse practitioner in charge of employee health in developing a back injury prevention program.

These same individuals may be complacent about such risks as radiation or clean air, which cannot be seen or felt as one works with clients.

Assessment of the workplace may require considerable data gathering to document the incidence of the problem and consultation with experts before a plan of action is drawn up. Healthcare organizations often create formal committees composed of experts from within the institution and representatives from the departments affected to assess these risks. It is important that staff members from various levels of the organization be allowed to give input into an assessment of safety needs and risks.

The third step is to *draw up a plan* to provide optimal protection for staff members. It is not always a simple matter to protect staff members without interfering with the provision of client care. For example, some devices that can be worn to prevent transmission of tuberculosis interfere with communication with the client ("Federal Agencies," 1993). There have also been some attempts to limit visits or withdraw home healthcare nurses from high-crime areas, but this leaves homebound clients without care (Nadwairski, 1992). A threat assessment team that evaluates problems and suggests appropriate actions may reduce the incidence and severity of problems with violent behavior but may also increase employees' fear of violence if not handled well.

Developing a safety plan includes the following:

- Consulting federal, state, and local regulations
- Distinguishing real from imagined risks
- Seeking administrative support and enforcement for the plan
- Calculating costs of a program

The final stage in developing a workplace safety program is *implementing the program*. Educating the staff, providing the necessary safety supplies and equipment, and modifying the environment will contribute to an effective program. Protecting client and staff confidentiality and monitoring adherence to control and safety procedures should not be overlooked in the implementation stage (CDC, 1992; Jankowski, 1992; "Federal Agencies," 1993).

An example of a safety program is the program for healthcare workers exposed to HIV instituted at the Department of Veteran's Affairs Hospital, San Francisco, California (Armstrong, Gordon, & Santorella, 1995). An HIV exposure can be stressful for both

---

Box 10–2 Responsibilities of the nurse: transmission of blood-borne pathogens

- Use universal precautions
- Respect sharps
- Immunize against hepatitis
- Report exposures
- Follow agency/OSHA regulations regarding post-exposure follow-up
- Participate with safety committees in developing ongoing safety programs
- Support peers who are potentially exposed to infectious diseases

Source: Adapted from American Nurses Association (1993). *HIV, Hepatitis-B, Hetatitis-C: Blood-borne Diseases.* Washington,DC: ANA.

---

healthcare workers and their loved ones. This employee assistance program includes as many as ten 60-minute individual counseling sessions on the meaning and experience of this traumatic event. Additional counseling sessions for couples are also provided. Information about HIV and about dealing with acute stress reactions is provided. Additional counseling assists workers to identify a plan to obtain help from their individual support systems, the healthcare worker's practice methods of dealing with blood-borne pathogens, and helping the client to return to work.

The American Nurses Association (ANA) has published a brochure entitled *HIV, Hepatitis-B, Hepatitis-C: Nurses' Risks, Rights, and Responsibilities* (ANA, 1993). A free copy of the brochure can be obtained by calling 1-800-274-4ANA. Box 10–2 lists the responsibilities of the nurse in dealing with transmission of blood-borne pathogens.

■ *Violence*

• • • • • • • • • • • • • • • • • • •

Violence in the workplace is a contemporary social issue. Newspapers and magazines have reported numerous incidences of vio-

lence in the workplace. Today, more assaults occur in the healthcare and social services industries than in any other (United States Department of Labor, 1996). The aggressor can be a disgruntled employee or employer, an unhappy significant other, or a person committing a random act of violence. Nurses have been identified as a group at risk of violence from clients, family members, and other staff members. Between 1983 and 1989, 69 registered nurses were killed at work. Homicide is the leading cause of traumatic occupational death among employees in nursing homes and personal care facilities. Nurses employed in psychiatric settings, emergency departments, and outpatient clinics are considered particularly vulnerable. Assault by a client is defined as "the act of a patient physically attacking or restraining a nurse with part of the patient's body or an object" (United States Department of Labor, 1996; Collins, 1994).

Ms. Jones works on the evening shift in the emergency department (ED) at a large, urban hospital. The ED frequently receives clients who have been victims of gunshot wounds, stabbings, and other gang-related incidents. Many of the clients entering the ED are high on alcohol or drugs. Ms. Jones has just interviewed a 21-year-old male client who is awaiting treatment as a result of a fight during an evening of heavy drinking. Because his injuries have been determined not to be life-threatening, he had to wait to see a doctor. "I'm tired of waiting. Let's get this show on the road," he screamed loudly as Ms. Jones walked by. "I'm sorry you have to wait, Mr. P., but the doctor is busy with another client and will get to you as soon as possible." She handed him a cup of juice she had been bringing to another client. He grabbed the cup, threw it in her face, and then grabbed her arm. Slamming her against the wall, he jumped off the stretcher and yelled obscenities at her. He continued to scream in her face until a security guard intervened.

Be aware of clues that may indicate a potential for violence (Box 10–3). These behav-

<table>
</table>

Box 10–3 Behaviors indicating a potential for violence

- History of violent behavior
- Delusional, paranoid, or suspicious speech
- Aggressive, threatening statements
- Rapid speech, angry tone of voice
- Pacing, tense posture, clenched fists, tightened jaw
- Alcohol or drug use
- Male gender, youth
- Policies that set unrealistic limits

Source: Adapted from Kinkle, S. (1993). Violence in the ED: How to stop it before it starts. *Am J Nurs, 93*(7), 22–24; Carroll, C. & Sheverbush, J. (1996). KANA violence assessment in hospitals provides basis for action. *American Nurse*, September 18.

TABLE 10–1
WHEN AN ASSAULT OCCURS: PLACING BLAME ON VICTIMS

Victim Gender
Women receive a higher degree of blame than men.

Subject Gender
Female victims receive a higher degree of blame from women than men.

Severity
The more severe the assault, the more often the victim is blamed.

Beliefs
The world is a just place and the person deserves the misfortune.

Age of Victim
The older the victim, the more he or she is held to blame.

Source: Adapted from Lanza, M.L., & Carifo, J. (1991). Blaming the victim: Complex (nonlinear) patterns of causal attribution by nurses in response to vignettes of a patient assaulting a nurse. *Journal of Emergency Nursing, 17*(5), 299–309.

iors may occur in clients, family members, visitors, or even other staff members.

Long waiting times, staff-to-staff conflicts, open access to client care areas, and unlimited visiting hours have also been linked to the potential for violence in healthcare facilities. Even clients with no past history of violent behavior may react violently to medication or pain (Carroll & Sheverbush, 1996; Lanza & Carifio, 1991).

Also of concern are the underreporting of violence and persistent misperception within the healthcare industry that assaults are part of the job or that the victim somehow caused the assault. Causes of underreporting may be a lack of institutional reporting policies or fear on the part of employees that the assault was a result of negligence or poor job performance (United States Department of Labor, 1996). Table 10–1 lists some of the faulty reasoning that leads to placing blame on the victim of the assault.

Actions to address violence in the workplace include (1) identifying the factors that contribute to violence and controlling as many as possible and (2) assessing staff attitudes and knowledge regarding violence in the workplace (Carroll & Sheverbush, 1996; Collins, 1994; Mahoney, 1991).

When you begin your new job, you may want to find out what the policies and procedures related to violence in the workplace are at your institution. Seeking information after an incident occurs may be too late. Preventing an incident is better than having to intervene after violence has occurred. Some of the strategies you can individually institute to prevent violence include the following (Carroll & Sheverbush, 1996; Collins, 1994; Mahoney, 1991):

- Look for clues indicating a potential for violence.
- Call clients, family members, and visitors by name; anonymity has been associated with a higher incidence of violence.
- Encourage the client or family to vent anger verbally by using effective communication techniques.
- Trust your intuition if you feel uncomfortable.
- Be knowledgeable regarding policies and procedures in your institution.

Violence in the workplace increases costs of care. Box 10–4 lists some additional ac-

---

Box 10–4 Increasing protection from violence in the workplace

- Security personnel and escorts
- Panic buttons in medication rooms, stairwells, activity rooms, and nursing stations
- Bullet-proof glass in reception, triage and admitting areas
- Locked or key-coded access doors
- Closed-circuit television
- Metal detectors
- Use of beepers and/or cellular car phones
- Hand-held alarms or noise devices
- Lighted parking lots
- Buddy system

Source: Adapted from Simonowitz, J. (1994). Violence in the workplace: You're entitled to protection. *RN, 57*(11), 61–63.

---

tions that can be taken to protect staff member and clients from violence in the workplace.

■ *Sexual Harassment*

A new supervisor was hired on the unit. After months of interviewing, the candidate selected was a young male nurse whom the staff members jokingly described as "a blond Tom Cruise." The new supervisor was an instant hit with the predominantly female executives and staff members. However, he soon found himself on the receiving end of sexual jokes and innuendos. He had been trying to prove himself a competent supervisor, with hopes of eventually moving up to a higher management position. He viewed the behavior of the female staff members and supervisors as undermining his credibility, in addition to being embarrassing and annoying. He attempted to have the unwelcome

conduct stopped by discussing it with his boss, a female nurse manager. She told him jokingly that it is nothing more than "good-natured fun" and besides, "men can't be harassed by women" (Outwater, 1994).

The laws that prohibit discrimination in the workplace are based on the Fifth and Fourteenth Amendments to the Constitution, mandating due process and equal protection under the law. The Equal Employment Opportunity Commission (EEOC) oversees the administration and enforcement of issues related to workplace equality. Although there may be exemptions from any law, it is important that the nurse recognize that there is significant legislation that prohibits employers from making workplace decisions based on race, color, sex, age, disability, religion, or national origin. The employer may ask questions related to these issues but cannot make decisions about employment based on them.

The EEOC issued a statement that sexual harassment is a form of sex discrimination prohibited by Title VII of the Civil Rights Act of 1964 in 1980. Two forms of sexual harassment are identified, both based on the premise that the action is unwelcome sexual conduct:

1. *Quid pro quo:* Sexual favors are given in exchange for favorable job benefits or continuation of employment. The employee must demonstrate that he or she was required to endure unwelcome sexual advances to keep the job or job benefits and that rejection of these behaviors would have resulted in deprivation of a job or benefits. Example: The administrator approaches a nurse for a date in exchange for a salary increase 3 months before the scheduled review.

2. *Hostile environment:* This is the most common sexual harassment claim and the most difficult to prove. The employee making the claim must prove that the harassment is based on gender and that it has affected conditions of employment or created an environment so offensive that the employee could not effectively discharge the re-

sponsibilities of the job (Outwater, 1994).

In 1993, the Supreme Court ruled that a plaintiff is not required to prove any psychological injury to establish a harassment claim. If the environment could be shown to be hostile or abusive, there was no further need to establish that it was also psychologically injurious. Although sexual harassment against women is more common, men can also become the victims of sexual harassment.

Since the 1991 allegations of sexual harassment by Anita Hill against Justice Clarence Thomas, the number of claims filed with the EEOC have increased dramatically: from 6892 in 1991 to over 12,500 in 1993. A study of female physicians conducted by the American Medical Association in 1993 indicated that more than 41 percent experienced sexual harassment in their practice (Outwater, 1994). Sexual harassment can cost an employer money, unfavorable publicity, expensive lawsuits, and large damage awards. Low morale caused by a hostile work environment can cause significant decreases in employee productivity, increased absenteeism, increases in sick leave and medical payments, and decreased job satisfaction.

Addressing the issue of sexual harassment in the workplace is important. As an employee, you should be familiar with the policies and procedures related to reporting sexual harassment incidents. If you supervise other employees, you should regularly review the agency's policies and procedures. Seek appropriate guidance from your human resources personnel. If an employee approaches you with a complaint, a confidential investigation of the charges should be initiated. Above all, do not dismiss any incidents or charges of sexual harassment involving yourself or others as "just having fun" or "there is nothing anyone can do." Responses like this can have serious consequences in the workplace (Outwater, 1994).

■ *Impaired Workers*

Alcohol and drug abuse continue to be major health problems in this country. Healthcare professionals are not immune to alcoholism or chemical dependency. In addition, mental illnesses of various kinds may also affect a nurse's ability to deliver safe, competent care. Impaired workers can adversely affect client care, staff retention, morale, and management time as team members try to "pick up the slack for the impaired worker" (Damrosch & Scholler-Jaquish, 1993). The most common signs of impairment are as follows (Damrosch & Scholler-Jaquish, 1993, pp. 154–160):

- Witnessed consumption of alcohol or other substances on the job
- Dress, appearance, posture, gestures
- Slurred speech, abusive/incoherent language
- Reports from clients and/or coworkers
- Witnessed unprofessional conduct
- Significant lack of attention to detail
- Witnessed theft of controlled substances

Mr. P., the unit manager, has noticed that Ms. J. has frequently been late for work. She arrives with a wrinkled uniform, dirty shoes, unkempt hair, and broken nails. Lately she has been overheard making terse remarks to clients such as, "Who do you think I am—your maid?", and spends longer and longer periods of time off the unit. The floor has a large number of surgical clients who receive intramuscular and oral medications for pain. Lately Ms. J.'s clients continue to complain of pain even after medication administration has been charted. She frequently "forgets" to waste her intramuscular narcotics in front of another nurse. Mr. P. is concerned that Ms. J. may be an impaired nurse.

Most employers and state boards of nursing have strict guidelines related to impaired nurses. Impaired nurse programs conducted by state boards of nursing work with the employer to assist the impaired nurse to remain licensed while receiving help for the addiction problem. It is important that you become aware of workplace issues surrounding the impaired worker: signs and symptoms of impairment and the policies and reporting procedures concerning an impaired worker. Compassion from coworkers and supervisors is of utmost importance in assisting the impaired worker to seek help (Damrosch & Scholler-Jaquish, 1993).

■ *Reporting Questionable Practices*

• • • • • • • • • • • • • • • • • • • •

Most employers have policies encouraging the reporting of behavior that may affect the workplace environment. These behaviors may include (1) endangering a client's health or safety; (2) abuse of authority; (3) violation of laws, rules, regulations, or standards of professional ethics; and (4) gross waste of funds (ANA, 1994).

The Code for Nurses (ANA, 1985, pp. 6–7) is very specific about nurses' responsibility to report questionable behavior that may impact the welfare of a patient:

> When the nurse is aware of inappropriate or questionable practice in the provision of health care, concern should be expressed to the person carrying out the questionable practice and attention called to the possible detrimental effect upon the client's welfare. When factors in the health care delivery system threaten the welfare of the client, similar action should be directed to the responsible administrative person. If indicated, the practice should then be reported to the appropriate authority within the institution, agency, or larger system.

The sources of various federal and state guidelines governing the workplace are listed in Box 10–5.

Protection by the agency should be afforded both the accused and the person doing the reporting. *Whistleblowers* is the term used to describe employees who report employer violations to outside agencies. Whistleblowers may be protected when they are

---

Box 10–5 Laws governing health care practices

• State nurse practice acts
• Federal and state health regulations
• State and federal pharmacy laws for controlled substances
• Occupational Safety and Health Administration (OSHA) state and federal standards and regulations
• State medical records and communicable disease laws
• Environmental laws regulating hazardous waste, air and water quality
• Centers for Disease Control and Prevention (CDC) guidelines
• Federal and state anti-discrimination laws
• State clinical laboratory regulations
• Joint Commission of Accreditation of Healthcare Organization (JCAHO) regulations

Source: Adapted from American Nurses Association (1994). *Guidelines on Reporting Incompetent, Unethical, or Illegal Practies.* Washington, DC: ANA.

---

involved in situations in which they refuse to perform illegal acts or when the employer sanctions acts that are illegal or unsafe or violate a code of professional ethics and could endanger the public health and safety (ANA, 1994). In May 1994, the U.S. Supreme Court ruled that nurses who direct the work of other employees may be found to be supervisors and therefore may not be covered by the protections guaranteed under the National Labor Relations Act. This ruling may cause nurses to have no protection from retaliation if they report illegal practices in the workplace (ANA, 1995). The 1995 brochure from the American Nurses Association, *Protect Your Patients—Protect Your License* states, "Be aware that reporting quality and safety issues may result in reprisals by an employer."

If attempts to resolve issues through appropriate workplace channels fail, the ANA has published information to assist the registered nurse in reporting quality concerns in the workplace (ANA, 1995). The brochure, item NP-105, may be obtained by calling 1-800-274-4ANA.

It is the responsibility of professional nurses to become acquainted with the state and federal regulations, standards of practice and professional performance, and agency protocols and practice guidelines governing their practice. Lack of knowledge will not protect you from ethical and legal obligations. Your state nurses association can assist you in seeking information related to incompetent, unethical, or illegal practices. When you join your state association, you will gain access to an opportunity to have input into policies and procedures designed to protect the public.

■ *Enhancing the Quality of Work Life*

• • • • • • • • • • • • • • • • • •

Both the social and physical aspects of a workplace can affect the way people work and how they feel about their jobs. The social aspects include working relationships, a climate that allows growth and creativity, and cultural diversity.

SOCIAL ENVIRONMENT

Working Relationships

Many aspects of the social environment have received attention in earlier chapters. Team building, effective communication, and development of leadership skills are essential to the development of effective working relationships. The day-to-day interactions with one's peers and supervisors have a major impact on the quality of the workplace environment.

Support of One's Peers and Supervisors

The difference between a supportive and nonsupportive environment is keenly felt by most employees.

Ms. B. came to work already tired. Her baby was sick and had been awake most of the night. Her team expressed concern about the baby when she told them she had a difficult night. Each team member voluntarily took an extra client so that Ms. B. could have a lighter assignment that day. When Ms. B. expressed her appreciation, her team leader said, "We know you would do the same for us." Ms. B. worked in a supportive environment.

Ms. G. came to work after a sleepless night. Her young son had been given a diagnosis of leukemia and she was very worried about him. When she mentioned her concerns, her team leader interrupted her saying, "Please leave your personal problems at home. We have a lot of work to do and expect you to do your share." Ms. G. worked in a nonsupportive environment.

Support from peers and supervisors involves professional concerns as well as personal ones. In a supportive environment, people are willing to make difficult decisions, take risks, and "go the extra mile" for team members and the organization. In contrast, in a nonsupportive environment, they are afraid to take risks, avoid making decisions, and usually limit their commitment.

Involvement in Decision Making

The importance of having a voice in the decisions made about one's work and one's patients cannot be overstated. Empowerment is a related phenomenon. It is a sense of having both the ability and the opportunity to act effectively (Kramer & Schmalenberg, 1993). Empowerment is the opposite of apathy and powerlessness. A number of actions can be taken to empower nurses: remove barriers to their autonomy and participation in decision making, publicly express confidence in their capability and value, reward initiative and assertiveness, and provide role models who demonstrate confidence and competence. The following illustrates the difference between empowerment and powerlessness:

> Soon after completing orientation, Nurse A heard a new nurse aide scolding a client for soiling the bed. Nurse A did not know how incidents of potential verbal abuse were handled in this institution, so she reported it to the nurse manager. The nurse manager asked Nurse A a few questions and thanked her for the information. The new aide was counseled immediately after their meeting. Nurse A noticed a positive change in the aide's manner with clients after this incident. Nurse A felt good about having contributed to a more effective client care team. Nurse A felt empowered and will take action again when another occasion arises.
>
> A colleague of Nurse B was an instructor at a nearby community college. This colleague asked Nurse B if students would be welcome on her unit. "Of course," replied Nurse B. "I'll speak with my head nurse about it." When Nurse B spoke with her head nurse, the response was that the unit was too busy to accommodate students. In addition, Nurse B received a verbal reprimand from the supervisor for overstepping her authority by discussing the placement of students. "All requests for student placement must be directed to the education department," she said. The supervisor directed Nurse B to write a letter of apology for having made an unauthorized commitment to the community college. Nurse B was afraid to make any decisions or public statements after this incident. Nurse B felt alienated and powerless.

PROFESSIONAL GROWTH AND INNOVATION

The difference between a climate that encourages staff growth and creativity and one that does not can be quite subtle. In fact, many people are only partly aware, if at all, of whether or not they work in an environment that fosters professional growth and learning. Yet the effect on the quality of the work done is pervasive, and it is an important factor in distinguishing the merely good healthcare organization from the excellent healthcare organization.

Much of the responsibility for staff development and promotion of innovation lies with upper-level management people, who can sponsor seminars, conduct organization-wide workshops, establish educational policies, promote career mobility, develop clinical ladders, initiate innovative projects, and reward suggestions.

Some of the ways in which the first-line manager can develop and support a climate of professional growth are to encourage critical thinking, provide opportunities to take advantage of educational programs, encourage new ideas and projects, and reward professional growth.

Encourage Critical Thinking

If you ever find yourself or other staff members saying, "Don't ask why; just go ahead and do it," you need to evaluate the type of climate in which you are functioning. An inquisitive frame of mind is relatively easy to suppress in a work environment. Clients and staff members quickly perceive a nurse's impatience or defensiveness when too many questions are raised. Their response will be to simply give up asking these questions.

On the other hand, if you support critical thinkers and act as a role model who adopts a questioning attitude, you can encourage others to do the same.

Seek Out Educational Opportunities

In most organizations, first-line managers do not have discretionary funds that can be allocated for educational purposes. However, they can usually support a staff member's request for educational leave or for financial support and often have a small budget that can be used for seminars or workshops.

Team leaders and nurse managers can make it easier or more difficult for staff members to further their education. They can make things difficult for the staff member who is trying to balance work, home, and school responsibilities. Or they can pitch in and help lighten the load of the staff member who has to finish a paper or take an exam. Unsupportive supervisors have even attacked staff members who pursue further education, criticizing every minor error and blocking their advancement. Obviously, such behavior should be dealt with quickly by upper-level management because it is a serious inhibitor of staff development.

Encourage New Ideas

The increasingly rapid accumulation of knowledge in the healthcare field mandates continuous learning for safe practice. Intellectual curiosity is a hallmark of the professional.

Every move up the professional ladder should bring new challenges that enrich one's work (Roedel & Nystrom, 1987). As a professional, you can be a role model for an environment in which every staff member is both challenged and rewarded for meeting these challenges. Participating in brainstorming sessions, group conferences, and discussions all encourage the generation of new ideas. Although new nurses may feel that they have nothing to offer, it is important to participate in activities that encourage staff members to look at fresh new ideas.

Reward Professional Growth

A primary source of discontent in the workplace is lack of recognition. Positive feedback and recognition of our contributions are important intangible rewards in the workplace. Regardless of how small a contribution is, everyone enjoys praise and recognition. A smile, a card or note, or a verbal "thank you" goes a long way with coworkers in recognizing a job well done. Staff recognition programs have also been identified as a means to increase self-esteem, social gratification, morale, and job satisfaction (Hurst, Croker, & Bell, 1994).

CULTURAL DIVERSITY

Ms. V. is beginning orientation for a new staff nurse position. She has been told that part of her orientation will be a morning class on cultural diversity. She says to the human resources person in charge of orientation, "I don't think I need to attend that class. I treat all people as equal. Besides, anyone living in the United States has an obligation to learn the language and ways of those of us who were born here, not the other way around."

Mr. M. is a staff nurse on a medical-surgical unit. A young man with HIV infection has been recently admitted. He is scheduled for surgery in the morning and has requested that his significant other be present for the preoperative teaching. Mr. M. reluctantly agrees but mumbles under his breath to a coworker, "It wouldn't be so bad if they didn't throw their homosexuality around and act like an old married couple. Why can't he act like a man and get his own preop instructions?"

Workforce diversity in terms of age, gender, culture, ethnicity, race, primary language, physical capabilities, and lifestyle presents a challenge to the workplace. By the year 2000, 47 percent of workers will be women and 26 percent minorities (Lappetito, 1994, p. 22). An organization that fosters diversity in the workplace encourages respect and understanding of human characteristics and acceptance of the similarities and differences that make us human.

As you begin your career, be alert to the signs of cultural diversity or insensitivity where you work. Signs that increased sensitivity and responsiveness to the needs of a culturally diverse workforce are needed on your team or in your organization would be a greater proportion of minorities or women in lower-level jobs, lower career mobility and higher turnover rates in these groups, and acceptance or even approval of insensitivity and unfairness (Malone, 1993). Observe interaction patterns, such as where people sit in the cafeteria or how they cluster during coffee breaks: are they mixing freely or can you see divisions by sex, race, language, or status in the organization (Moch & Diemert, 1990; Ward, 1992)? Other indications of an organization's diversity "fitness" include the following (Mitchell, 1995, pp. 44–48):

◆ The personnel mix reflects the current and potential population being served.

◆ Individual cultural preferences pertaining to issues of social distance, touching, voice volume and inflection, silence, and gestures are respected.

◆ There is awareness of special family and holiday celebrations important to people of different cultures.

◆ The organization communicates through action that people are individuals first and members of a particular culture second.

Effective management of cultural diversity requires considerable time and energy. Although organized cultural diversity programs are usually the responsibility of middle- and upper-level managers, you can play a part in raising awareness. You can be a culturally competent practitioner and a role model for others by becoming:

◆ Aware of and sensitive to your own culture-based preferences

◆ Willing to explore your own biases and values

◆ Knowledgeable about other cultures

◆ Respectful of and sensitive to diversity among individuals

◆ Skilled using and selecting culturally sensitive intervention strategies

Some additional dos and don'ts for managing diversity are listed in Table 10–2.

PHYSICAL ENVIRONMENT

This aspect of workplace improvement is not as well developed as the social aspect, especially in nursing. However, with the increase in technology in health care, we may see more attention to this area of work life. The use of lighting, colors, and music in improving the workplace environment is increasing. Computer workstations designed to promote efficiency in the client care unit are becoming a common fixture. Modifications to various elements of the physical environment such as the floors, chairs, desks, beds, and workstations can decrease the incidence of back and upper extremity injuries. Relocation of supplies and substations closer to client rooms to reduce steps, easier visual and auditory scanning of clients from the nurses' station, better light and ventilation, a unified information system, and reduced need for client transport are all possible with changes in the physical environment.

■ *Conclusion*

Workplace safety is an increasing concern. Staff members have a right to be informed of any potential risks in the workplace. Employers have a responsibility to provide adequate equipment and supplies to protect employees and programs and policies to inform employees to minimize risks to the extent possible. Issues of workplace violence, sexual harassment, and impaired workers

TABLE 10–2
DOS AND DON'TS FOR MANAGING DIVERSITY

Do . . .	Don't . . .
Recognize diversity	Pretend everyone is alike
Value diversity	Expect everyone to conform to the prevailing culture
Develop informal supports	Seek a quick solution
Ensure fairness	Develop different standards of performance
Make these principles an integral part of your individual philosophy	Expect one workshop to solve the problem

should be addressed to protect both employees and patients.

A social environment that promotes professional growth and creativity and a physical environment that offers comfort and maximum work efficiency should be considered in improving the quality of work life. Cultural awareness, a respect for the diversity of others, and increased contact between groups should be the goals of the workforce for the next century.

Many waking hours are spent in the workplace. It can offer a climate of companionship, professional growth, and excitement. You can be part of the solution if you remain aware of workplace issues.

？ *Study Questions*

1. Why is it important for nurses to understand the major federal laws enacted to protect the individual in the workplace?

2. What actions could nurses take if they believed that OSHA guidelines were not being followed in the workplace?

3. What are nurses' responsibilities in dealing with transmission of blood-borne pathogens in the workplace?

4. Describe the difference between a supportive and nonsupportive social environment in the workplace.

5. How could you, as a new nurse, raise awareness related to cultural diversity issues in the workplace?

Critical Thinking Exercise

You have been hired as a new registered nurse on a busy pediatric unit in a large metropolitan hospital. The hospital provides services for a culturally diverse population including African-American, Asian, and Hispanic people. Family members often attempt alternative healing practices specific to their culture and bring special foods from home to entice the sick child to eat. One of the more experienced nurses said to you,

"We need to discourage these people from fooling with all this hocus-pocus. We are trying to get their sick kid well in the time allowed under their managed care plans, and all this medicine-man stuff is only making the kid sick longer. Besides, all this stuff stinks up the rooms and brings in bugs." You have observed how important these healing rituals and foods are to the clients and families and believe both the families and the children have benefited from this nontraditional approach to healing.

1. What are your feelings about nontraditional healing methods?

2. How should you respond to the experienced nurse?

3. How can you be a client advocate without alienating your coworkers?

4. What could you do to assist your coworkers to become more culturally sensitive to their clients and families?

5. How can healthcare facilities incorporate both Western and nontraditional medicine? Should they do this? Why?

REFERENCES

American Nurses Association. (1985). *Code for Nurses.* Washington, D.C.: American Nurses Association.

American Nurses Association. (1993). *HIV, Hepatitis-B, Hepatitis-C: Blood-borne Diseases.* Washington, D.C.: American Nurses Association.

American Nurses Association. (1994). *Guidelines on Reporting Incompetent, Unethical, or Illegal Practices.* Washington, D.C.: American Nurses Association.

American Nurses Association. (1995). *Protect Your Patients—Protect Your License.* Washington, D.C.: American Nurses Association.

American Nurses Association. (1995). *The Supreme Court Has Issued the Ultimate Gag Order for Nurses.* Washington, D.C.: American Nurses Association.

Armstrong, K., Gordon, R., & Santorella, G. (1995). Occupational exposure of healthcare workers to HIV. *Social Work in Health Care, 21*(3), 61–80.

Carroll, C., & Sheverbush, J. (1996, September). Violence assessment in hospitals provides basis for action. *American Nurse,* p. 18.

Centers for Disease Control and Prevention (CDC). (1992). Surveillance for occupationally acquired HIV infection—United States, 1981–1992. *MMWR, 41*(43), 823–825.

Chisholm, R.F. (1992). Quality of working life: A crucial management perspective for the year 2000. *Journal of Health and Human Resources Administration, 15*(1), 6–34.

Collins, J. (1994). Nurses' attitudes toward aggressive behavior following attendance at "The Prevention and Management of Aggressive Behavior Programme." *J Adv Nurs, 20,* 117–131.

Damrosch, S., & Scholler-Jaquish, A. (1993). Nurses' experiences with impaired nurse coworkers. *Applied Nursing Research, 6*(4), 154–60.

Federal agencies clash as TB workplace safety debate rages. (1993). *The Nation's Health, 23*(1), 1, 24.

Flarey, D.L. (1993). The social climate of work environments. *J Nurs Adm, 23*(6), 9–15.

Herring, L.H. (1994). *Infection Control.* New York: National League for Nursing.

Himali, U. (1995). Caring for the caregivers. *American Nurse, 27*(6), 8.

Hurst, K.L., Croker, P.A., & Bell, S.K. (1994). How about a lollipop? A peer recognition program. *Nursing Management, 25*(9), 68–73.

Jankowski, C.B. (1992). Radiation protection for nurses: Regulations and guidelines. *J Nurs Adm, 22*(22), 30–34.

Kinkle, S. (1993). Violence in the ED: How to stop it before it starts. *Am J Nurs, 93*(7), 22–24.

Kramer, M., & Schmalenberg, C. (1993). Learning from success: Autonomy and empowerment. *Nursing Management, 24*(5), 58–64.

Lanza, M.L., & Carifio, J. (1991). Blaming the victim: Complex (nonlinear) patterns of casual attribution by nurses in response to vignettes of a patient assaulting a nurse. *Journal of Emergency Nursing, 17*(5), 299–309.

Lappetito, J. (1994). Workplace diversity: A leadership challenge. *Health Progress, 75*(2), 22–27, 33.

Mahoney, B. (1991). The extent, nature, and response to victimization of emergency nurses in Pennsylvania. *Journal of Emergency Nursing, 17*(5), 282–292.

Malone, B.L. (1993). Caring for culturally diverse racial groups: An administrative matter. *Nursing Administration Quarterly, 17*(2), 21–29.

Mitchell, A. (1995). Cultural diversity: The future, the market, and the rewards. *Caring, 14*(12), 44–48.

Moch, S.D., & Diemert, C.A. (1987). Health promotion within the nursing work environment. *Nursing Administration Quarterly, 11*(3), 9–12.

Nadwairski, J.A. (1992). Inner-city safety for home care providers. *Journal of Nursing Administration, 22*(9), 42–47.

National Safety Council (1992). *Accident Prevention Manual for Business and Industry.* Chicago: National Safety Council.

Outwater, L.C. (1994). Sexual harassment Issues. *Caring, 13*(5), 54–56, 58, 60.

RNs cite physical and verbal abuse. (1993). *Am J Nurs, 93*(1), 81–84.

Roche, E. (1993, February 23). Nurses' risks and their rights. *Vital Signs,* p. 3.

Roedel, R.S., & Nystrom, P.C. (1987). Clinical ladders and job enrichment. *Hospital Topics, 65*(2), 22–24.

Simonowitz, J. (1994). Violence in the workplace: You're entitled to protection. *RN, 57*(11), 61–63.

Strader, M.K., & Decker, P.J. (1995). *Role Transition to Patient Care Management.* Norwalk, Conn.: Appleton & Lange.

United States Department of Labor (OSHA). (1995). *Employee Workplace Rights and Responsibilities.* OSHA 95-35. Available: Internet.

United States Department of Labor (OSHA). (1996). *Guidelines for Preventing Workplace Violence for Health Care and Social Service Workers.* OSHA 3148-1996. Available: Internet.

Ward, L.B. (1992, December 27). In culturally diverse work place, language may alienate. *Miami Herald.*

UNIT III

Professional Issues

CHAPTER 11

Nursing Practice and the Law

OBJECTIVES   *After reading this chapter, the student will be able to:*

◆ Identify three major sources of laws.
◆ Explain the differences between various types of laws.
◆ Differentiate between negligence and malpractice.
◆ Explain the difference between an intentional and unintentional tort.
◆ Explain how standards of care are used in determining negligence and malpractice.
◆ Discuss advance directives and how they pertain to clients' rights.

The courtroom was cold and sterile. Scanning her surroundings with nervous eyes, Marie decided she knew how Alice must have felt when the Queen of Hearts screamed for her head. The image of the White Rabbit running through the woods, looking at his watch, yelling, "I'm late! I'm late!" flashed before her eyes. For a few moments, she indulged herself in thoughts of being able to turn back the clock and rewrite the past. The future certainly looked grim at the moment.

The calling of her name broke her reverie. Mr. Jefferson, the attorney for the plaintiff, wanted her undivided attention regarding the fateful day when she injected a client with 40 mEq of potassium chloride in error. That day the client died following cardiac arrest because Marie failed to check the appropriate dosage and route for the medication. She had administered 40 mEq of potassium chloride by IV push. Her 15 years of nursing experience meant little to the court. Because she had not followed hospital protocol and had violated an important standard of practice, Marie stood alone. She was being sued for malpractice.

As client advocates, nurses have a responsibility to deliver safe care to their clients. This expectation requires that nurses have professional knowledge at their expected level of practice and be proficient in technological skills. A working knowledge of the legal system, client rights, and behaviors that may result in lawsuits helps nurses to act as client advocates. As long as nurses practice nursing according to the established standards of care, they will be able to avoid the kind of day in court that Marie was experiencing.

■ *General Principles*
• • • • • • • • • • • • • • • • • • • •

MEANING OF LAW

The word "law" has several different meanings. For the purposes of this chapter, "law" means those rules that prescribe and control social conduct in a formal and legally binding manner (Bernzweig, 1994). Laws are created in one of three ways:

◆ *Statutory laws* are created by various legislative bodies such as state legislatures or the Congress.

◆ *Common law* develops within the court system as judicial decisions are made in various cases and precedents for future cases are set. In this way, a decision made in one case can affect decisions made in later cases of a similar nature. This portion of American law is based on the English tradition of case law. This is "judge-made law" (Black, 1957). Many times one judge will follow another's reasoning in a subsequent case. Therefore, one case sets a *precedent* for another.

◆ *Administrative law* is established through the authority given to government agencies such as the state boards of nursing by a legislative body.

SOURCES OF LAW

The Constitution

The Constitution is the foundation of American law. The Bill of Rights, composed of the first 10 amendments to the United States Constitution, is the basis for protection of individual rights. These laws define and limit the power of the government and protect citizens' freedom of speech, freedom of assembly, religious freedom, freedom of the press, and freedom from unwarranted intrusion by government into personal choices. State constitutions can expand individual rights but cannot deprive people of rights guaranteed by the United States Constitution.

Constitutional law evolves. As persons or groups bring suit to challenge interpretations of the Constitution, decisions are made concerning application of the law to that particular event. An example is the protection of freedom of speech. Are obscenities protected? Can one person threaten another person? Criticize another person? The freedom to criticize is protected; threats are not. The definition of what constitutes "obscenity" is often debated and has not been fully clarified by the courts.

Statutes

Statutes are created by localities, state legislatures, and the United States Congress. These can be found in multivolume sets of books.

At the federal level, conference committees comprising representatives of both houses of Congress negotiate the resolution of any differences between the houses on wording of the final bill before it becomes law. If the bill does not meet with the approval of the executive branch of government, the president can veto it. If that occurs, the legislative branch must have enough votes to override the veto or the bill will not become law.

Nurses have an opportunity to influence the development of statutory law both as citizens and as healthcare providers. Writing or meeting with state legislators or members of Congress is a way to demonstrate interest in such issues and their outcome in terms of the laws passed. Passage of a new law is often a long process that includes compromise of the various viewpoints of the interested individuals.

Administrative Law

The Department of Health and Human Services, the Department of Labor, and the Department of Education are federal agencies that have been given the responsibility for administering healthcare-related laws. At the state level are the departments of health and mental health and the licensing boards. Administrative agencies are staffed with professionals who develop the specific rules and regulations that direct the implementation of statutory law. These rules must be reasonable and consistent with the existing statutory law and the intent of the legislature. Usually they go into effect only after review and comment by affected persons or groups.

■ *Types of Laws*
• • • • • • • • • • • • • • • • • •

Another way to look at the legal system is to divide it into two categories: criminal law and civil law.

CRIMINAL LAW

Criminal laws were developed to protect society from actions that threaten its existence. Criminal acts, although directed toward individuals, are considered offenses against the state. The perpetrator of the act is punished, and the victims receive no compensation for injury or damages. There are three categories of criminal law:

◆ *Felony*, which is the most serious and includes such acts as homicide, grand larceny, and violating a nurse practice act.

◆ *Misdemeanor*, which is a lesser offense such as a traffic violation or shoplifting of a small dollar amount.

◆ *Juvenile*, which is a crime carried out by individuals under the age of 18. The specific age varies by state and crime.

There may be occasions where a nurse breaks a law and is tried in criminal court. A nurse who illegally distributes controlled substances, either for personal use or the use of others, for example, is violating the law. Falsification of records of controlled substances is also a criminal action. In some states, altering a client record may be a misdemeanor (Northrop & Kelly, 1987). For example:

> Nurse V. needed to administer a blood transfusion. Because she was in a hurry, she did not properly check the paperwork and violated the standard of practice established for blood administration. Because the nurse failed to follow the designated protocol, the patient was transfused with incompatible blood, suffered from a transfusion reaction, and died. Nurse V. attempted to conceal her conduct and falsified the records. She was found guilty of manslaughter. (*State of New Jersey v. Winter*)

CIVIL LAW

Areas of civil law that particularly affect nurses are tort law, contract law, antitrust law, employment discrimination, and labor laws.

Tort

The remainder of this chapter focuses primarily on tort law. A tort is "a legal or civil wrong committed by one person against the person or property of another" (Black, 1957, p. 1660). Tort law recognizes that individuals in their relationships with each other have a general duty not to harm others (Cushing, 1988). For example, as drivers of automobiles, each of us has a duty to drive safely so that others will not be harmed. A roofer has a duty to place a roof properly so that it will not collapse and injure individuals within the structure. Nurses have a duty to deliver care in such a manner that the consumers of care are not harmed. These legal duties of care may be violated intentionally or unintentionally.

Negligence

Negligence is the unintentional tort of acting or failing to act as an ordinary, reasonable, prudent person, resulting in harm to the person to whom the duty of care is owed (Black, 1959). The legal elements of negligence consist of duty, breach of duty, causation, and harm or injury (Cushing, 1988). All four elements must be present in the determination. For example, if a nurse administers the wrong medication to a client but the client is not injured, the element of harm has not been met. However, if a nurse administers appropriate pain medication and fails to put up the side rails and the client falls and breaks a hip, all four elements have been satisfied. The duty of care is the standard of care. The law defines the standard of care as that which a reasonable, prudent practitioner with similar education and experience would do or not do in similar circumstances (Prosser, 1971).

Malpractice

"Malpractice" is the term used for *professional negligence*. When fulfillment of duties requires specialized education, the term "malpractice" is used.

An important principle in understanding negligence is *respondeat superior*, or the captain of the ship doctrine. Translated literally, this phrase means "let the master speak."

The doctrine of respondeat superior holds employers liable for any negligence by their employees when the employees were acting within the realm of employment and when the alleged negligent acts happened during employment (Prosser, 1971). Consider the following scenario:

> A nursing instructor on a clinical unit in a busy metropolitan hospital instructed his students not to administer any medications unless he was present. Luis, a second-level student, was unable to find his instructor, so he decided to administer digoxin to his client without supervision. The dose was 0.125 mg. The unit dose came as digoxin 0.5 mg/mL. Luis administered the entire amount without checking the digoxin dose, the client's blood level, or the potassium level. The client became toxic, developed a dysrhythmia, and was transferred to the intensive care unit. The family sued the hospital and the nursing school for malpractice. The nursing instructor was sued under the principle of respondeat superior, even though specific instructions to the contrary had been given to the students.

■ Other Laws Relevant to Nursing Practice

• • • • • • • • • • • • • • • • •

GOOD SAMARITAN LAWS

In the past, fear of being sued often prevented trained professionals from assisting during an emergency. To encourage physicians and nurses to respond to emergencies, many states developed what are now known as the Good Samaritan laws. When administering emergency care, nurses and physicians are protected from civil liability by Good Samaritan laws as long as the individual behaves in the same manner as an ordinary, reasonable, and prudent professional would have done in the same or similar circumstances (Prosser, 1971). In other words, nurses must still observe professional standards of care when assisting during an emergency.

CONFIDENTIALITY

It is possible for nurses to be involved in lawsuits other than those involving negligence. For example, clients have the right to confidentiality, and it is the duty of the professional nurse to ensure this right. This assures the client that information obtained while giving care will not be communicated to anyone who does not have a need to know (Cushing, 1988). For example:

> Leonard was admitted for pneumonia. With Leonard's permission, an HIV test was performed and returned with a positive result. Several nurses were discussing the situation in the cafeteria and were overheard by one of Leonard's coworkers, who had come to visit him. This individual reported the test results to Leonard's supervisor. When Leonard returned to work, he was fired for "poor job performance," although he had had superior job evaluations. In the process of filing a discrimination suit against his employer, Leonard discovered that the information on his health status had come from a group of nurses. A lawsuit was filed against the hospital and the nurses involved based on a breach of confidentiality.

SLANDER AND LIBEL

Nurses rarely think of themselves as being guilty of slander or libel. The term *slander* refers to the spoken word, *libel* to the written word. Making a false statement about a client's condition that may result in an injury to that client is considered slander. Putting a false statement into writing is libel. For example, stating that a client who had blood drawn for drug testing has a substance abuse problem when in fact the client does not carry that diagnosis could be considered a slanderous statement. This could result in harm or injury if the client is fired from his or her job because this statement was overheard and repeated (remember Leonard).

FALSE IMPRISONMENT

False imprisonment means confining individuals against their will by either physical (restraining) or verbal (detaining) means. The following examples fall within the definition of false imprisonment:

- Using restraints on individuals without the appropriate written consent
- Restraining mentally handicapped individuals who do not represent a threat to themselves or others
- Detaining unwilling clients in an institution when they desire to leave
- Keeping persons who are medically cleared for discharge for an unreasonable amount of time
- Removing the clothing of clients to prevent them from leaving the institution
- Threatening clients with some form of physical, emotional, or legal action if they insist on leaving.

There are times when clients are a danger to themselves and to others. Nurses often need to decide on the appropriateness of restraints as a protective measure. Nurses should try to obtain the cooperation of the client prior to applying any type of restraints. The first step is to attempt to identify a reason for the risky behavior and resolve the problem. If this fails, documentation of the need for restraints, consultation with the physician, and carefully following the institution's policies and standards of practice are indicated. A failure to follow the preceding guidelines may result in greater harm to the client and possibly a lawsuit for the staff. Consider the following:

> Mr. Harrison, an 87-year-old man, was admitted through the emergency department with severe lower abdominal pain of 3 days' duration. Physical assessment revealed a severely dehydrated man in acute distress. A surgeon was called, and an abdominal laparotomy was performed, revealing a ruptured appendix. Surgery was successful, and the client was sent to the intensive care unit for 24 hours.

On transfer to the surgical floor the next day, Mr. Harrison was in stable condition. Later that night, he became confused, irritable, and anxious. He attempted to climb out of bed and pulled out his indwelling urinary catheter. The nurse restrained him. The next day, his irritability and confusion continued. Mr. Harrison's nurse placed him in a chair, tying him in and restraining his hands. Three hours later he was found in cardiopulmonary arrest.

A lawsuit of wrongful death and false imprisonment was brought against the nurse manager, the nurses caring for Mr. Harrison, and the institution. During discovery, it was determined that the primary cause of Mr. Harrison's behavior was hypoxemia. A violation of law occurred with the failure of the nursing staff to notify the physician of the client's condition and to follow the institution's standard of practice on the use of restraints.

To protect themselves against charges of negligence or false imprisonment in such cases, nurses should discuss safety needs with patients, their families, or other members of the healthcare team. Careful assessment and documentation of client status are also imperative; confusion, irritability, and anxiety often have metabolic causes that need correction, not restraint.

There are also statutes and case laws specific to the admission of clients to psychiatric institutions. Most states have guidelines for emergency involuntary hospitalization for a specific time period. Involuntary admission is considered necessary when clients are a danger to themselves or others. Specific procedures must be followed. A determination by a judge or administrative agency or certification by a specified number of physicians that a person's mental health justifies detention and treatment may be required. Once admitted, these clients may not be restrained unless the guidelines established by state law and the institution's policies are followed. Clients who voluntarily admit themselves to psychiatric institutions are also protected against false imprisonment. Nurses need to make themselves aware of the policies of their state and employing institution.

ASSAULT AND BATTERY

Assault is a threat to harm. *Battery* is actual touching without consent. Most medical treatments, particularly surgery, would be battery if it were not for informed consent from the client. The significance of an assault is in the threat. "If you don't stop pushing that call bell, I'll give you this injection with the biggest needle I can find" is considered an assaultive statement. Battery would occur if the injection were actually given when it was refused, even if medical personnel deemed it was for the "client's good." Holding down a violent client against his or her will and injecting a sedative is battery. With few exceptions, clients have a right to refuse treatment.

■ *Standards of Practice*

Concern for the quality of care is a major part of nursing's responsibility to the public. Therefore the nursing profession is accountable to the consumer for the quality of its services. One of the defining characteristics of a profession is the ability to set its own standards. *Nursing standards* were established as guidelines for the profession to ensure acceptable quality of care (Beckman, 1995).

Standards of practice are also used as criteria to determine whether appropriate care has been delivered. In practice, they represent the minimum acceptable level of care. Nurses are judged on generally accepted standards of practice for their level of education, experience, position, and specialty areas.

Standards of the profession may take many forms. Some are written and may be included in recommendations by professional organizations, job descriptions, agency policies and procedures, and textbooks. Others, which may be intrinsic to the custom of practice, are not found in writing (Beckman, 1995).

Standards of practice are established by statute, professional organizations, and healthcare institutions. The Nurse Practice Acts of the individual states define the boundaries of nursing practice within the state. The American Nurses Association also has specific standards of practice in general and in several clinical areas (see Appendix 1).

With the expansion of advanced nursing practice, it has become particularly important to clarify the legal distinction between nursing and medical practice. It is important to be aware of the boundaries between these professional domains because crossing them can result in legal consequences and disciplinary action. The Nurse Practice Acts and related regulations developed by most state legislatures and state nursing boards help to clarify nursing roles at the varying levels of practice.

PATIENT'S BILL OF RIGHTS

In 1973, the American Hospital Association approved a statement called "A Patient's Bill of Rights." These standards were derived from the ethical principle of autonomy (see Appendix 5).

INFORMED CONSENT

Without consent, many of the procedures performed on clients in a healthcare setting may be considered battery or unwarranted touching. When they consent to treatment, clients give healthcare personnel the right to deliver care and perform specific treatments without fear of prosecution. Although physicians are responsible for obtaining the informed consent, nurses often find themselves involved in the process. It is also the physician's responsibility to give information to a client about a specific treatment or medical intervention. This information should contain all the possible negative outcomes as well as the positive. Nurses may be asked to obtain the signatures on the informed consent. The following are some helpful criteria for ensuring that a client has actually given an informed consent (Northrup & Kelly, 1987; Kozier, Erb, Blois, & Wilkinson, 1995):

- The consent has been given voluntarily by a mentally competent adult.
- The client understands exactly what he or she is consenting to.

- The consent includes the risks involved in the procedure, alternative treatments that may be available, and the possible outcome if the treatment is refused.
- The consent is written.
- Consent to treatment for a minor is usually given by a parent or guardian.

Ideally, the nurse should be present when the physician is explaining the treatment to the client. Before getting a signature, the nurse should ask the client to recall exactly what the physician has told him or her about the treatment. If at any point the nurse feels that the client does not understand the treatment or the expected outcome, the nurse needs to notify the physician of this fact. To give informed consent, the client must be fully informed. Clients have the right to refuse treatment, and we must respect this right. If recommended treatment is refused, a client must be informed of the possible consequences of this decision.

■ *Staying Out of Court*

PREVENTION

Unfortunately, the public's trust in the medical profession has declined over recent years. Consumers are better informed and more assertive in their approach to health care. They demand good and responsible care.

If clients and their families feel that behaviors are uncaring, or attitudes are impersonal, they are more likely to sue for what they view as errors in treatment. The same applies to nurses. If nurses demonstrate an interest in and caring behaviors toward clients, a relationship develops. Individuals do not sue those they view as "caring friends." The potential to change attitudes of the healthcare consumer lies within the power of healthcare personnel. Demonstrating care and concern and making clients and families aware of choices and methods can assist in decreasing liability. When nurses involve clients and their families in decisions about care, it reduces the likelihood of a lawsuit. Tips to prevent legal problems are listed in Box 11–1.

Box 11–1 Tips to avoid legal problems

- Keep yourself informed regarding new research findings related to your area of practice.
- Insist that the health care institution keep personnel apprised of all changes in policies and procedures and in the management of new technological equipment.
- Always follow the standards of care or practice for the institution.
- Delegate tasks and procedures only to appropriate personnel.
- Identify patients at risk for problems such as falls or the development of decubiti.
- Establish and maintain a safe environment.
- Document precisely and carefully.
- Write detailed incident reports and file them with the appropriate personnel or department.
- Recognize certain patient behaviors that may indicate the possibility of a lawsuit.

All healthcare personnel are accountable for their own actions and adherence to the accepted standards of health care. Most negligence and malpractice cases arise out of a violation of the accepted standards of practice and the policies of the employing institution. Common causes of negligence are listed in Table 11–1. Expert witnesses on both sides are called to cite the accepted standards and assist attorneys in formulating the legal strategies pertaining to those standards. For example, most medication errors can be traced back to a violation of the accepted standard of medication administration, the *five rights* (Kozier, Erb, & Blois, 1995):

- Right drug
- Right dose
- Right route
- Right time
- Right patient

In the case of Luis, the nursing student violated the *right dose* principle and therefore made a medication error. When nurses sign off medications on all their clients for the shift before they are administered, they leave themselves open to charges of medication error.

TABLE 11–1
COMMON CAUSES OF NEGLIGENCE

Problem	Prevention
Client falls	Identify clients at risk. Place notices instituting fall precautions. Follow institutional policies on the use of restraints. Always be sure beds are in their lowest positions. Use siderails appropriately.
Equipment injuries	Check thermostats and temperature in equipment used for heat or cold application. Check wiring on all electrical equipment.
Failure to monitor	Observe IV infusion sites as directed by institutional policy. Obtain and record vital signs, urinary output, cardiac status, etc. as directed by institutional policy and more often if client condition dictates. Check pertinent laboratory values.
Failure to communicate	Report pertinent changes in client status to appropriate personnel. Document changes accurately. Document communication with appropriate source.
Medication errors	Follow the Five Rights. Monitor client responses. Check client medications for multiple drugs for the same actions.

In the case of Mr. Harrison, the institutional personnel were found negligent because of a direct violation of the institution's standards on the application of restraints.

Nursing units are busy and often understaffed. These situational realities exist but should not be allowed to interfere with the safe delivery of health care. Clients have a right to safe and effective health care, and nurses have an obligation to deliver this care.

IF A PROBLEM ARISES

When served with a summons or complaint, people often panic, allowing fear to overcome reason and sanity. First of all, you are required to answer the complaint. Failure to do this may result in a default judgment, causing greater distress and difficulties.

In addition, there is much you can do to protect yourself if you are named in a lawsuit. You may want to obtain legal representation to protect personal property. Never sign any documents without consulting your malpractice insurance carrier or your legal representative. If you are personally covered by malpractice insurance, notify the company immediately, and follow their instructions carefully. Institutions usually have lawyers to defend themselves and their employees. Whether or not you are personally insured, the legal department of the institution should be contacted. You need to keep a file of all papers, proceedings, meetings, and telephone conversations about the case. Although a pending or ongoing legal case should not be discussed with coworkers or friends, do not withhold any information you have from your attorneys, even if you believe that it may be harmful to you. Let the attorneys and the insurance company help you decide how to handle the difficult situation. They are in charge of damage control. Concealing information usually causes more damage than disclosing it.

Sometimes nurses feel that they are not being adequately protected or represented by the attorneys from their employing institution. If this happens, consider hiring a personal attorney who is experienced in malpractice. This information can be obtained through either the State Bar Association or the local Trial Lawyer's Association.

■ *Professional Liability Insurance*

• •

Various forms of professional liability insurance are available to nurses. These policies have been developed to protect nurses against personal financial losses should they be involved in a medical malpractice suit. If a nurse is charged with malpractice and found guilty of the charges, the employing institution has the right to sue for reclaiming of damages. Professional malpractice insurance protects the nurse in these situations.

■ *End-of-Life Decisions and the Law*

• •

When a heart ceases to beat, a client is in a state of cardiac arrest. Both in modern healthcare institutions and in the community, it is common to begin cardiopulmonary resuscitation when cardiac arrest occurs. In healthcare institutions, an elaborate mechanism is put into action when a client "codes." Much controversy exists concerning when these mechanisms should be used and whether individuals who have no chance of regaining full viability should be resuscitated.

DO NOT RESUSCITATE (DNR) ORDERS

A DNR is a specific directive to healthcare personnel not to initiate cardiopulmonary resuscitative measures. Only physicians can write a DNR order, usually after consulting with the client or family. Other members of the healthcare team are expected to comply with the order. Clients have the right to request a DNR order. However, they may make this request without a full understanding of what it really means. Take the following example:

> When Mrs. Vincent, 58 years old, was admitted to the hospital for a hysterectomy, she explicitly stated, "I want to be made a DNR." The nurse, rather concerned by the statement, ques-

tioned Mrs. Vincent's understanding of a DNR. The nurse asked the client, "Do you mean that if you are walking down the hall after your surgery and you have a heart attack, you do not want the nurses or physicians to do anything? You want us to just let you die?" Mrs. Vincent responded with a resounding, "No, that is not what I mean. I mean if something happens to me and I won't be able to be the way I am now, I want to be a DNR!" The nurse then explained the concept of a DNR. Apparently Mrs. Vincent had been watching too much television.

Do Not Resuscitate orders are common in many acute- and long-term care facilities. Every facility should have a written policy regarding the initiation of such orders (ANA, 1992). The client or, if the client is unable to speak for himself or herself, a family member or guardian should make clear his or her preference for either having as much as possible done or withholding treatment (see the next section on advance directives). Elements to include in a DNR order are listed in Box 11–2.

Box 11–2 Elements to include in a Do Not Resuscitate (DNR) order

- Statement of the policy of the institution that resuscitation will be initiated unless there is a specific order to withhold resuscitative measures
- Statement from the client regarding specific desires
- Description of the client's medical condition to justify a DNR order
- Statement about the role of the family members or significant others
- Definition of the scope of the DNR order
- Delineation of the roles of various caregivers

Source: ANA (1992). Position Statement on Nursing Care and Do Not Resuscitate Decisions. Washington, DC: ANA, with permission.

ADVANCE DIRECTIVES

The legal dilemmas that may arise in relation to DNR orders often require court decisions. For this reason, in 1990, Senator Danforth of Missouri and Senator Moynihan of New York introduced the Patient Self-Determination Act to address questions regarding life-sustaining treatment. The act was created to allow people the opportunity to make decisions about treatment in advance of a time when they might become unable to participate in the decision-making process. Through this mechanism, families can be spared the burden of having to decide what the family member would have wanted.

Federal law requires that healthcare institutions that receive federal money (from Medicare, for example) inform clients of their right to create advance directives. The Patient Self Determination Act provides guidelines for developing advance directives concerning what will be done for individuals if they are no longer able to actively participate in making decisions about care options. The Patient Self-Determination Act (S.R. 13566) states that institutions must do several things:

- **PROVIDE INFORMATION TO EVERY CLIENT.** On admission, all clients must be informed in writing of their rights under state law to accept or refuse medical treatment while competent to make decisions about their care. This includes the right to execute advance directives.

- **DOCUMENTATION.** All clients must be asked if they have a living will or have chosen a durable power of attorney for health care (also known as a healthcare surrogate). The response must be indicated on the medical record and a copy of the documents, if available, should be placed on the client's chart.

- **EDUCATION.** Nurses, other healthcare personnel, and the community need to understand what the Patient Self-Determination Act requires, as well as the state laws regarding advance directives.

- **CLIENT'S RIGHTS.** All clients are to be treated with respectful care regardless of their decision regarding life-prolonging treatments.

The Living Will and a Durable Power of Attorney for Health Care (Healthcare Surrogate)

The two most common forms of advance directives are living wills and durable power of attorney for health care (also known as a healthcare surrogate). See Appendix D for samples of these documents.

The living will is a legally executed document that states individuals' wishes regarding the use of "life-prolonging" medical treatment in the event that they are no longer competent to make informed treatment decisions on their own behalf and are suffering from a terminal condition (Flarey, 1991). A condition is considered terminal when, to a reasonable degree of medical certainty, there is little likelihood of recovery or the condition may be expected to cause death. It may also refer to a persistent vegetative state characterized by a permanent and irreversible condition of unconsciousness in which there is (Marshall, Marshall, Vos, & Chestnut, 1990):

- Absence of voluntary action or cognitive behavior of any kind
- An inability to communicate or interact purposefully with the environment

Another form of advance directive is the appointment of a healthcare surrogate. Chosen by the client, the healthcare surrogate is usually a family member or close personal friend. The role of the healthcare surrogate is to make the client's wishes known to medical and nursing personnel. Imperative in the designation of a healthcare surrogate is a clear understanding of an individual's wishes should this situation arise.

There are situations in which clients are not able to adequately or competently express themselves although they are not terminally ill. For example, clients with advanced Alzheimer's disease or other forms of dementia cannot communicate their wishes; clients under anesthesia are temporarily unable to communicate effectively; the condition of comatose clients does not allow for expression of healthcare wishes. In these situations, healthcare surrogates can make treatment decisions on the behalf of the clients. However, when clients regain the ability to make their own decisions and are capable of expressing them effectively, they resume control of all decision-making pertaining to medical treatment (Reigle, 1992).

NURSING IMPLICATIONS

The Patient Self-Determination Act does not specify who should discuss treatment decisions or advance directives with clients. Because the directives are often implemented on nursing units, however, nurses need to be knowledgeable about living wills and healthcare surrogates and to be prepared to answer questions that clients may have about directives and the forms used by the healthcare institution.

As client advocates, the responsibility for creating an awareness of individual rights often falls on nurses. It is the responsibility of the healthcare institution to educate personnel on the policies of the institution so that nurses and others involved in client care can inform the healthcare consumers of their choices. Nurses who are unsure of the policies in their healthcare institution should contact the appropriate department.

Conclusion

Nurses need to understand the legalities involved in the delivery of safe health care. It is important to know the standards of care established within your institution because these will be the standards to which you will be held accountable. Healthcare consumers have a right to quality care, and nurses have an obligation to deliver it. Caring for clients safely and avoiding legal difficulties require nurses to adhere to the expected standards of care and carefully document changes in client status.

Study Questions

1. How do federal laws, court decisions, and state boards of nursing affect nursing practice? Give an example of each.
2. The next time you are on your clinical unit, look at the nursing documentation done by several different staff members. Do you feel it is adequate? Explain your rationale.

3. How does your institution handle medication errors?

4. If a nurse is found to be less than proficient in the delivery of safe care, how should the nurse manager remedy the situation?

5. Look at the forms for advance directives and DNR policies in your institution. Do they follow the guidelines of the Patient Self-Determination Act?

6. What should a practicing nurse do to stay out of court? What should a nurse *not* do?

Critical Thinking Exercise

Mr. Evans, a 40-year-old man, was admitted to the medical-surgical unit from the emergency department with a diagnosis of acute abdomen. He had a 20-year history of Crohn's disease and had been on prednisone, 20 mg, every day for the last year. Because he was allowed nothing by mouth (NPO), total parenteral nutrition was started through a triple-lumen central venous catheter line, and his steroids were changed to Solu-medrol, 60 mg by intravenous push q6h. He was also receiving several intravenous antibiotics as well as medication for pain and nausea. Over the next several days, his condition worsened. He was in severe pain and needed more analgesics. One evening at 9 P.M., it was discovered that his central venous catheter line was out. The registered nurse notified the physician, who stated that a surgeon would come in the morning to replace it. The nurse failed to ask the physician what to do about the intravenous steroids, antibiotics, and fluid replacement because the patient was still NPO. At 7 A.M., the night nurse noted that the client had had no urinary output since 11 P.M. the night before. She failed to report this information to the day shift.

The client's physician made rounds at 9 A.M. The nurse for Mr. Evans did not discuss the fact that the client had not voided since 11 P.M. the previous night, nor did she request orders for alternative delivery of the steroids and antibiotics. At 5 P.M. that evening, while Mr. Evans was having a computed tomography scan, his blood pressure dropped to 70 mm Hg, and because no one was in the scan room with him, he coded. He was transported to the intensive care unit and intubated. He developed sepsis and acute respiratory distress syndrome.

1. List all the problems you can find with the nursing care in this case.

2. What were the nursing responsibilities in reporting information?

3. What do you think was the possible cause of the drop in Mr. Evans's blood pressure and his subsequent code?

4. If you worked in risk management, how would you discuss this situation with the nurse manager and the staff?

REFERENCES

American Nurses Association. (1992). *Position Statement on Nursing Care and Do Not Resuscitate Decisions.* Washington, D.C.: American Nurses Association.

Badzek, L. (1992). What you need to know about advance directives. *Nursing 92, 22* (6), 57–60.

Beckman, J.P. (1995). *Nursing Malpractice: Implications for Clinical Practice and Nursing Education.* Seattle: Washington University Press.

Bernzweig, E.P. (1994). *The Nurse's Liability for Malpractice.* New York: McGraw-Hill.

Black, H.C. (1957). *Black's Law Dictionary.* St. Paul: West Publishing.

Cushing, M. (1988). *Nursing Jurisprudence.* Norwalk, Conn.: Appleton & Lange.

Flarey, D. (1991). Advanced directives: In search of self-determination. *J Nurs Adm, 21*(11), 17.

Kozier, B., Erb, G., Blois, K., & Wilkinson, J.M. (1995). *Fundamentals of Nursing: Concepts, Process and Practice* (ed. 15). Menlo Park, Calif.: Addison-Wesley.

Marshall, S.B., Marshall, L.F., Vos, H.R., & Chestnut, R.M. (1990). *Neuroscience Critical Care: Pathophysiology and Patient Management.* Philadelphia: W.B. Saunders.

Northrop, C.E., & Kelly, M.E. (1987). State of New Jersey v. Winter. *Legal Issues in Nursing.* St. Louis: C.V. Mosby.

Patient Self-Care Determination Act. (1989). S.R. 13566, *Congressional Record.*

Prosser, W.L. (1971). *Handbook of the Law of Torts.* St. Paul: West Publishing.

Reigle, J. (1992). Preserving patient self-determination through advance directives. *Heart Lung, 21*(2) 196–98.

CHAPTER 12

Questions of Values and Ethics

OBJECTIVES   *After reading this chapter, the student will be able to:*
- Discuss the way values are formed.
- Differentiate between personal ethics and professional ethics.
- List the seven basic ethical principles and give an example of each.
- Identify an ethical dilemma in the clinical setting.
- Discuss current ethical issues in health care and possible solutions.

It is 1961. In a large metropolitan hospital, a group of 10 healthcare professionals is meeting to consider the cases of three different individuals. Ironically, they all have something in common. Larry Jones, aged 66, Irma Kolnick, aged 31, and Nancy Roberts, aged 10, are all suffering from chronic renal failure and are in need of hemodialysis. Equipment is scarce, the cost of the treatment is prohibitive, and it is doubtful whether it will be covered by health insurance. The hospital is able to provide this treatment to only one of these individuals. Who shall live, and who shall die? In a novel of the same name, Noah Gordon called this decision-making group the "Death Committee" (Gordon, 1965). Today they are referred to as ethics committees.

Not so long ago, we had neither the knowledge nor the technology to prolong life. The main role of nurses and physicians was to support patients through the time of illness, helping them toward recovery or keeping them comfortable until death. There were few "who shall live, and who shall die?" decisions.

In the late 1960s, technological advances made the intensive care unit possible. Health care could keep alive people who would die without intervention. The development of new drugs and advances in biomechanical technology permitted physicians and nurses to challenge nature. This progress also brought new perplexing questions. The ability to prolong life has created some heartbreaking situations for families and terrible ethical dilemmas for healthcare professionals. How does one decide when it is time to "pull the plug," that is, turn off the life support machines, on someone's beloved son or daughter kept alive on these machines after an auto accident? Families and professionals alike are faced with some of the most difficult ethical decisions at times like this. How do we define death? How do we know when it has occurred? Perhaps we also need to ask, "What is life? Is there ever a time when life is no longer worth living?" Healthcare professionals have looked to

philosophy, especially the branch that deals with human behavior, for resolution of these issues. A field known as bioethics (Mappes & Zembaty, 1991), a subdiscipline of the area known as ethics, or the philosophical study of morality, has evolved. In essence, bioethics is the study of medical morality, the moral and social implications of health care and science in human life (Mappes & Zembaty, 1991).

To understand biomedical ethics, we need to consider first the basic concepts of values, belief systems, and morality. We will then discuss the resolution of ethical dilemmas in health care.

■ *Values*

• •

The dictionary defines *values* as the "estimated or appraised worth of something, or that quality of a thing that makes it more or less desirable, useful" (*Webster's New World Dictionary*, 1990). Values, then, are judgments about the importance or unimportance of objects, ideas, attitudes, and attributes. They become a part of a person's conscience and world view. Values provide a frame of reference and act as pilots to guide behaviors and assist people in making choices.

VALUE SYSTEMS

A value system is a set of related values. For example, one person may value (believe to be important) material things such as money, objects, and social status. Another person may value more abstract concepts such as kindness, charity, and caring. One's system of values frequently affects how people make decisions. For example, while one person may base a decision on cost, another person placed in the same situation may base the decision on kindness. There are different kinds of values:

◆ *Intrinsic values* are those related to sustaining life, such as food and water (Steele & Harmon, 1983).

◆ *Extrinsic values* are not essential to life. Things, people, and ideas such as kindness, understanding, and material items are extrinsically valuable.

- ◆ *Personal values* are qualities that people consider valuable in their private lives. Such things as strong family ties and acceptance by others are personal values.

- ◆ *Professional values* are qualities considered important by a professional group. Autonomy, integrity, and commitment are examples of professional values.

People's behavior is motivated by values. Individuals take risks, relinquish their own comfort and security, and generate extraordinary efforts because of their values (Edge & Groves, 1994). Stroke patients may overcome tremendous barriers because they value independence. Race car drivers may risk death or other serious injury because they value competition and winning.

Values are also the basis of standards by which people judge others. For example, if you value work over leisure activities, you will look unfavorably on the coworker who refuses to work over the weekend. If you believe that health is more important than wealth, you would approve of spending money on a relaxing vacation rather than putting it in the bank.

Often people adopt the values of individuals whom they admire. For example, a nursing student may begin to value humor after observing it used effectively with clients. You can see that values provide a guide for decision making and give additional meaning to life. Individuals develop a sense of satisfaction when they work toward achieving values they feel are important.

HOW VALUES ARE DEVELOPED

Values are learned (Wright, 1987). Values can be taught directly, or they can be modeled through one's behavior. Children learn by watching their parents, friends, teachers, and religious leaders. By continuous reinforcement, children eventually learn about and then adopt these values as their own. Because of the values they hold dear, people often make great demands on themselves, ignoring the personal cost. Here is an example:

> David grew up in a family in which educational achievement was highly valued. Not surprisingly, he adopted this as one of his own values. At school, he worked very hard because some of the subjects did not come easily to him. When his grades did not reflect his great effort, he felt as if he had disappointed his family as well as himself. By the time David reached the age of 15, he had developed severe migraine headaches.

Values change with experience and maturity. For example, young children often value objects such as a favorite blanket or stuffed animal. Older children are more likely to value a particular event such as a scouting expedition. As they enter adolescence, they may value peer opinion over the opinions of their parents. Young adults often value certain ideals such as beauty and heroism. The values of adults are formed from all of these past experiences, learning, and thought.

The number of values that people hold is not as important as what values they hold to be important. Choices are influenced by values. The way people use their own time and money, choose friends, and pursue a career are all influenced by values.

VALUES CLARIFICATION

Values clarification is a method through which people become more aware of what they believe is important. Values clarification is a process that helps people become aware of their own values. Values play an important role in everyday decision making. For this reason, nurses need to be aware of what they value and what they do not. This process helps them to behave in a manner consistent with their values. Both personal and professional values can affect nurses' decisions. Understanding your values makes it easier to solve problems, come to decisions, and develop better relationships with others. Raths, Harmon, and Simmons (1979) suggested using a three-step model of choosing, prizing, and acting with seven substeps to identify your own values (Table 12–1).

TABLE 12–1
VALUES CLARIFICATION

I. Choosing
  1. Free choice
  2. Choosing from alternatives
  3. Deciding after giving consideration to the consequences of each alternative

II. Prizing
  4. Being satisfied about the choice
  5. Being willing to declare the choice to others

III. Acting
  6. Making the choice a part of one's world view and incorporating it into behavior
  7. Repetition of the choice

Source: Adapted from Raths, L.E., Harmon, M., & Simmons, S.B. (1979). *Values and Teaching.* New York: Charles E. Merrill.

You may have used this method when making the decision to return to school. Today many career options are available to men and women. For some of you, nursing is a first career; for others, it may be a second career. Using the model in Table 12–1, let's analyze the valuing process:

1. *Choosing*: After researching different career options, you freely chose nursing school out of a whole range of options. This choice was most likely influenced by factors such as educational achievement and abilities, finances, support and encouragement from others, time factors, and feelings about people.
2. *Prizing*: Once the choice was made, you were satisfied with it and told your friends about it.
3. *Acting*: You have entered school and begun the journey to your new career. Later in your career, you may decide to return to school for a bachelor's degree or master's degree.

As you progress through school, you have probably begun to develop a new set of values, your professional values. Professional values are those established as being impor-

tant in your practice, such as caring, quality of care, and ethical behaviors.

■ *Belief Systems*

Belief systems are an organized way of thinking about why people exist within the universe. The purpose of belief systems is to explain such mysteries as life and death, good and evil, health and illness. Usually these systems include an ethical code that specifies appropriate behavior. People may have a personal belief system or participate in a religion that provides such a system, or both.

Members of primitive societies worshiped events in nature. Unable to understand the science of weather, for example, early civilizations believed these things to be under the control of "someone" or "something" that needed to be appeased. They developed rituals and ceremonies to appease these unknown faces. In doing this, they named these faces gods, believing that certain behaviors either pleased or angered the gods. As these societies associated certain behaviors with specific outcomes, they created a belief system that enabled them to function as a group.

As higher civilizations evolved, belief systems became more complex. Archeology has provided us with evidence of the religious practices of ancient civilizations (Wack, 1992). The Aztecs, Mayans, Incas, and Polynesian cultures each had a religious belief system composed of numerous gods and goddesses for the same functions. The Greek, Roman, Egyptian, and Scandinavian societies believed in a hierarchy of gods as well as individual gods and goddesses. Interestingly, although given different names by different cultures, most of the deities had similar purposes. For example, Zeus was the Greek king of the gods and Thor the Norse god of thunder. Both used a thunderbolt as their symbol. Sociologists believe that these religions developed to explain what was then unexplainable. Human beings have a deep need to create order from chaos and to have logical explanations regarding events. Religion explains theologically what objective science cannot.

Along with the creation of the rites and rituals, religions also developed codes of behaviors or ethical codes. These codes contribute to the social order. There are rules regarding how to treat members of the family, neighbors, the young, and the old. Many religions have also developed rules regarding marriage, sexual practices, business practices, the ownership of property, and rules of inheritance.

The advancement of science certainly has not made belief systems any less important. In fact, the technology explosion has created an even greater need for these systems. Technological advances often place people in situations that justify religious convictions rather than oppose them. Many religions, particularly within Christianity, focus on the will of a supreme being, and technology is a gift that allows healthcare personnel to maintain the life of a loved one. Other religions, such as certain branches of Judaism, focus on free choice or free will, leaving the decisions in the hands of humankind. Genetic testing provides an example of this. Many religious leaders believe that if genetic testing indicates an infant will be born with a disease such as Tay-Sachs, which causes severe suffering and ultimately death, an abortion may be an acceptable option. Belief systems often help survivors in making decisions and living with them afterward. So far, more questions than answers have emerged from these technological advances. As science explains more and more previously unexplainable phenomena, we need beliefs and values to guide our use of this new knowledge.

■ *Ethics and Morals*

• • • • • • • • • • • • • • • • • • •

MORALS

Although the terms *morals* and *ethics* are often used interchangeably, ethics usually refers to a standardized code as a guide to behaviors, whereas morals usually refers to an individual's own code for acceptable behavior. Morals arise from an individual's conscience. They act as a guide for individual behavior and are learned through instruc-

tion and socialization. You may find, for example, that you and your clients disagree on the acceptability of certain behaviors such as premarital sex, taking drugs, or gambling. Even in your nursing class, you will probably find some disagreements because each of you has developed your own personal code that defines acceptable behavior.

ETHICAL PRINCIPLES

Ethics is the part of philosophy that deals with the rightness or wrongness of human behavior. It is also concerned with the motives behind the behavior. *Bioethics* is the application to issues that pertain to life and death. The implication is that judgments can be made about the rightness or goodness of healthcare practices.

Ethical codes are based on principles that can be used to judge behavior. Ethical principles assist decision making because they are a standard for measuring actions. They may be the basis for laws, but they themselves are not laws. Laws are rules created by a governing body. Laws can operate because the government has the power to enforce them. They are usually quite specific, as are the punishments for disobeying them. Ethical principles are not confined to specific behaviors. They act as guides for appropriate behaviors. They also take into account the situation in which a decision must be made. You might say that ethical principles speak to the essence or fundamentals of the law, rather than the exactness of the law (Macklin, 1987). Here is an example:

> Mrs. Van Gruen, 82 years old, was admitted to the hospital in acute respiratory distress. She was diagnosed with an aspiration pneumonia and soon became septic, developing adult respiratory distress syndrome (ARDS). She had a living will, and her attorney was her designated healthcare surrogate. Her competence to make decisions was uncertain because of her illness. The physician presented the situation to the attorney, indicating that without a feeding tube and tracheostomy, Mrs. Van

Gruen would die. According to the laws governing living wills and healthcare surrogates, the attorney could have made the decision to withhold all treatments. However, he felt he had an ethical obligation to still discuss the situation with his client. The client requested that the tracheostomy and the feeding tube be inserted, which was done.

In some situations, two or more principles may conflict with each other. Making a decision under these circumstances is very difficult. We consider several of the ethical principles that are most important to nursing practice—autonomy, nonmaleficence, beneficence, justice, confidentiality, veracity, and accountability—and then look at some of the ethical dilemmas nurses encounter in clinical practice.

Autonomy

Autonomy is the freedom to make decisions for oneself. This ethical principle requires that nurses respect clients' rights to make their own choices about treatment. Informed consent before treatment, surgery, or participation in research is an example. To be able to make an autonomous choice, individuals need to be informed of the purpose, benefits, and risks of the procedures to which they are agreeing. Nurses accomplish this by providing information and supporting clients' choices.

Nurses are often in a position to protect a client's autonomy. They do this by ensuring that others do not interfere with the client's right to proceed with a decision. If a nurse observes that a client has insufficient information to make an appropriate choice, is being forced into a decision, or is unable to understand the consequences of the choice, then the nurse may act as a client advocate to ensure the principle of autonomy.

There are times when nurses have difficulty with the principle of autonomy because it also means respecting another's choice even if you disagree with it. According to the principle of autonomy, nurses cannot replace a client's individual decision with their own even when they honestly believe that the client has made the wrong

choice. Nurses can, however, discuss concerns with their clients and make sure they have thought about the consequences of the decision they are about to make.

Nonmaleficence

The ethical principle of nonmaleficence requires that no harm be done, either deliberately or unintentionally. This rather complicated word comes from Latin roots:

non=not
male=bad
facere=to do

The principle of nonmaleficence also requires that nurses protect from danger individuals who are unable to protect themselves because of their physical or mental condition. An infant, a person under anesthesia, and a person with Alzheimer's disease are examples of people with limited ability to protect themselves. We are ethically obligated to protect our clients when they are unable to protect themselves.

This obligation to do no harm extends to the nurse who for some reason is not functioning at an optimal level. For example, a nurse who is impaired by alcohol or drugs is knowingly placing clients at risk. Other nurses who observe such behavior have an ethical obligation to protect the client according to the principle of nonmaleficence.

Beneficence

The principle of beneficence comes from similar Latin roots:

bene=well
facere=to do

This principle demands that nurses do good for the benefit others. For nurses, this is more than delivering competent physical or technical care. It means helping clients meet all of their needs, physical, social, or emotional. Beneficence means caring in the truest sense, and caring fuses thought, feeling, and action—knowing and being truly understanding of the situation and the thoughts and ideas of the individual (Benner & Wrubel, 1989).

Sometimes physicians, nurses, and families withhold information from clients in the name of beneficence. The problem with this is that it does not allow competent individuals to make their own decisions based on all available information. In an attempt to be beneficent, the principle of autonomy is violated. This is just one of many examples of the ethical dilemmas encountered in nursing practice.

> Mrs. Gonzalez has just been admitted to the oncology unit with a diagnosis of ovarian cancer. She is scheduled to begin chemotherapy treatment. Her two children and her husband have requested that she not be told her diagnosis because they feel she would not be able to deal with it. The information is communicated to the nursing staff.

After the first treatment, Mrs. Gonzalez becomes very ill. She refuses the next treatment, stating that she didn't feel sick until she came to the hospital. She asks the nurse what could possibly be wrong with her that she needs a medicine that makes her sick when she doesn't feel sick. Only people who get cancer medicine get this sick! Mrs. Gonzalez then asks the nurse, "Do I have cancer?"

As the nurse, you understand the order that the client is not to be told her diagnosis. You also understand your role as a patient advocate.

1. To whom do you owe your duty—the family or the client?
2. How do you think you may be able to be a client advocate in this situation?
3. What information would you communicate to the family, and how could you assist them in dealing with their mother's concerns?

Justice

The principle of justice obliges nurses and other healthcare professionals to treat every person equally regardless of gender, religion, ethnicity, disease, or social standing (Edge & Groves, 1994). This principle also applies in the work and educational setting. Everyone should be treated and judged by the same criteria according to this principle.

> Found on the street by the police, Mr. C.P. Johnson was admitted through the emergency room to a medical unit. He was in deplorable condition: wearing dirty, ragged clothes, unshaven, and covered with blood. His diagnosis was chronic alcoholism, complicated by esophageal varices and end-stage liver disease. Several nursing students overheard the staff discussing Mr. Johnson. The essence of the conversation was that no one wanted to care for him because he was "dirty, smelly, and brought this condition on himself." The students, upset by what they heard, went to their instructor about the situation. The instructor explained that every individual has a right to good care despite his or her economic or social position. This is the principle of justice.

Confidentiality

The principle of confidentiality states that anything said to nurses and other healthcare providers by their clients must be held in the strictest confidence. Exceptions exist only when clients give permission for the release of information or when the law requires the release of specific information. Sometimes just sharing information without revealing an individual's name can be a breach in confidentiality because the situation and the individual are identifiable. It is important to realize that what seems like a harmless statement can become harmful if other people can piece together bits of information and identify the client. Nurses come into contact with people from different walks of life. When working within communities, people are bound to know other people, who know people, and so on. Individuals have lost families, jobs, and insurance coverage because nurses have shared confidential information and others have acted on that knowledge (AIDS Update Conference, 1995).

Veracity

Veracity requires nurses to be truthful. Intentionally deceiving or misleading a client is a violation of this principle. Deliberately omitting a part of the truth is deception and violates the principle of veracity. This principle often creates ethical dilemmas. When is it okay to lie? Some ethicists will say it is never appropriate to deceive another individual. Others say that if another ethical principle overrides veracity, then lying is permissible.

> Ms. Allen has just been told that her father has Alzheimer's disease. The nurse practitioner wants to come into the home to discuss treatment. Ms. Allen refused, saying that the nurse practitioner should under no circumstances tell her father the diagnosis. She explained to the practitioner that she is sure he will kill himself if he learns he has Alzheimer's disease. She bases this on statements he has made regarding this disease.
>
> The nurse practitioner replied that a medication is available that might help her father. However, it is only available through a research study being conducted at a nearby university. To participate in the research, the client must be informed of the purpose of the study, the medication to be given, its side effects, and follow-up procedures. Ms. Allen continued to refuse to allow her father to be told his diagnosis because she is positive he will commit suicide.
>
> The nurse practitioner faces a dilemma: does he abide by Ms. Allen's wishes based on the principle of beneficence, or does he abide by the principle of veracity and inform his client of the diagnosis. What would you do?

Accountability

Accountability means accepting responsibility for one's own actions. Nurses are accountable to their clients and to their colleagues. When providing care to clients, nurses are responsible for their own actions, good and not so good. If something was not done, do not chart or tell a colleague that it was. An example of violating accountability is the story of Anna:

> Anna was a registered nurse who worked nights on an acute-care unit. She was an excellent nurse, but as the acuity of the clients' condition increased, she was unable to keep up with both clients needs and the technology, particularly IVs. She began to chart that all the IVs were infusing as they should even when they were not. Each morning, the day shift would find that the actual infused amount did not agree with the paperwork. One night Anna allowed an entire liter to be infused into a client with congestive heart failure in 2 hours. When the day staff came on duty, they found the client expired, the bag empty, and the tubing filled with blood. Anna's IV sheet showed 800 ml left in the bag. It was not until a lawsuit was filed that Anna took responsibility for her behavior.

The idea of a standard of care evolves from this principle. Standards of care provide a ruler for measuring nursing actions.

ETHICAL CODES

A code of ethics is a formal statement of the rules of ethical behavior for a particular group of individuals. A code of ethics (see Chap. 15 and Appendix 1) is one of the hallmarks of a profession. This code makes clear the behavior expected of its members.

Ethical codes are dynamic. They reflect the values of the profession and the society for which they were developed. Changes occur as society and technology evolve. For example, years ago no thought was ever given to do not resuscitate (DNR) orders or withholding food and fluids. These were not issues then, but the technological advances that have made it possible to keep people in a kind of twilight life, comatose and unable to participate in living in any way, have made these very important issues in health care.

It is not the purpose of ethical codes to change with every little breeze but to maintain a steady course, evolving as needed, but continuing to emphasize the basic ethical principles. Technology has increased our knowledge and skills, but our ability to make decisions regarding ourselves and those we care for is still guided by the principles of autonomy, maleficence, beneficence, justice, accountability, and veracity.

ETHICAL DILEMMAS

What is a dilemma? Where did the term "dilemma" originate? The word "dilemma" is of Greek origin. A lemma was an animal resembling a ram, having two horns. Thus came the saying "stuck on the horns of dilemma." The story of Hugo illustrates a hypothetical life or death dilemma with a touch of humor:

> One day Hugo, dressed in a bright red cape, walked through his village into the countryside. The wind had caught the corners of the cape, and it was being whipped in all directions. As he walked down the dusty road, he happened to pass by a lemma. Hugo's bright red cape caught the lemma's attention.
>
> Lowering its head with its two horns poised in attack position, the animal began to chase poor Hugo down the road. Panting and exhausted, Hugo reached the end of the road to find himself blocked by a huge stone wall. He turned to face the lemma, which was ready to charge. A decision needed to be made, and Hugo's life depended on this decision. If he moved to the left, the lemma would gore his heart. If he moved to the right, the lemma would gore his liver. Alas, no matter what his decision, our friend Hugo would be stuck on the horns of "da lemma."

Like Hugo, nurses are often faced with difficult dilemmas. Also, as Hugo found, an ethical dilemma can be a choice between two unpleasant alternatives.

An ethical dilemma occurs when a problem exists that forces a choice between one or more ethical principles. Deciding in favor of one principle will violate another. Both sides have goodness and badness to them, but neither decision satisfies all the criteria that apply. Ethical dilemmas also have the added burden of emotions. Feelings of anger, frustration, and fear often override rationality in the decision-making process.

> Mr. Sussman, 80 years old, was admitted to the neuroscience unit after suffering left hemispheric bleeding. He had total right hemiplegia and was completely nonresponsive, with a Glasgow Coma Scale score of 8. He had been on IV fluids for 4 days, and the question of placing a percutaneous endoscopic gastrostomy (PEG) tube for enteral feedings was raised. The eldest of the two children asked what the chances of recovery were, and the physician explained that this was probably the best Mr. Sussman could attain but that miracles happen every day. However, there were tests that could help in determining the prognosis. The family asked that these be performed.
>
> After the rest of the results were in, the physician explained that the prognosis was grave, but that IV fluids were insufficient to sustain life. The PEG tube would be a necessity if the family wished to continue with food and fluids.
>
> As the physician went down the hall, the family pulled in the nurse, Gail, who had been with Mr. Sussman during the last 3 days and asked, "If this were your father, what would you do?" This situation became an ethical dilemma for Gail as well. If you were Gail, what would you say? Depending on your answer, what would be the possible principles that you might violate?

■ *Resolving Ethical Dilemmas Faced by Nurses*

• • • • • • • • • • • • • • • • • •

Ethical dilemmas can occur in any aspect of our lives, personal or professional. Here we focus on the resolution of professional dilemmas. The nursing process provides a helpful mechanism for finding solutions to

Box 12–1 Questions to help resolve ethical dilemmas
- What are the medical facts?
- What are the psychosocial facts?
- What are the patient's wishes?
- What values are in conflict?

ethical dilemmas. The first step is assessment, including identification of the problem. The simplest way to do this is to create a statement that summarizes the issue. The remainder of the process evolves from this statement (Box 12–1).

ASSESSMENT

Ask yourself, am I directly involved in this dilemma? An issue is not an ethical dilemma for nurses unless they are directly involved or have been asked for input on the situation. Some nurses involve themselves in situations when their opinion has not been solicited. This is generally unwarranted unless the issue is a violation of the professional code of ethics.

Nurses are often in the position of hearing both sides of an ethical dilemma. Often all that is asked for is an empathetic listener. Other times, when guidance is requested, we can help people work through the decision (remember the principle of autonomy).

Collecting data from all of the decision makers helps in identifying the reasoning process being used by these individuals as they struggle with the issue. The following questions assist in the information-gathering process:

What are the medical facts? Find out how the physicians, physical and occupational therapists, dietitians, and your fellow nurses view the client's condition and treatment options. Speak with the client if possible, and determine his or her understanding of the situation.

What are the psychosocial facts? In what emotional state is the client right now? The client's family? What kind of relationship exists between the client and the family? What are the client's living conditions? Who are the individuals who form that client's sup-

port system? How are they involved in the client's care? What is the client's ability to make medical decisions about his or her care? Are there financial considerations that need to be taken into account? What concepts or things does the client value? What does the client's family value? The answers to these questions will give you a better understanding of the situation. You may also find yourself asking more questions to complete the picture.

The social facts of a situation also include institutional policies, legal aspects, and economic factors. The personal belief systems of physicians and other healthcare professionals will also influence this aspect.

What are the client's wishes? Remember the ethical principle of autonomy. With very few exceptions, if the client is competent, his or her decisions take precedence. Too often, the family's or physician's world view and belief system overshadow that of the client. Nurses can assist by maintaining the focus on the client.

If the client is unable to communicate, try to discover if the individual has discussed the issue in the past. If the client has completed a living will or designated a healthcare surrogate, this will also help in divining the client's wishes. Often by interviewing family members, the nurse can discover conversations in which the client voiced his or her feelings about treatment decisions. Through guided interviewing, the nurse can encourage the family to tell anecdotes that provide relevant insights into what the client's values and beliefs are.

What values are in conflict? To assess this, begin by listing each person involved in the situation. Then identify the values represented by each person. You can do this by asking questions such as "What do you feel is the most pressing issue here?" and "Tell me more about your feelings regarding this situation." In some cases, you may find little disagreement among the people involved, just a different way of expressing their beliefs. In others, however, you may discover a serious value conflict.

PLANNING

For planning to be successful, everyone involved in the decision must be included in the process. According to Thompson and

Thompson (1985), there are three very specific but integrated phases to this planning:

1. **Determine goals of treatment.** Is cure the goal? Or is it keeping the client comfortable? Is it life at any cost, or is it a peaceful death at home? These goals need to be client-focused, centered on reality, and attainable. They should be consistent with current medical treatment and, if possible, be measurable according to an established time frame.

2. **Identify the decision makers.** As mentioned earlier, nurses may or may not be decision makers in these health-related ethical dilemmas. It is important to know who the decision makers are and what their belief systems are. When the client is a capable participant, this task is much easier. However, people who are ill are often too exhausted to speak up for themselves or to ensure that their voices are heard. When this happens, the client needs an advocate. Family, friends, spiritual advisors, and nurses often act as advocates for clients. If the client is unable to speak for himself or herself, then someone else must speak for him or her. A family member may need to be designated as the primary decision maker, a role often called the *healthcare surrogate*.

   The creation of living wills, establishment of advance directives, and appointment of a healthcare surrogate while a person is still healthy often ease the burden for the decision makers during a later crisis. Clients can exercise autonomy through these mechanisms even though they may no longer be able to directly communicate their wishes. When these documents are not available, the information gathered during the assessment of social factors helps identify those individuals who may be able to act in the person's best interest.

3. **List and rank all the options.** Performing this task involves all the decision makers. Sometimes it is helpful to begin with the least desired choice and methodically work toward the preferred treatment choice that is most likely to lead to the desired outcome.

Asking all participating parties to discuss what they feel are reasonable outcomes to be attained with the use of available medical treatment often helps in the decision process. By listening to others in a controlled situation, family members and healthcare professionals discover that they actually want the same thing as the client; they just had different ideas about how to achieve their goal.

IMPLEMENTATION

During the implementation phase, the client or the surrogate (substitute) decision makers and members of the healthcare team reach a mutually acceptable decision. This occurs through open discussion and sometimes negotiation. An example of negotiation may be as follows:

> Elena's mother has metastatic ovarian cancer. She and Elena have discussed treatment options. Her physician suggested the use of Taxol, an experimental chemotherapeutic agent that has demonstrated success in many cases. But Elena's mother says emphatically that she has had enough and would just like to spend her remaining time doing whatever she chooses. Elena would like her mother to try the drug.
>
> To resolve the dilemma, the oncology nurse practitioner and the physician sat down to talk with Elena and her mother. Everyone reviewed the facts and expressed their feelings about the situation. Seeing Elena's distress over her decision, Elena's mother said, "OK, I will try the Taxol for 1 month. If there is no improvement after this time, I want to stop all treatment and live out the time I have with my daughter and her family." All agreed that this was a reasonable decision.

The role of the nurse during the implementation phase is to ensure that communication does not break down. Ethical dilemmas are often emotional issues, filled with guilt, sorrow, anger, and other strong emotions. These strong feelings can cause communication failures among decision makers. Remind yourself, "I am here to do what is best for this client."

Keep in mind that an ethical dilemma is not always a choice between two attractive alternatives. Many are between two unattractive, even unpleasant choices. Elena's mother's options did not include the choice she really wished for: good health and a long life.

Once an agreement is reached, the decision makers must live with it. Sometimes an agreement is not reached because the parties cannot reconcile their conflicting belief systems or values. Other times, caregivers are unable to recognize the worth of the client's point of view. Occasionally, the client or the surrogate may make a request that is not institutionally or legally possible. In some cases, a different institution or physician may be able to honor the request. In other cases, the client or surrogate may request information from the nurse regarding illegal acts. When this happens, the nurse should sit down with the client and family and ask them to consider the consequences of their proposed actions. It may be necessary to bring other counselors into the discussion (with the client's permission) to negotiate an agreement.

EVALUATION

As in the nursing process, the purpose of evaluation in resolving ethical dilemmas is to determine whether the desired outcomes have occurred. In the case of Mr. Sussman, some of the questions that could be posed by Gail to the family are as follows:

- ◆ "I have noticed the amount of time you have been spending with your father. Have you observed any changes in his condition?"

- ◆ "I see Dr. Washburn spoke to you about the test results and your father's prognosis. How do you feel about the situation?"

- ◆ "Now that Dr. Washburn has spoken to you about your father's condition, have you considered future alternatives?

Changes in client status, availability of medical treatment, and social facts may call

for re-evaluation of the situation. The course of treatment may need to be altered. Continued communication and cooperation among the decision makers are essential.

CURRENT ETHICAL ISSUES

The well-known Dr. Jack Kevorkian (sometimes called "Dr. Death" in the press) has raised the consciousness of the American people and the healthcare system about the issues of euthanasia and assisted suicide. Do individuals have the right to consciously end their own lives when they are suffering from terminal conditions? If they are unable to perform the act themselves, should others assist them in ending their lives? Should this be illegal? We do not have answers to these difficult questions, yet these same questions are faced daily by clients and their families across the country.

The primary goal of nursing and other healthcare professions is to keep people alive and well or, if we cannot do this, to help them live with their problems and die peacefully. To do this, we struggle to improve our knowledge and skills so that we can care for our clients, provide them with some quality of life, and bring them back to the state known as wellness. The costs involved in achieving this can be astronomical. Questions are being raised more and more often about who should receive the benefits of this technology. Other difficult questions, such as who should pay for care when the illness may have been due to poor healthcare practices such as smoking or substance abuse, are also being debated.

Most of this chapter has dealt with client issues, but ethical problems may involve leadership and management issues as well. What do you do about an impaired coworker? Personal loyalties often cause conflict with professional ethics, creating an ethical dilemma. For this reason, most nurse practice acts address this problem today, requiring the reporting of impaired professionals and providing rehabilitation for them.

Other professional dilemmas may involve working with incompetent personnel. This may be frustrating for both staff and management. Regulations created to protect individuals from unjustified loss of position and the enormous amount of paperwork, remediation, and time that must be exercised to terminate an incompetent healthcare worker often make management "look the other way." Employing institutions providing nursing services have an obligation to establish a process for the reporting and handling of practices that jeopardize client safety (American Nurses Association, 1994). The behaviors of incompetent staff place both clients and other staff members in jeopardy. Eventually the incompetency may lead to legal action, which may have been avoidable.

■ *Conclusion*

Ethical dilemmas become issues in the changing healthcare environment. More questions will be raised, with fewer answers available. New guidelines will need to be developed to assist in finding these answers. Technology has given us enormous power to keep the human organism alive; economics may force us to answer the questions of what is living and when people should be allowed to die. Again and again the question is raised, "Who shall live, and who shall die?" What is your answer?

? *Study Questions*

1. What is the difference between intrinsic and extrinsic values? Make a list of your intrinsic values.

2. Consider a decision you made recently that was based on your values. How did you make your choice?

3. Describe how you could use the valuing process of choosing, prizing, and acting in making the decision.

4. Which of your personal values would be primary if you were assigned to care for a microcephalic infant whose parents have decided to withhold all food and fluids?

5. If the parents confronted you and asked you, "What would you do if this were your baby?" what do you feel would be the most important thing to consider in responding to them?

Critical Thinking Exercise

Andy is employed in a hospital where nurses are now responsible for giving respiratory therapy treatments. To save money, his nurse manager has decided that they will wash out the suction traps and reuse them on other clients. All suction tubing will be fresh. Andy realizes that this is a breach of universal precautions.

1. To whom should Andy speak to about this problem?

2. If he gets no response from the selected individual or individuals, where does he go next?

3. Which, if any, ethical principles have been violated?

4. What is Andy's responsibility in this situation?

REFERENCES

AIDS Update Conference (1995), Hollywood Memorial Hospital, Hollywood, Fla.

American Nurses Association. (1994). *Guidelines on Reporting Incompetent, Unethical, or Illegal Practices.* Washington, D.C.: American Nurses Association.

Benner, P. & Wrubel, J. (1989). *The Primary of Caring: Stress and Coping in Health and Illness.* Menlo Park, Calif.: Addison Wesley.

Edge, R.S., & Groves, J.R. (1994). *The Ethics of Healthcare: A Guide for Clinical Practice.* Albany, N.Y.: Delmar.

Gordon, N. (1963). *The Death Committee.* New York: Fawcett Crest.

Macklin, R. (1987). *Mortal Choices: Ethical Dilemmas in Modern Medicine.* Boston: Houghton Mifflin.

Mappes, T.A., & Zembaty, J.S. (1991). *Biomedical Ethics* (3rd ed.). St. Louis: McGraw-Hill.

Raths, L.E., Harmon, M., & Simmons, S.B. (1979). *Values and Teaching.* New York: Charles E. Merrill.

Steele, S.M., & Harmon, V. (1983). *Values Clarification in Nursing.* New York: Appleton-Century-Crofts.

Thompson, J., and Thompson, H. (1985). *Bioethical Decision Making for Nurses.* New York: Appleton-Century-Crofts.

Wack, J. (1992). *Sociology of Religion.* Chicago: University of Chicago Press.

Webster's New World Dictionary. (1990). New York: Simon & Schuster.

Wright, R.A. (1987). *Human Values in Health Care.* St. Louis: McGraw-Hill.

CHAPTER 13

Your Nursing Career

OBJECTIVES *After reading this chapter, the student will be able to:*

◆ Evaluate personal strengths, weaknesses, opportunities, and threats using a SWOT analysis.

◆ Develop a resume including objectives, qualifications, skills experience, work history, education, and training.

◆ Compose job search letters including cover letter, thank-you letter, and acceptance and rejection letters.

◆ Discuss components of the interview process.

◆ Discuss the factors involved in selecting the right position.

◆ Explain why the first year is critical to the planning of a career.

◆ Distinguish between the novice, advanced beginner, competent, proficient, and expert practitioner.

By now, you have invested considerable time, expense, and emotion in preparing for your new career. Your educational preparation, technical and clinical expertise, interpersonal and management skills, personal interests and needs, and commitment to the nursing profession will all contribute to meeting your career goals. Changes in technology and healthcare reform will continue to affect the way in which nursing care is delivered. However, as these changes eventually work out, we believe that nurses will continue to play a major role in the delivery of health care. Successful nurses view nursing as a lifetime pursuit, not an occupational stepping stone. As a professional nurse, the sky is the limit in terms of the opportunities and challenges available to you.

What steps are important in strategizing your career path? This chapter deals with a most important endeavor—finding and keeping your first nursing position. The chapter begins with planning your initial search, developing a strengths, weaknesses, opportunities, and threats (SWOT) analysis, searching for available positions, and researching organizations. There is a section on writing a resume and employment-related information about the interview process and selecting the first position. The chapter concludes with information from Dr. Benner's book, *From Novice to Expert* (1984), explaining how this historic work can help the new graduate understand the path to excellence in our profession.

■ *Getting Started*

• • • • • • • • • • • • • • • • • • •

Most of the students who have graduated from associate degree programs did not have the luxury of checks from "Mom and Dad" as they paid for college tuition, books, uniforms, and miscellaneous supplies for their nursing education. On graduating with an associate degree in nursing, you may still have student loans and continued responsibilities for supporting a family. If this is so, you may be so focused on job security and a steady source of income that the idea of career planning has not even entered your mind. Besides, isn't the idea just to "get the first job"? Not exactly. The idea is to find the job that fits you, and that is a good first step in the path to a lifelong career in nursing.

Searching for a job is a consideration of not only who will hire you for the first position but also what career path you will pursue. Yes, you do need to prepare for the first job, but in doing so you also need to prepare yourself for your future as a professional nurse. Doing this first will decrease your chances of burnout, frequent position changes, and dissatisfaction with your chosen profession.

SWOT ANALYSIS

Many students assume that their first position will be as a staff nurse on a medical-surgical floor. They see themselves as "putting in their year" and then moving on to what they really want to do. However, as the healthcare system continues to evolve and reallocate resources, this may no longer be the automatic first step for new graduates. Instead, the new graduate should focus on long-term career goals and the different avenues by which they can be reached.

Many times your past experiences will be an asset in presenting your abilities for a particular position. A strengths, weakness, opportunities, and threats (*SWOT*) analysis plan, borrowed from the corporate world, can guide you through your own internal strengths and weaknesses and an analysis of external opportunities and threats that may help or hinder your job search and career planning. Your SWOT analysis may include these factors (Prutt, 1994):

Strengths

- Relevant work experience
- Advanced education
- Additional product knowledge
- Good communications/people skills
- Computer skills
- Self-managed learner
- Flexibility

Weaknesses

- History of frequent job changes
- Poor communication/people skills
- Inflexibility
- Lack of interest in further training
- Difficulty adapting to change
- Inability to see health care as a business

Opportunities

- Expanding markets in health care
- New applications of technology

- New products and diversification
- Increasing at-risk populations

Threats

- Increased competition among healthcare facilities
- Changes in government regulation

Take some time to personalize the preceding SWOT analysis. What are *your* strengths? What are the things you are not so good at? What weaknesses do you need to minimize or strengths do you need to develop as you begin your job search? What opportunities and threats exist in the healthcare community you are considering? Doing a SWOT analysis will help you make an initial assessment of the job market. It can be used again after you narrow down your search for that first nursing position.

BEGINNING THE SEARCH

The saying "Once you have a degree, you can get a job anywhere" is no longer true for many college graduates. Hospital mergers, emphasis on increased staff productivity, budget crises, staffing shifts, and changes in job market availability affect the numbers and types of nurses employed in various facilities and agencies. What do employers think you need to be ready to work for them? Besides passing the NCLEX examination, employers cite the following skills as desirable in job candidates (Shingleton, 1994):

- Oral and written communication skills
- Ability to assume responsibility
- Interpersonal skills
- Proficiency in field of study/technical competence
- Teamwork abilities
- Willingness to work hard
- Leadership abilities
- Motivation, initiative, and flexibility

◆ Analytical skills

◆ Computer knowledge

◆ Problem-solving and decision-making abilities

◆ Self-discipline

◆ Organizational skills

Active job searches may include looking in a variety of places (Beatty, 1991):

◆ Public employment agencies

◆ Private employment agencies

◆ Human resource departments

◆ Information from friends or relatives

◆ Newspaper, professional journals

◆ College and university career centers

◆ Career/job fairs

Regardless of where you begin your search, you should explore the market vigorously and thoroughly. Looking only in the classified ads on Sunday morning is a limited search. Instead, speak to everyone you know about your job search. Encourage classmates and colleagues to share contacts with you, and do the same with them. Also, when possible, try to speak directly with the person who is looking for a nurse when you hear of a possible opening. The people in human resources offices (personnel) may reject a candidate on a technicality that a nurse manager would realize does not affect that person's ability to handle the job if he or she is otherwise a good match with the position. For example, experience in day surgery would prepare a person to work in other surgery-related settings, but a human resources interviewer may not know this.

Try to obtain as much information as you can about the position advertised. Is there a match between your skills and interests and the position available? Ask yourself whether you are applying for this position because you really want it or just to gain interview experience. Be careful about going through the interview process and receiving job offers only to turn them down. Employers may share information with one another, and you could end up being denied the position you really want.

RESEARCHING YOUR POTENTIAL EMPLOYER

You have spent time taking a look at yourself and the climate of the healthcare job market. You have narrowed your choice to those organizations that really interest you. Now the time has come to find out as much as possible about these organizations.

Ownership of the company may be public or private, foreign-owned or American-owned. The company may be a local, regional, or small corporation or a division of a much larger corporation. Depending on the size and ownership of the company, information may be obtained from the public library, chamber of commerce, or government offices. A telephone call or letter to the corporate office or local human resources department may also furnish you with valuable information on organizations of interest (Crowther, 1994). Has the organization recently gone through a merger, reorganization, or downsizing? Information from current and past employees is valuable and may provide you with more detailed information on whether or not the organization would be suitable for you. Be wary of gossip and half-truths that may emerge, however, as they may discourage you from applying to an excellent healthcare facility. In other words, if you hear something negative about an organization, check it out for yourself.

You may want to obtain the mission statement of organizations that interest you. The mission statement reflects what the institution sees as important to its public image. A look at the department of nursing philosophy and objectives indicates how the nursing department defines nursing and outlines the objectives for the department—what are the important goals for nursing? The nursing philosophy and goals should reflect the mission of the organization. Where is nursing administration on the organizational chart of the institution? To whom does the chief nursing administrator report? Although much of this information may not be obtained until an interview, a preview of how the institution views itself and the value it places on nursing will help you to decide if your philosophy of health care and nursing is compatible with a particular organization.

■ *Writing a Resume*

Your resume is your self-advertisement and will be the first impression the recruiter or your potential employer will have of you. Through the resume you are selling yourself—your skills, talents, and abilities. You may decide to prepare your own resume or have it prepared by a professional service. Regardless of who prepares your resume, the purpose is clear: to get you a job interview!

ESSENTIALS OF A RESUME

Resumes most frequently follow three formats: chronological order, functional, or a combination. The chronological resume is easiest to prepare. This resume allows you to document your work history in reverse chronological order, using dates of employment. Frequently the chronological resume includes an objective that indicates the type of work you are seeking. This resume focuses on what you have done in the past, not what you can or feel you will do in the future. It is easy to read and can be prepared so that your past work experience relates to your current job objective. The functional resume starts with a job objective and documents your accomplishments, abilities, and transferable skills under headings such as "leadership skills." Most people prepare a combination of functional and chronological resumes by documenting skills and abilities as well as a chronological education and work history (Vogel, 1993; Dadich, 1992; Collins, 1991).

Most professional recruiters and placement services agree on the following tips in preparing a resume (Anderson, 1992; Rodriquez & Robertson, 1992):

◆ **MAKE SURE YOUR RESUME IS READABLE.** Although most professionals recommend a resume of no more than two pages, the length does not appear to be as important as the need for the reader to find the critical information easily. Is the type large enough for easy reading? Are paragraphs indented or bullets used to set off information, or does the entire page look like a gray blur? Using bold headings and appropriate spacing can offer relief from lines of gray type, but be careful not to get so carried away with graphics that your resume becomes a new art form. The paper should be an appropriate color such as cream, white, or off-white. Use appropriate fonts and a laser printer. If a good computer and printer are not available to you, most printing services will prepare resumes at a reasonable cost.

◆ **MAKE SURE THE IMPORTANT FACTS ARE EASY TO SPOT.** Education, current employment, responsibilities, and facts to support the experience you have gained from past experience are important. Put the strongest statements at the top. Avoid excessive use of "I." If you are a new nursing graduate with little or no job experience, list your educational background first. Remember that positions you held in your "other life" can frequently support experience that will be relevant in your nursing career. Do let your prospective employer know how you can be reached.

◆ **DO A GRAMMAR CHECK.** Use simple terms, action verbs, and descriptive words. Check your finished resume for spelling, typing, or grammar errors. If you are not sure how something sounds, get another opinion.

◆ **FOLLOW THE DON'TS.** Don't include pictures, fancy binders, or personal references. Don't include salary information or hobbies (unless they have contributed to your work experience). Don't include personal information such as weight, marital status, and number of children. Don't repeat yourself just to make the resume longer. A good resume is lean and to the point and focuses on your strengths and accomplishments.

Whatever format you use, it is essential to include the following (Parker, 1989):

◆ A clearly stated job objective
◆ Highlighted qualifications

◆ Presentation of directly relevant skills experience

◆ Chronological work history

◆ Listing of relevant education and training

TABLE 13–1
ACTION VERBS

Management Skills
attained
improved
increased
strengthened
developed
planned
organized
recommended
strengthened
supervised

Communication Skills
collaborated
convinced
developed
formulated
negotiated
recruited
promoted
reconciled
enlisted

Accomplishments
achieved
expanded
improved
reduced (losses)
resolved (problems)
restored
coordinated
adapted
developed
facilitated
instructed
implemented

Helping Skills
assessed
assisted
clarified
demonstrated
diagnosed
expedited
facilitated
motivated
represented

Source: Adapted from Parker, Y. (1989). *The Damn Good Resume Guide.* Berkeley, California: Ten Speed Press.

HOW TO BEGIN

Begin by writing down everything you can think of in the preceding five categories. Work history is usually the easiest place to begin. Arrange your work history in reverse chronological order, listing your current job first. Account for all your employable years. Short lapses in employment are acceptable, but longer periods should be accounted for with an explanation. Each position should include employer, dates worked (years only, i.e., 1991–1993), city, and state. Briefly describe duties and responsibilities of each position. This is the place to emphasize your accomplishments, any special techniques you learned, or changes you implemented. Use action verbs such as those listed in Table 13–1 to describe your accomplishments. Also cite any special awards or committee chairmanships. If the position is not health-related, try to relate your duties and accomplishments to the position you are seeking.

EDUCATION

Next, focus on your *education*. Include the name and location of every educational institution, dates you attended, and the degree, diploma, or certification attained. Start with your most recent degree. Include your license number and state(s) of licensure. If you are awaiting licensure, indicate when you will sit for the NCLEX examination. If you are seeking additional training such as IV certification, include only what is relevant to your job objective.

YOUR OBJECTIVE

It is now time to write your job objective. Don't panic over the thought of writing a clearly stated, brief job objective. Ask yourself: What do I want to do? For whom or with whom? When? At what level of responsibility? For example (Parker, 1989):

What: registered nurse
For whom: pediatric patients
Where: large metropolitan hospital
At what level: staff

The new graduate's objective might read: "Position as staff nurse on a pediatric unit" or "Graduate nurse position on a pediatric unit." *Do not* include phrases such as "advancing to NICU." Employers are looking at what positions *they can fill* and do not want be seen as a stepping-stone in your career.

SKILLS AND EXPERIENCE

Relevant skills and experience are included not to describe your past but to present a "word picture of you in your proposed new job, created out of the best of your past experience" (Parker, 1989, p. 13). Begin by jotting down the major skills required for the position you are seeking. Include five or six major skills such as:

◆ Administration/management

◆ Teamwork/problem solving

◆ Patient relations

◆ Proficiency in a specialty

◆ Technical skills

What if you were "just a housewife" for many years? First, let's do an attitude adjustment. You were not "just a housewife" but a family manager. Explore your role in work-related terms such as community volunteerism, personal relations, fund raising, counseling, and teaching. College career offices, women's centers, or professional resume businesses can offer assistance with analyzing the skills and talents you shared with your family and community. If you are a student with no work experience, do not despair. Examples of nonwork experience that show marketable skills include (Parker, 1989; Eubanks, 1991:

◆ Working on school paper or yearbook

◆ Serving in student government

◆ Leadership positions in clubs, bands, church activities

◆ Community volunteerism

◆ Coaching sports or tutoring academic areas

Now that you have jotted down everything relevant about yourself, it is time to develop the *highlights of your qualifications*. This area could also be called the *summary of qualifications* or just *summary*. These are your unmodest one-liners designed to let your prospective employer know that you are qualified and talented and absolutely the best choice for the position! A typical group of highlights might include (Parker, 1989):

◆ How much relevant experience you have

◆ What your formal training and credentials are, if relevant

◆ Significant accomplishments, very briefly stated

◆ One or two outstanding skills or abilities

◆ A reference to your values, commitment, or philosophy if appropriate

A new graduate's highlights could read:

◆ Five years of experience as an LPN in a large nursing home

◆ Excellent client/family relationship skills

◆ Experience with chronic psychiatric patients

◆ Strong teamwork and communication skills

◆ Special certification in rehabilitation and reambulation strategies

Tailor the resume to the job you are seeking. Include only relevant information such as internships, summer jobs, intersemester experiences, and volunteer work. Even if your previous experience is not directly related to nursing, your previous work experience can show transferable skills, motivation, and your potential to be a great employee.

Regardless of how wonderful you sound on paper, if the paper itself is not presentable your resume may end up in the circular file (trash can!). Do tell your perspective employer if you have an answering machine or fax for leaving messages.

A portion of a sample resume is shown in Fig. 13–1.

Delores Wheatley
5734 Foster Road
Middleton, Indiana 46204
(907) 123-4567

Objective: Position as staff registered nurse on medical-surgical unit

HIGHLIGHTS OF QUALIFICATIONS

EDUCATION:

High School Diploma 1995
Coral Ridge High School
Dolphin Beach, Florida

Associate of Science Degree in Nursing 1997
Howard Community College
Middleton, Indiana
Currently enrolled in 30-hour IV certification course at HCC

EXPERIENCE:

Volunteer, Association for the Blind 1993–1995
Nursing Assistant, Howard Community Hospital 1995–1997
(Summer Employment)
Special Olympics Committee 1996–1997

QUALIFICATIONS:

Experience with blind and disabled children
Pediatric inpatient experience
Ability to work as part of an interdisciplinary team
Experience with families in crisis

FIGURE 13-1 Sample resume.

■ *Job Search Letters*

• • • • • • • • • • • • • • • • • • •

The most common job search letters are the cover letter, thank-you letter, and acceptance letter. Job search letters should be linked to the SWOT analysis you prepared earlier. Regardless of the purpose, the letters should follow basic writing principles (Banis, 1994):

◆ Identify the purpose of the letter.

◆ State the most important items first.

◆ Support these comments with facts.

◆ Keep the letter organized.

◆ Group similar items together in a paragraph; then organize paragraphs to flow logically.

◆ Although business letters are formal, keep the letters personal and warm but professional.

◆ Avoid sending the same letter to everyone. Instead, tailor your form letter to meet each individual situation.

◆ As you write the letter, keep it work-centered and employee-centered, not self-centered.

◆ Be direct and brief. Keep your letter to one page.

◆ Use the active voice and action verbs with a positive, optimistic tone.

◆ If possible, address your letters to a specific individual, using the correct title and business address. Letters addressed "To Whom It May Concern" do not indicate much research (or interest) in your prospective employer.

◆ A timely (rapid) response demonstrates your knowledge of how to do business.

◆ Be honest. Use specific examples and evidence from your experience to back up your claims.

COVER LETTER

You have spent time preparing the resume that best "sells" you to your prospective employer. What about your cover letter? The cover letter is your introduction. If it is true that first impressions are lasting impressions, the cover letter will have a significant impact on your prospective employer. The purposes of the cover letter include (Beatty, 1989):

◆ Acting as a transmittal letter for your resume

◆ Presenting you and your credentials to the prospective employer

◆ Generating interest in interviewing you

Regardless of whether your cover letter will first be read by the human resource personnel or by the individual nurse manager, the effectiveness of your cover letter cannot be overemphasized. A poor cover letter can eliminate you from the selection process before you ever have an opportunity to compete. A sloppy, unorganized cover letter and resume may suggest that you are sloppy and unorganized at work. A lengthy, wordy cover letter may suggest a verbose, nonfocused individual (Beatty, 1991). The cover letter should include the following (Anderson, 1992):

◆ State the purpose. Indicate your purpose in applying and your interest in a specific position. Identify how you learned about the position.

◆ Emphasize your strongest qualifications, those that match the requirement for the position. Provide evidence of experience and accomplishments that relate to the available position. Refer to your enclosed resume.

◆ Sell yourself! Convince this employer that you have the qualifications and motivation to perform in this position.

◆ Express appreciation to the reader for consideration.

Fig. 13–2 is an example of a cover letter.

THANK-YOU LETTER

Thank-you letters are an important yet seldom implemented tool in a job search. Everyone who has helped in any way in your job search should get a thank-you letter. As indicated earlier, promptness is important. Thank-you letters should be sent out within 24 hours to anyone who has interviewed you. The thank-you letter (Banis, 1994, p. 4a) should be used to:

◆ Express appreciation

◆ Reemphasize your qualifications and the match between your qualifications and the position required

◆ Restate your interest in the position

◆ Provide supplemental information if not previously stated

A sample thank-you letter is found in Fig. 13–3.

ACCEPTANCE LETTER

The acceptance letter is used to accept the position, confirm the terms of employment such as salary and starting date, and reiterate the employer's decision to hire you. Many times the acceptance letter follows a telephone conversation in which the terms of employment were discussed. A sample acceptance letter is found in Fig. 13–4.

5734 Foster Road
Middleton, Indiana 46204

April 15, 1996

Ms. Joan Smith
Human Resource Manager
All Care Nursing Center
4431 Lakeside Drive
Middleton, Indiana 46204

Dear Ms. Smith:

 I am applying for the registered nurse position that was advertised in the Fort Lauderdale News on April 14. The position seems to fit very well with my education, experience, and career interests.

 Your position requires interest and experience in caring for the elderly and IV certification. In addition to my clinical experience in the nursing program at Howard Community College, I have worked as a certified nursing assistant at St. Mary's Nursing Home 25 hours/week during the 2 years I was enrolled in the Howard Community College nursing program. My responsibilities included assisting the elderly clients with activities of daily living, including special range-of-motion and reambulation exercises. The experience of serving as a team member under the supervision of the registered nurse and physical therapist was invaluable. I am currently enrolled in the 30-hour IV certification course at HCC. My enclosed resume provides more details on my qualifications and education.

 My background and career goals seem to match your job requirements. I am confident that I can perform the duties of a registered nurse at All Care Nursing Center. I am genuinely interested in pursuing a nursing career in care of the aging. Your agency has an excellent reputation in the community, and your parent company is likewise highly respected.

 I am requesting a personal interview to discuss the possibilities of employment. I shall call you during the week of April 21 to request an appointment. Should you need to reach me, please call me at 123-4567. My telephone has an answering machine. I will return your call promptly. Thank you for your consideration. I look forward to talking with you.

Sincerely yours,

Delores Wheatley

FIGURE 13-2 Sample cover letter.

April 27, 1998

Ms. Martha Berrero
Nurse Manager, 3 East
All Care Nursing Center
4431 Lakeside Drive
Middleton, Indiana 46204

Dear Ms. Berrero:

Thank you very much for interviewing me yesterday for the registered nurse position at All Care Nursing Center. I enjoyed meeting you and learning more about the role of the registered nurse in long-term care with Jefferson Corporation.

My enthusiasm for the position and my interest in working with the elderly are increased as a result of the interview. I feel that my education and experience in long-term care fit with the job requirements. I know I can make a contribution to the care of the residents and as a nursing team leader over time.

I wish to reiterate my strong interest in working with you and your staff. I know All Care Nursing Center can provide the kind of opportunities I am seeking. Please call me at 123-4567 if I can provide you with any additional information.

Again, thank you for the interview and for considering me for the registered nurse position.

Sincerely yours,

Delores Wheatley

FIGURE 13-3 Sample thank-you letter.

April 28, 1998

Ms. Martha Berrero
Nurse Manager, 3 East
All Care Nursing Center
4431 Lakeside Drive
Middleton, Indiana 46204

Dear Ms. Berrero:

I am writing to confirm my acceptance of your employment offer of April 27. I am delighted to be joining All Care Nursing center. I feel confident that I can make a significant contribution to your team and I appreciate the opportunity you have offered me.

As we discussed, I will report to the Personnel Office at 8AM for new employee orientation on May 15. I will have the medical exam, employee, and insurance forms completed when I arrive. I understand the starting salary will be $19.10/hour with full benefits beginning May 15. Overtime salary in excess of 40 hours/week will be paid if overtime hours are requested by you.

I appreciate your confidence in me and look forward to joining your team.

Sincerely yours,

Delores Wheatley

FIGURE 13-4 Sample acceptance letter.

April 28, 1998

Ms. Martha Berrero
Nurse Manager, 3 East
All Care Nursing Center
4431 Lakeside Drive
Middleton, Indiana 46204

Dear Ms. Berrero:

Thank you for offering me the position of staff nurse with
All Care Nursing Center. I appreciate your taking the time to give
me such extensive information about the position.

There are many aspects of the position that appeal to me.
Jefferson Corporation is an excellent provider of health care
services throughout this area and nationwide. However, after
giving it much thought, I have decided to accept another offer
and must therefore decline your offer.

Again, thank you for your consideration and the courtesy
extended to me. I enjoyed meeting with you and your staff.

Sincerely yours,

Delores Wheatley

FIGURE 13-5 Sample rejection letter.

REJECTION LETTER

Although not as common as the first three job search letters, a rejection letter should be sent if you are declining an employment offer. When rejecting an employment offer, indicate that you have given the offer careful consideration but have decided that the position does not fit your career objectives and interest at this time. As with your other letters, thank the employer for his or her consideration and offer. A sample rejection letter is found in Fig. 13–5.

■ *The Interview Process*

INITIAL INTERVIEW

Congratulations! Your superb resume got you (and perhaps 10 others) through the door for an interview. Your first interview may be with the nurse manager, someone in the human resources office, or an interviewer at a job fair or even over the phone. Regardless of with whom or where you interview, preparation is the key to success.

You began the first step in the preparation process with your SWOT analysis. If you did not obtain any of the following information regarding your prospective employer at that time, it is imperative that you do it now:

- Key people in the organization
- Size in terms of clients and employees
- Types of services provided
- Reputation in the community

You also need to review your qualifications for the position. What does your interviewer want to know about you? Consider the following:

- Why should I hire you?
- What kind of employee will you make?
- Will you get things done?
- How much will you cost the company?
- How long will you stay?
- What haven't you told us about yourself or your weaknesses?

The exchange of information between you and the interviewer will go more smoothly if you keep the following points in mind when answering questions (Bischof, 1993; Mascolini & Supnick, 1993; Krannich & Krannich, 1993):

- Be brief. Stop talking when you feel you have said enough.
- Don't be overly modest, but don't exaggerate.
- Talk in concrete terms.
- Be specific. Responses should be in behavioral terms supported by personal experience and specific examples.
- Do not defend or argue your view.
- Make connections for the interviewer. Relate your responses to the needs of the individual organization.

ANSWERING QUESTIONS

Interview questions may include background questions, professional questions, and personal questions.

Background Questions

Background questions usually relate to information on your resume. Again, if you have no nursing experience, relate your prior school and work experience and other accomplishments relevant to the position you are seeking without going through your entire autobiography with the interviewer. You may be asked to expand on the information in your resume about your formal nursing education. Here is your opportunity to relate specific courses or clinical experiences you enjoyed, academic honors, and participation in extracurricular activities or research projects.

Professional Questions

Many recruiters today are looking for specifics, especially those related to skills and knowledge needed in the position available. They may start with questions related to your education, career goals, strengths, weaknesses, philosophy of nursing, style, and abilities. Interviewers often open their questioning with words such as "review," "tell me," "explain," and "describe," followed by such phrases as "How did you do it?" or "Why did you do it that way?" (Mascolini & Supnick, 1993). How will you be successful with these types of questions?

When answering "what if" questions, it is especially important that you remain specific, citing your own experiences and relating these behaviors to a demonstrated skill or strength. Examples of questions in this area include the following (Bischof, 1993):

- **What is your philosophy of nursing?** This is a frequently asked question, so you may want to think about how you would answer it. Your response should relate to the position you are seeking.
- **What is your greatest weakness? Your greatest strength?** Don't be afraid to present a weakness, but present it to your best advantage, making it sound like a desirable characteristic. Even better, discuss a weakness that is already apparent such as lack of nursing experience, stating that you recognize your lack of nursing experience but that your

prior work or management experience has taught you skills that will assist you in this position. These skills might include organization, time management, being part of a team, and communication. If you are asked for both strengths and weaknesses, start with your weakness, and end on a positive note with your strengths. Don't be too modest, but don't exaggerate. Relate your strengths to the prospective position. Skills such as interpersonal relationships, organization, and leadership are usually broad enough to fit most positions.

- **Where do you see yourself in 5 years?** Most interviewers want to gain insight into your long-term goals, as well as a feel for whether you are only using this position as a brief stop on the path to another job. Here it is helpful for you to have some history regarding the position in question. How long have others usually remained in this position? Your answer should reflect a career plan in tune with the organizational needs.

- **What are your educational goals?** Be honest and specific. Include both professional education such as RN to BSN and continuing education courses. If you want to pursue further education in related areas such as a foreign language or computers, include this as a goal. Indicate schools to which you have applied or in which you are already enrolled.

- **Describe your leadership style.** Be prepared to discuss your style in terms of how effectively you work with others, and give examples of how you have implemented your leadership in the past.

- **What can you contribute to this position?** Review your SWOT analysis as well as the job description for the position before the interview. Be specific in relating your contributions to the position.

- **What are your salary requirements?** You may be asked about minimum salary range. Try to find out the prospective employer's salary range before this question comes up. Be honest about your expectations, but make it clear that you are willing to negotiate.

- **"What if" questions.** Prospective employers are increasingly using competency-based interview questions to determine people's preparation for a job. There is often no single correct answer to these questions. The interviewer may be assessing your clinical decision-making and leadership skills. Again, be concise, focusing your answer in line with the organizational philosophy and goals. If you do not know the answer, tell the interviewer how you would go about finding the answer. You cannot be expected to have all the answers before you begin a job, but you can be expected to know how to obtain the answers once you are in the position.

Personal Questions

Personal questions deal with your personality and motivation. Common questions include the following:

- **How would you describe yourself?** This is a standard question. Most people find it helpful to think about an answer in advance. You can repeat some of what you said in your resume and cover letter. You do not have to provide an in-depth analysis of your personality. In fact, you should not do this.

- **How would your peers describe you?** Ask them! Again, be brief, describing several strengths. Forget about your weaknesses unless you are asked about them.

- **What would make you happy with this position?** Be prepared to discuss your needs related to your work environment. Do you enjoy self-direction, flexible hours, strong leadership support? Now is the time to cite specifics related to your ideal work environment.

- **Describe your ideal work environment.** Give this question some thought before the interview. Be specific but realistic. If the norm in your community is two RNs to a floor with LPN and other ancillary support, don't say that you feel a total RN staff is needed for good client care!

◆ **Describe hobbies, community activities, and recreation.** Again, brevity is important. Many times this question is used to further observe the interviewee's communication and interpersonal skills.

Never pretend to be someone or something other than who or what you are. If this is necessary to obtain the position, then the position is not right for you.

ADDITIONAL POINTS ABOUT THE INTERVIEW

There are federal, state, and local laws governing questions related to employment questions. Questions asked on the job application and in the interview must be related to the position advertised. Questions or statements that may lead to discrimination on the basis of age, sex, race, color, religion, or ethnicity are illegal. If you are asked a question that appears illegal, you may wish to take one of several approaches:

◆ You may answer the question, realizing that it is not a job-related question. Make it clear to the interviewer that you will answer the question even though you know it is not job-related.

◆ You may refuse to answer. You are within your rights but may be seen as uncooperative or confrontational.

◆ Examine the intent of the question, and relate it to the job.

Just as important as the actual verbal exchange of the interview are the nonverbal aspects of appearance, handshake, eye contact, posture, and listening skills.

Appearance

Dress in business attire. For women, a skirted suit or tailored jacket dress is appropriate. Men should wear a classic suit, light-colored shirt, and conservative tie. For both men and women, gray or navy is rarely

wrong. Shoes should be polished, with appropriate heels. Nails and hair for both men and women should reflect cleanliness, good grooming, and willingness to work. The 2-inch red dagger nails worn on prom night will not support an image of the professional nurse. Paint stains on the hands from a weekend of house maintenance are equally unsuitable for presenting a professional image.

Handshake

Arrive at the interview 10 minutes before your scheduled time (allow yourself a little extra time to find the place if you have not been there before). Introduce yourself courteously to the receptionist. Stand when your name is called, smile, and shake hands firmly. If you perspire easily, wipe your palms just before handshake time.

Eye Contact

During the interview, use the interviewer's title and last name as you speak. Never use the interviewer's first name unless specifically requested to do so. Use good listening skills (all those leadership skills you've just learned). Smile and nod occasionally, making frequent eye contact. Do not fold your arms across your chest, but keep your hands at your sides or in your lap. Pay attention, and sound sure of yourself!

Posture and Listening Skills

Phrase your questions appropriately, and relate them to yourself as a candidate: "What would be my responsibility?" instead of "What are the responsibilities of the job?" Use appropriate grammar and diction. Words like "yeah," "uh-huh," "uh," "you know," or "like" are too casual for an interview.

Don't say "I guess" or "I feel" about anything. These words make you sound indecisive and wishy-washy. Remember your action verbs—I analyzed, I organized, I developed. Don't evaluate your achievements as mediocre or unimpressive. Of course that walkathon you organized was a huge success!

ASKING QUESTIONS

At some point in the interview, you will be asked if you have any questions. Knowing what questions you want to ask is just as important as having prepared answers for their questions. The interview is as much a time for you to find out the details of the job as it is for your potential employer to find out about you. You will need to obtain specific information about the job itself, including the type of clients you will be caring for, the people with whom you would be working, the salary and benefits, and your potential employer's expectations of you.

Jot down a few questions on an index card before going for the interview. You will want to ask questions about the following (Bischof, 1993):

- What is this position's key responsibility?
- What kind of person are you looking for?
- What are the challenges of the position?
- Why is this position open?
- To whom would I report directly?
- Why did the previous person leave this position?
- What is the salary for this position?
- What opportunities are there for advancement?
- Are there opportunities for continuing education? What kind?
- What are your expectations of me as an employee?
- How, when, and by whom are evaluations done?
- What other opportunities for professional growth are available here?
- How are promotion and advancement handled within the organization?

The following are a few additional tips about asking questions during a job interview:

- *Do not* begin with questions about vacations, benefits, or sick time. This would leave the impression that these are the most important part of the job to you, not the work itself.

- *Do* begin with questions about the employer's expectations of you. This will leave the impression that you want to know how you can contribute to the organization.
- *Be sure* you know enough about the position to make a reasonable decision about accepting an offer when one is made.
- *Do* ask questions about the organization as a whole. The information is useful to you and demonstrates that you are able to see the big picture.
- *Do bring* a list of important points to discuss to help if you are nervous.

There are a few "red flags" to be alert for during the interview process (Tyler, 1990):

- Lots of turnover in the position
- A newly created position without a clear purpose
- An organization in transition
- A position that is not feasible for a new graduate
- A gut feeling that things are not what they seem

AFTER THE INTERVIEW

If the interviewer does not offer the information, ask about the next step in the process. Thank the interviewer, shake hands, and exit. If the receptionist is still there, you may quickly smile and say thank you and good-bye. Don't linger and chat, and do not forget your follow-up thank-you letter.

THE SECOND INTERVIEW

If you are invited back for a second interview, it means that the first interview went well and you made a favorable impression. Second visits may include a tour of the facility and meetings with a higher-level executive or supervisor of the department for which you are interviewing and several colleagues. In preparation for the second interview, review the information on the organization and your own strengths. It doesn't hurt to have a few resumes and potential references available. Pointers to make your second visit successful include the following (Muha & Orgiefsky, 1994):

♦ Continue to dress professionally.

♦ Be professional and pleasant with everyone, including secretaries, and housekeeping and maintenance personnel.

♦ Do not smoke.

♦ Remember table manners.

♦ Avoid controversial topics for small talk.

♦ Obtain answers to questions you might have thought of since your first visit.

In most instances, the personnel director or nurse manager will let you know how long it will be before you are contacted again. It is appropriate to get this information before you leave. If you do receive an offer during this visit, graciously say thank you and ask for a little time to consider the offer (even if this is the offer you have anxiously been awaiting!).

If the organization does not contact you by the agreed-on date, don't panic. It is appropriate to call your contact person and tactfully explain your continued interest and the need to know the status of your application so that you can respond to other deadlines.

■ *Making the Right Choice*
• • • • • • • • • • • • • • • • • • • •

You have interviewed well, and now you have to decide among several job offers. Your choice not only will affect your immediate work but will also influence your future career opportunities. There are several factors to consider.

JOB CONTENT

The immediate work you will be doing should be a good match to your skills and interests. Although your work may be personally challenging and satisfying this year, what are the opportunities for growth? How will your desire for continued growth and challenge be satisfied?

DEVELOPMENT

You should have learned from your interviews if the initial training and orientation seem sufficient and well organized. Don't forget to inquire regarding continuing education to keep you current in your field. Is tuition reimbursement available for further education? Is management training provided, or are supervisory skills learned on the job?

DIRECTION

Good supervision and mentors are especially important in this first position. You may be able to judge prospective supervisors throughout the interview process, but you should also try to get a broader view of the overall philosophy of supervision. You may not be working for the same supervisor in a year, but the overall management philosophy is likely to remain consistent.

WORK CLIMATE

The day-to-day work climate must make you feel comfortable. Your preference may be formal or casual, structured or unstructured, complex or simple. It is easy to observe the way people dress, layout of the unit, and lines of communication. It is more difficult to observe company values—factors that will affect your work comfort and satisfaction over the long term. Try to look beyond the work environment to get a "feel" for values. What is the unwritten message? Is there an open-door policy that sends a message that "everyone is equal and important," or does the nurse manager appear too busy to be concerned with the needs of the employees?

COMPENSATION

In evaluating the compensation package, starting salary should be less important than the organization's philosophy on future compensation. What is the potential for salary growth? How are individual increases determined?

■ *The Critical First Year*

Why a section on the "first year"? Don't you just get a nursing license and go to work? Aren't nurses always in demand? You have worked hard to succeed in college—won't those lessons help you to succeed in your new position? Of course they will, but some of the behaviors that were rewarded in school are not rewarded at work. There are no syllabi, study questions, or extra credit points. Only "As" are acceptable, and there do not appear to be many completely correct answers. Discovering this has been called "reality shock" (Kramer, 1974), which is discussed elsewhere in this book. Voluminous care plans and meticulous medication cards are out; multiple responsibilities and thinking on your feet are in. What is the new graduate to do?

Your first year will be a transition year. You are no longer a college student, but you are not yet a full-fledged professional. You are the new kid on the block, and people will respond to you differently and judge you differently than when you were a student. To be successful, you have to respond differently. You may be thinking, "Oh, they always need nurses—it doesn't matter." Yes, it does matter. Many of your career opportunities will be influenced by the early impressions you make. The following paragraphs discuss what you can do to help ensure first-year success.

ATTITUDE AND EXPECTATIONS

Adopt the right attitudes and adjust your expectations. Now is the time to learn the art of being new. You felt like the most important, special person during the recruitment process. Now, in the real world, neither you nor the position may be as glamorous as you once thought. In addition, although you thought you learned a lot in school, your decisions and daily performance do not always warrant an "A." Above all, people shed the "company manners" that they put on when you were interviewing, and organizational politics eventually surface. Your leadership skills and commitment to teamwork will get you through this transition period.

IMPRESSIONS AND RELATIONSHIPS

Manage a good impression and build effective relationships. Remember, you are being watched—by peers, subordinates, and superiors. Because you have no track record to fall back on, impressions are magnified. Although every organization is different, most are looking for someone with good judgment, a willingness to learn, readiness to adapt, and a respect for the expertise of more experienced employees. Most people expect you to "pay your dues" to earn respect from them.

ORGANIZATIONAL SAVVY

Develop organizational savvy. The most important person in this first year is your immediate supervisor. Support this person. Find out what is important, what your supervisor needs and expects from the team. Become a team player. Present solutions, not problems, as often as you can. You want to be a good leader someday; learn first to be a good follower.

SKILLS AND KNOWLEDGE

Master the skills and knowledge of the position. Technology is constantly changing, and contrary to popular belief, you did not learn everything in school. Be prepared to seek out new knowledge and skills on your own. This may entail extra hours of preparation and study, but who said that learning stopped after graduation (Holton, 1994; Johnson, 1994)?

■ *I Can't Find a Job*

It is often said that finding the first job is the hardest. Many employers prefer to hire seasoned nurses who do not require a long orientation and mentoring. Some require new graduates to do postgraduate internships. Changes in skill mix with the implementation of various types of care delivery influence the market for the professional nurse. The new graduate may need to be armed with a variety of skills such as IV certification, home assessment, advanced rehabilitation skills, and various respiratory modalities to even warrant an initial interview. Keep informed of the demands of the market in your area, and be prepared to be flexible in seeking this first position.

■ *From Novice to Expert*

In 1984, Dr. Patricia Benner published a book entitled *From Novice to Expert*. In this book, she described five levels of competency in clinical nursing practice: novice, advanced beginner, competent, proficient, and expert. For example, the statement "He doesn't look right to me" has caused many expert nurses to take immediate action even though the objective signs that the novices had learned from their textbooks had not yet emerged.

NOVICE

The novice is the beginner. You were a novice as a beginning nursing student, and you will be a novice in your first position. As a novice, you use rules to guide your actions. These rules are typically limited and inflexible and are related to the theory you learned in school.

ADVANCED BEGINNER

The advanced beginner has handled enough real situations to have prior experience to apply to new situations. The advanced beginner can now sift through the inflexible, rigid rules to assess situations through the eyes of past experience. Both novices and advanced beginners need support in the clinical area. They are still unable to set their own priorities and identify meaningful recurrent patterns without help from more competent nurses.

COMPETENT

The competent nurse usually has been in the same or similar situation for 2 to 3 years. The competent nurse is able to develop long-range plans and proceed accordingly. Although not as quick or flexible as the proficient nurse, the competent nurse is beginning to achieve efficiency, organizational skills, and ability to cope with the complex needs of multiple clients.

PROFICIENT

The proficient nurse has learned from experience and can look at the whole picture at once. Perception is important, and the proficient nurse no longer has to consciously think through why a client "doesn't look right to me."

EXPERT

The expert nurse has an enormous background of experience and an intuitive grasp of each situation. This expert nurse is able to assess a situation quickly, forming an accurate picture of the current and long-term implications and solutions. Along with possessing finely tuned analytical skills, the expert nurse is a role model and mentor for the novice. Someday you will be the expert, and a new novice will obtain from you the support, guidance, and nurturing needed to provide care for clients in the complex health-care environment.

■ *Advancing Your Career*

Many of the ideas presented in the preceding pages will continue to be helpful as you advance in your nursing career. Continuing to develop your leadership and client care skills through practice and further education will be the key to your professional growth. According to a survey by *Hospitals and Health Networks* (Sherer, 1993), the future looks bright for nursing into the 21st century. Although the delivery of care is expected to continue to move from acute-care centers to subacute-care centers, long-term care facilities, and the home, the need for the registered nurse to be the care manager and provider of care will continue to advance. "As we move toward the end of the 20th century, nurses will not just be asked to acclimate to new roles and participate in new movements. They will be encouraged to lead them as well. The benefactors of this new-found leadership will ultimately be patients, better served by nursing's advancement" (Sherer, 1993).

■ Conclusion
• • • • • • • • • • • • • • • • • • •

Finding that first position is more than being at the right place at the right time. It is a complex combination of learning about yourself and the organizations you are interested in and presenting your strengths and weaknesses in the most positive manner possible. Keeping the first position and using the position to grow and learn are also a planning process. Recognize that the skills of independence and the ability to "do your own thing" through college may not be the skills you need to keep you in your first position. There is an important lesson to be learned. Becoming a team player and savvy in organizational politics is as important as becoming proficient in your nursing skills. As you move through the steps of novice to expert, good luck and good planning!

❓ Study Questions

1. Develop a SWOT analysis. How will you articulate your strengths and weaknesses during an interview?

2. Design a one-page resume to use in seeking your first position. Develop a cover letter, thank-you letter, acceptance letter, and rejection letter that you could potentially use during the interview process.

3. Review the questions discussed in this chapter that a potential employer might ask during an interview. Formulate responses to the questions. How comfortable do you feel in answering these questions?

4. Evaluate the job prospects in the community where you now live. What areas could you explore in seeking your first position?

5. What plans do you have for advancing your career? How can Dr. Benner's work assist you?

Critical Thinking Exercise

Paul Delane is interviewing for his first nursing position after obtaining his registered nurse license. He has been interviewed by the nurse recruiter and is now being interviewed by the nurse manager on the pediatric floor. After a few minutes of social conversation, the nurse manager begins to ask some specific nursing-oriented questions: How would you respond if a mother of a seriously ill child asks you if her child will die? What attempts do you make to understand different cultural beliefs and their importance in health care when planning nursing care? How does your philosophy of nursing affect your ability to deliver care to children whose mothers are HIV-positive?

Paul is very flustered by these questions and responds with "it depends on the situation," "it depends on the culture," and "I don't ever discriminate."

What responses would have been more appropriate in this interview? How could Paul have used these questions to demonstrate his strengths, experiences, and skills?

REFERENCES

Anderson, J. (1992). Tips on resume writing. *Imprint, 39*(1), 30–31.

Banis, W. (1994). The art of writing job-search letters. In College Placement Council, Inc. (Ed.). *Planning Job Choices* pp. 44–51). Philadelphia: College Placement Council.

Beatty, R. (1989). *The Perfect Cover Letter*. New York: John Wiley & Sons.

Beatty, R. (1991). *Get the Right Job in 60 Days or Less*. New York: John Wiley & Sons.

Benner, P. (1984). *From Novice to Expert: Excellence and Power in Clinical Nursing Practice*. Menlo Park, CA: Addison Wesley.

Bischof, J. (1993). Preparing for job interview questions. *Critical Care Nurse, 13*(4), 97–100.

Collins, M. (1991). Resume is key to getting a job. *American Nurse, 23*(2), 18.

Crowther, K. (1994). How to research companies. In College Placement Council, Inc. (Ed.). *Planning Job Choices* (pp. 27–32). Philadelphia: College Placement Council.

Dadich, K.A. (1992). Your resume. *Health Care Trends and Transition, 3*(2), 20, 21, 96.

Eubanks, P. (1991). Experts: Making your resume an asset. *Hospitals, 5*(20), 74.

Holton, E. (1994). The critical first year on the job. In College Placement Council, Inc. (Ed.). *Planning Job Choices* (pp. 68–71). Philadelphia: College Placement Council.

Johnson, K. (1994). Choose your first job with your whole future in mind. In College Placement Council, Inc. (Ed.). *Planning Job Choices* (pp. 65–67). Philadelphia: College Placement Council.

Kramer, M. (1974). *Reality Shock: Why Nurses Leave Nursing*. St. Louis: C.V. Mosby.

Krannich, C. & Krannich, R. (1993). *Interview for Success*. New York: Impact Publications.

Mascolini, M., & Supnick, R. (1993). Preparing students for the behavioral job interview. *Journal of Business and Technical Communication, 7*(4), 482–88.

Muha, D., & Orgiefsky, R. (1994). The 2nd interview: The plant or office visit. In College Placement Council, Inc. (Ed.). *Planning Job Choices* (pp. 58–60). Philadelphia: College Placement Council.

Parker, Y. (1989). *The Damn Good Resume Guide*. Berkeley, California: Ten Speed Press.

Pratt, C. (1994). Successful job-search strategies for the 90's. In College Placement Council, Inc. (Ed.). *Planning Job Choices* (pp. 15–18). Philadelphia: College Placement Council.

Rodriquez, K., & Robertson, D. (1992). Selling your talents with a resume. *American Nurse, 24*(10), 27.

Sherer, J.L. (1993). Next steps for nursing. *Hospital and Health Networks, 8*(20), 26–28.

Shingleton, J. (1994). The job market for '94 grads. In College Placement Council, Inc. (Ed.). *Planning Job Choices* (pp. 19–26). Philadelphia: College Placement Council.

Tyler, L. (1990). Watch out for "red flags" on a job interview. *Hospitals, 64*(14), 46.

Vogel, D. (1993). Writing a resume. *Imprint, 40*(1), 35–36.

CHAPTER 14

Historic Leaders in Nursing

OBJECTIVES   *After reading this chapter, the student will be able to:*

◆ Discuss Florence Nightingale's contribution to the development of modern nursing.

◆ Describe the effect Lillian Wald and the Henry Street Settlement had on community health care.

◆ Describe the contributions that Margaret Sanger made to women's health and social reform.

◆ Describe Adelaide Nutting's contributions to nursing education.

◆ Discuss the common characteristics of these four historic leaders in nursing.

◆ Discuss some of the issues faced by the nursing profession over the last 100 years.

In its history, the nursing profession has had many great leaders. From these, we have chosen just four who not only demonstrate the strengths of our historic leaders but also reflect some of the most important issues that the profession has had to face over the last hundred years or so. Each of these leaders initiated change within the social environment of their time using the theories of change and conflict resolution discussed earlier in the text.

Florence Nightingale is probably the best known of the four. She is considered the founder of modern nursing. Ms. Nightingale changed not only the care of soldiers in the military but also hospital record keeping, the status of nurses, even the profession itself. Her concepts of nursing care became the basis of modern theory development in nursing. Lillian Wald, founder of the Henry Street Settlement, is a role model for contemporary community health nursing. Ms. Wald developed a model for bringing health care to the people. Her social conscience and determination to make changes in health care have been a model for the modern day healthcare revolution. Margaret Sanger, a political activist like the others, is best known for her courageous fight to make birth control information available to everyone who needed it or wanted it. Her fight to make Congress aware of the plight of children in the labor force is less well known but led to important changes in the child labor laws. Ms. Sanger was perhaps the first nurse lobbyist. Finally, Adelaide Nutting is probably the best known example of early leaders in nursing education in the United States.

As you read this chapter, you will see how each of these famous women exemplifies leadership in the nursing profession. Many of their characteristics—intelligence, courage, foresight—are the same ones needed in today's nursing leaders.

■ *Florence Nightingale*

• •

BACKGROUND

Florence Nightingale was born in the city for which she was named, Florence, Italy, on May 12, 1820. She was the second daughter of William and Frances Nightingale. Her father was a well-educated, wealthy man who put considerable effort into the education of his two daughters (Donahue, 1985). Florence Nightingale learned French, German, and Italian in addition to her native English. Mr. Nightingale personally instructed her in mathematics, classical art, and literature. The family made extended visits to London every year, which provided opportunities for contact with people in the highest social circles. These contacts were very valuable to Ms. Nightingale in later years.

In spite of her family's ability to shelter her from the meaner side of life, Nightingale had always shown an interest in the welfare of those with less good fortune than she had. She was driven to improve herself and the world around her. It seems that she was never quite content with herself, as she was described as a "sensitive, introspective, and somewhat morbid child" (Schuyler, 1992). She was driven to improve herself and the world around her. When she expressed an interest in becoming a nurse, her parents objected strenuously. They wanted her to assume the traditional role of well-to-do women of the time: marry, have children, and take her "rightful" place in society.

BECOMING A NURSE

In the fall of 1847, Nightingale left England for a tour of Europe with family friends. In Italy, she entered a convent for a retreat. This strengthened her religious beliefs, although she never converted from Church of England to Catholicism. After this retreat, she felt that she had been called by God to help others. This experience made her more determined than ever to pursue nursing.

In 1851, Nightingale insisted on going to Kaiserswerth in Germany to obtain training in nursing. Her family gave her their permission on the condition that no one would know where she was. When she returned from Kaiserswerth, she began to work on her plan to make an impact in the healthcare field.

Nightingale soon left for France to work with several Catholic nursing sisters. While in France, she received an offer from the committee that regulated the Establishment for Gentlewomen During Illness, a nursing home in London for governesses who became ill. She was appointed superintendent of the home and soon had it well organized, although she did have some difficulties with the committee.

Because of her knowledge of hospitals, Nightingale was often consulted by social reformers and by those physicians who also recognized the need for this new type of nurse. Nightingale was offered a position as superintendent of nurses at King's College Hospital, but her family objected so strongly that she remained at home instead until she went to the Crimea.

THE NEED FOR REFORM

Fortunately for Nightingale, it was fashionable to become involved in the reform of medical and social institutions in the middle of the nineteenth century. After completing the reorganization of the nursing home, she began visiting hospitals and collecting information about nurses' working conditions. In the course of doing this, she realized that to improve nurses' working conditions, she would first have to improve the nurses.

Up to this time, the guiding principle of nursing had revolved around charity. Nursing services in Europe were provided primarily by the family or by members of religious orders. These Catholic organizations experienced a decline during the Reformation, when the government closed churches and monasteries. Hospitals were no longer run for charitable reasons but because of social necessity.

Nursing lost its social standing when the religious orders declined. Nurses were no longer recruited from the respectable classes but from the lower classes of society. Women who needed to earn their keep entered domestic service, and nursing was considered a form of domestic service. Other women who could no longer earn a living by gambling or selling themselves also turned to nursing. Many came from the criminal classes. They lacked the spirit of self-sacrifice found in the religious orders, and they often abused clients. Many consoled themselves with alcohol and snuff.

The duties of a nurse in those days were to take care of the physical needs of clients and to make sure they were reasonably clean. The conditions under which they had to accomplish this were less than ideal. The hospitals were dirty and unventilated. They were contaminated with infection and actually spread diseases instead of preventing them. The same bedsheets were used on several clients. The nurses dealt with people suffering from unrelenting pain, hemorrhage, infections, and gangrene (Kalisch & Kalisch, 1986).

To accomplish the needed reforms, Nightingale realized that she had to recruit her nurses from higher strata of society, as had been done in the past, and then educate them well. She concluded that this could be accomplished only by organizing a school to prepare reliable, qualified nurses.

THE CRIMEAN WAR

A letter written by war correspondent W.H. Russell comparing the nursing care in the British army unfavorably with that given to the French army created a tremendous stir in England. There was demand for change. In response, the Secretary of War, Sir Sidney Herbert, commissioned Nightingale to go to the Crimea (a peninsula in southeastern Ukraine) to investigate conditions there and make improvements.

On October 21, 1854, Nightingale left for the Crimea with a group of nurses on the steamer Vectis (Griffith & Griffith, 1965). They found a disaster when they arrived. The hospital that had been built to accommodate 1700 soldiers was filled with over 3000 wounded and critically ill men. There were no plumbing or sewage disposal facilities. The mattresses, walls, and floors were wet with human waste. Rats, lice, and maggots thrived in this filthy environment (Kalisch & Kalisch, 1986).

The nurses went right to work. They set up a kitchen, rented a house and converted it into a laundry, and hired soldiers' wives to do the laundry. Money was difficult to obtain, so Nightingale used the *Times* relief fund and her own personal funds to purchase medical supplies, food, and equipment. After the hospital had been cleaned and organized, she began to set up social services for the soldiers.

Nightingale rarely slept. She spent hours giving nursing care, wrote letters to families, prepared requests for more supplies, and reported back to London on the conditions that she had found and improved. At night, she made rounds accompanied by an 11-year-old boy who held her lamp when she sat by a dying soldier or assisted during emergency surgery. This is how she earned the title "The Lady with the Lamp" from the poet Longfellow (1868).

Despite their strenuous efforts and enormous accomplishments, the nurses were resented by the physicians and army officers. They regarded these nurses as intruders who interfered with their work and undermined their authority. There was also some conflict between Nightingale and Dr. John Hall, the chief of the medical staff. At one time, after Dr. Hall had been awarded the K.C.B. (Knight Commander of the Order of the Bath), Nightingale sarcastically referred to him as "Dr. Hall, K.C.B., Knight of the Crimean Burial Grounds." When Nightingale contracted Crimean fever, Hall used this as an excuse to send her back to England. However, Nightingale thwarted his resistance and eventually won over the medical staff by creating an operating room and supplying the instruments with her own resources. Although she returned to duty, she never fully recovered from the fever. She returned to England in 1865 a national heroine but remained a semi-invalid for the rest of her life.

A SCHOOL FOR NURSES

After her return from the Crimea, Nightingale pursued two goals: reform of military health care and establishment of an official training school for nurses. More than $220,000 was contributed by the British public to the Nightingale Fund for the purpose of establishing the school.

Although opposed by most of the physicians in Britain, Nightingale continued her efforts, and the Nightingale Training School for Nurses opened in 1860. The school was an independent educational institution financed by the Nightingale Fund. Fifteen probationers were admitted to the first class. Their training took 1 year.

Although Nightingale was not an instructor at the school, she was consulted on all of the details of student selection, instruction, and organization. Her book, *Notes on Nursing: What It Is and What It Is Not*, established the fundamental principles of nursing. The following is an example of her writing:

On What Nursing Ought to Do

I use the word nursing for want of a better. It has been limited to signify little more than the administration of medicines and the application of poultices. It ought to signify the proper use of air, light, warmth, cleanliness, quiet and the proper selection and administration of diet—all at the least expense of vital power to the patient. (Nightingale, 1859)

This book was one of the first nursing textbooks and is still widely quoted today. Many nursing theorists have used Nightingale's thoughts as a basis for constructing their view of nursing.

The basic principles on which the Nightingale school was founded are the following:

1. Nurses should be technically trained in schools organized for that purpose.
2. Nurses should come from homes that are of good moral standing.

Nightingale believed that schools of nursing must be independent institutions and that those women who were selected to attend the school should be from the higher levels of society. Many of Nightingale's beliefs about nursing education are still applicable today, particularly those involved with the progress of students, the use of diaries kept by students, and the need for integrating theory into clinical practice (Roberts, 1937).

The Nightingale school served as a model for nursing education. Its graduates were sought worldwide. Many established other schools and became matrons (superintendents) in hospitals in other parts of England, the Commonwealth, and the United States. However, very few schools were able to remain financially independent of the hospitals, and therefore they lost much of their autonomy. This was in contradiction to Nightingale's philosophy that the training schools were educational institutions, not part of any service agency.

HEALTHCARE REFORM

Nightingale's second goal was the improvement of military health care. As a result of her documentation of the conditions in the Crimea and the nurses' efforts to improve them, reforms were undertaken. Her work marked the beginning of modern military nursing.

Nightingale's statistics were so accurate and clearly reported that she was elected a member of the British Statistical Society, the first woman to hold this position. At their conference in 1860, she presented a paper entitled, "Miss Nightingale's Scheme for Uniform Hospital Statistics." Before this, each hospital had used its own names and classification systems for diseases.

Nightingale's continuous efforts to study and improve health care made her an expert in her day. Her opinions were constantly sought after in regard to this area. This led to another publication, *Notes on Hospitals.*

For over 40 years, Nightingale played an influential part in most of the important healthcare reforms of her time. At the turn of the century, however, her energies had waned, and she spent most of the next 10 years confined to her home on South Street. She died in her sleep on August 13, 1910.

NIGHTINGALE'S CONTRIBUTIONS

There are only two areas in which Nightingale is believed to have been in error. The first is that she did not believe in or appreciate the significance of the germ theory of infection, although her insistence on fresh air, physical hygiene, and environmental cleanliness certainly did a great deal to decrease the transmission of infectious diseases. Second, she did not support a central registry or testing for nurses similar to what was in place for physicians. She was convinced that this would undermine the profession and that a letter of recommendation from the school matron was sufficient to attest to the skill and character of the nurse.

Florence Nightingale was a woman of vision and determination. Her strong belief in herself and her abilities allowed her to pursue and achieve her goals. She was a political activist and a revolutionary in her time. Her accomplishments went beyond the scope of nursing and nursing education, penetrating into all aspects of healthcare and social reform.

Although many memorials have been established in honor of Florence Nightingale, it is the legacy she has left to all of us who followed in her footsteps that perpetuates her name. Through today's nurses, Nightingale's spirit and determination remain alive. She has handed her lamp to each of us, and we have become the keepers of the lamp.

■ *Lillian Wald*

BACKGROUND

Born in 1897, Lillian Wald moved from Cincinnati, Ohio, to Rochester, New York, where she spent most of her childhood. She received her education at Miss Crittenden's English and French Boarding and Day School for Young Ladies and Little Girls. Her relatives were physicians and had a tremendous influence on her. They encouraged her to choose nursing as a career.

Wald attended the New York Hospital School of Nursing. After graduation, she worked as a nurse in the New York Juvenile Asylum. She felt a need for more medically oriented knowledge, so she entered the Women's Medical College in New York.

TURNING POINT

During this time, Wald and a colleague, Mary Brewster, were asked to go to New York's Lower East Side to give a lecture to immigrant mothers on care of the sick. They were shocked by what they discovered there.

While showing a group of mothers how to make a bed, a child came up to Wald and asked for help. The boy took her to a squalid tenement apartment where nine poorly nourished people were living in two rooms. A woman lay on a bed. Although she was seriously ill, it was apparent that no one had attended to her needs for several days (Kalisch & Kalisch, 1986). Miss Crittenden's School had not prepared Wald for this, but she went right to work anyway. She bathed the woman, washed and changed the bed-clothes, sent for a physician, and cleaned the room.

This incident was a turning point in her life. Wald left medical school and began a career as advocate and helper of the poor and sick, joined by her friend Mary Brewster. They soon found that there were thousands of cases such as the first one, just in one small neighborhood.

THE VISITING NURSES

Wald and Brewster established a settlement house in 1893 in a rented tenement apartment in a poor section of the Lower East Side of New York. To be closer to their clients, they gave up their comfortable living quarters and moved into a smaller, upper floor apartment there.

It did not take long for the women to build up a nursing practice. At first they had to seek out the sick, but within weeks calls came to them by the hundreds. The people of the neighborhood trusted them and relied on them for help. Gradually they also developed a reputation among the physicians and hospitals of the area, and requests to see clients came from these sources as well.

Lillian Wald and her nursing colleagues brought basic nursing care to the people in their home environments. These nurses were independent practitioners who made their own decisions and followed up on their own assessments of the families' needs. Like Nightingale, they were very aware of the effect of the environment on the health of their clients and worked hard to improve their surroundings.

Wald was convinced that many of the illnesses resulted from causes outside of individual control and that treatment needed to be holistic. She claimed that she chose the title *public health nurse* to emphasize the value of the nurse whose work was built on an understanding of the social and economic problems that inevitably accompanied the clients' ills (Bueheler-Wilkerson, 1993).

Because she had the freedom to explore alternatives for care during numerous births, illnesses, and deaths, Wald began to organize an impressive group of services ranging from private relief to services from the medical establishment. She developed cooperative relationships with various organizations, and this allowed her access to goods and jobs for her clients. News of her successes spread. Private physicians sought her out and referred their clients to her for service.

THE HENRY STREET SETTLEMENT HOUSE

Within 2 years, the nurses had outgrown their original quarters. They needed larger facilities and more nurses. With the help of Jacob Schiff, a banker and philanthropist, they moved to a larger building at 265 Henry Street. This became known as the Henry Street Settlement House (Mayer, 1994). Nine graduate nurses moved in soon after.

By 1909, the Henry Street Settlement had grown into a well-organized social services system with many departments. The staff included 37 nurses, 5 of whom were managers, and other men and women involved in carrying out the many activities of the settlement house.

OTHER ACCOMPLISHMENTS

Wald is also credited with the development of school health nursing. Health conditions were so bad in the New York City schools that 15 to 20 children per school were sent home every day. The children sent home ill were returned to school by their parents in the same condition. As a result, illnesses spread from child to child. Ringworm, scabies, and pediculosis were common.

To prove her point about the value of community health nurses, Wald set up an experiment using one nurse for 1 month in one school. In that time, the number of children dismissed from classes dropped from over 10,000 to 1100. The New York Board of Health was so impressed that they hired nurses to continue the nurse's work. Wald's nurses treated problems, explained the modes of transmission, and explained when children had to be excluded from class and when they did not. The nurses also followed the children at home to prevent the recurrence of illnesses.

Wald was also responsible for organizing the Children's Bureau, the Nursing Service Division of the Metropolitan Life Insurance

Company, and the Town and Country Nursing Service of the American Red Cross. Her dreams of expanding public health nursing, obtaining insurance coverage for home-based preventive care, and developing a national health nursing service have not become a reality. However, in view of the healthcare demands of today, she was a visionary who believed that health care belonged in the community and that nurses had a vital role to play in community-based care. She died in 1940 and has been remembered as one of the foremost leaders in public health nursing.

Margaret Sanger

BACKGROUND

Margaret Sanger was born in Corning, New York, on September 14, 1883. After recovering from tuberculosis, which she contracted while caring for her mother, she attended nursing school at the White Plains Hospital School of Nursing. In her autobiography, Sanger described the school as rigid and at times inhuman, perhaps an indication of where her future interests would take her (Sanger, 1938). During her affiliation at the Manhattan Eye and Ear Hospital, she met William Sanger. They married and moved to a suburb of New York, where she stayed at home to raise three children.

LABOR REFORMER

Sanger was very concerned about the working conditions faced by people living in poverty. Many workers were barely paid enough to buy food for themselves or their families. At that time, the income for a family with both parents working was about $12 to $14 a week. If only the father worked, earnings dropped to $8 a week. If only the mother worked, it was even less. A portion of this income was paid back to the company as rent for company housing. Food was often purchased through a company store. Very little was left for any other expenses, including health care.

A major strike of industrial workers in Lawrence, Massachusetts, marked the beginning of Sanger's career as an advocate and social reformer. The workers had attempted a strike for better conditions before but failed because of threatening starvation. If the workers went on strike, there was no money for food. Strike sympathizers in New York offered to help the workers and to take the children from Lawrence into their homes. Because of her interest in the situation of the underpaid workers and her involvement with New York laborers, Sanger was asked to assist in the evacuation of children from the unsettled and sometimes violent conditions in Lawrence. Following another outbreak of serious rioting, she was called to Washington to testify before the House Committee on Rules about the condition of the children. She testified that the children were poorly nourished, ill, ragged, and living in worse conditions than those seen in the impoverished city slums.

Two months later, the owners of the mills sat down to talk with the workers and conceded to their demands. Sanger's interventions on behalf of the children had brought the workers' plight to the attention of the public and the people in Washington.

A NEW CONCERN FOR SANGER

In the spring of 1912, Sanger returned to work as a public health nurse. She was assigned to maternity cases on the lower east side of New York City. One case that she encountered became a turning point in her life. Sanger was caring for a 28-year-old mother of three children who had attempted to self-abort. She and her husband were already struggling to feed and clothe the children they had and could not afford any more. After 3 weeks, the woman had regained her health. However, during his final visit to her home, the physician told the young woman that she had been lucky to survive this time but that if she tried to self-abort again, she would not need his services but those of a funeral director. The young woman pleaded with him for a way to prevent another pregnancy. The doctor replied, "Tell your husband to sleep on the roof." (Sanger, 1938). The young woman turned then to Sanger, who remained silent.

Three months later, Sanger was called to the same home. This time, the woman was in a coma and died within minutes of Sanger's arrival. It was at this moment that Sanger dedicated herself to learning about and disseminating information on birth control.

CONTRACEPTION REFORM

This task turned out to be far more difficult than Margaret Sanger had expected. The Comstock Act of 1873 classified birth control information as obscene. Unrewarding research at the Boston Public Library, the Library of Congress, and the New York Academy of Medicine only heightened her frustration. Very little information on birth control was available anywhere in the United States at that time.

But contraception was widely practiced in many European countries, so Sanger went to Europe. She studied methods of birth control in France, and when she returned to the United States, she began to publish a journal called *The Woman Rebel*. This journal carried articles about contraception, family planning, and other matters related to women's rights.

The first birth control clinic in the United States opened at 46 Amboy Street in Brooklyn in 1916. Sanger operated the clinic with her sister, Ethel Byrne, and another nurse, Fania Mindell. On the first day, over 150 women asked them for help. Everything went smoothly until a policewoman masquerading as a client arrested the three women and recorded the names of all the by-now frightened clients. To bring attention to their plight and to the closing of the clinic, Sanger refused to ride in the police wagon. Instead, she walked the mile to the courthouse.

Several weeks later, Sanger returned to a courthouse overflowing with friends and supporters to face the charges that had been filed against her. The public found it difficult to believe that this attractive mother, flanked by her two sons, was either demented or oversexed, as her adversaries had claimed. She did not deny the charges of disseminating birth control information but challenged the law that made this information illegal. Because she refused to abide by that law, the judge sentenced her to 30 days in the workhouse.

After completing her 30 days, Sanger continued her work for many years. She solicited the support of wealthy women and used their help to gain financial backing to continue her fight. She delivered talks and organized meetings. In 1921, she organized the Birth Control Conference in New York (Kalisch & Kalisch, 1986). In 1928, she established the National Committee on Federal Legislation for Birth Control, which eventually became the Planned Parenthood Foundation. Sanger was also an accomplished author, writing *What Every Girl Should Know, What Every Mother Should Know*, and *Motherhood in Bondage*.

Conservative religious and political groups were the most vocal in their opposition to Sanger's work. In the end, however, Sanger won. Planned Parenthood is a thriving organization, and birth control information is available to anyone who seeks it, although there are still groups who oppose its availability on religious and political grounds.

Sanger could fairly be labeled an early example of the liberated woman. She was independent and assertive in a time when it was not considered "politically correct" for a woman to behave in such a manner. Perhaps her most important contributions to the community at large were her tenacity and her ability to bring to society's attention the needs of the poor, not just the favored few who had sufficient money. As a nurse, she represented that part of caring that operates in the political arena to bring about change to improve people's health and save lives.

■ *Adelaide Nutting*
• • • • • • • • • • • • • • • • • • •

BACKGROUND

Adelaide Nutting was Canadian by birth. She was the first graduate of the Johns Hopkins School of Nursing. During her student days, the journal *Trained Nurse* offered a 10-dollar prize for an essay on a typhoid fever case. Nutting submitted her essay and won the prize. Her essay was printed in the March 1910 issue, just the beginning for this dynamic nurse leader.

Nutting was a close friend of Isabel Hampton, the director of the Johns Hopkins School of Nursing. When Hampton resigned her position, Nutting became the superintendent of nurses and the principal of the School of Nursing at the Johns Hopkins Hospital in Baltimore, Maryland.

NURSING EDUCATION

Nutting established the 3-year, 8-hour-day program that became the prototype for diploma school education in nursing. She later felt that more background in the basic sciences was a necessity and developed a 6-month course that also became a model for other schools. Although associated with a hospital school of nursing, Nutting was convinced that nursing education would advance only if the profession developed more autonomy. Like Nightingale, Nutting believed that schools of nursing should be independent of hospital control or ownership.

HIGHER EDUCATION

Nutting is probably best known for her work in the creation of the Department of Nursing and Health at Teachers College, Columbia University. After leaving Johns Hopkins in 1907 to take the first chair in nursing at Columbia University, she became the first professor of nursing in the world. She held this position until 1925. She was succeeded by a former student and colleague, Isabel Stewart.

OTHER INTERESTS

Nutting was interested in many aspects of nursing. In 1918, she approached the Rockefeller Foundation to request funds for her alma mater, Johns Hopkins. During the interview, she stressed the need for improvement in the education of public health nurses. This meeting led to the formation of a blue-ribbon committee that studied the situation and released a report emphasizing the need for university education of nurses.

Nutting also recognized the importance of cultivating benefactors for nursing. For example, she became very close to Frances Payne Bolton, a wealthy and influential citizen of Cleveland, Ohio. She convinced Bolton to fund an Army Nurse Training School at a time when women were being trained as aides rather than professional nurses. Nutting opposed their training as aides, believing that soldiers with war wounds needed professionals to care for them. The three major nursing organizations of the time supported the establishment of the school, but the U.S. War Department rejected the idea. In response, Frances Payne Bolton went to Washington to persuade the War Department to prepare the women as nurses. The Frances Payne Bolton School of Nursing at Case Western Reserve University in Cleveland, Ohio, is named after this supporter of nursing.

Nutting was committed to the promotion of nursing and nursing education. She was in the forefront of educational reform, first by establishing standards of diploma education and later by supporting the move to the university setting. One of her greatest achievements was improvement in the preparation of teachers of nursing. She realized early that the quality of the nurse is greatly influenced by the quality of the teachers of nursing students.

■ *Conclusion*

• • • • • • • • • • • • • • • • • •

As nursing moves into the twenty-first century, the need for courageous and innovative nurse leaders is greater than ever. Society's demand for quality health care at affordable cost is a contemporary force for change. We began in hospitals, moved to the community, moved back into the hospitals, and are now seeing a move back to the community. We will be the Nightingales, Walds, Sangers, and Nuttings of the future. The creativity and dedication of these nurses are part of all of us.

? *Study Questions*

1. Read *Notes on Nursing: What It Is and What It Is Not*, by Florence Nightingale. How much of it is true today?

2. If Margaret Sanger were alive today, how do you think she would view the issue of teaching schoolchildren about AIDS?

3. What do you think Lillian Wald would say about the status of hospitals and health care today?

4. How do you think Florence Nightingale would deal with a physician who is verbally abusive to the nursing staff?

5. If you had been Margaret Sanger, would you have decided to stop teaching women about birth control? Explain your answer.

6. If Adelaide Nutting visited your nursing school, what do you think she would say about it? What advice do you think she would give to your graduating class?

Critical Thinking Exercise

Jason went to school on a navy scholarship. He has now received his assignment, which is to establish a comprehensive primary care and health promotion program clinic on board the navy's newest atomic-powered submarines, which are able to remain submerged for 6 months at a time. The crew will consist of all professional military men and women. The maiden voyage is to be submerged under the South Pole for a minimum of 3 months.

1. What medical and nursing equipment should Jason plan to have in this center?

2. What would the physical environment on board need to have to satisfy Florence Nightingale and Lillian Wald?

REFERENCES

Bueheler-Wilkerson, K. (1993). Bring care to the people: Lillian Wald's legacy to public health nursing. *Am J Public Health, 83*(12), 1778–1785.

Donahue, H.P. (1985). *Nursing the Oldest Art*. St. Louis: C.V. Mosby.

Griffith, G.J., & Griffith, H.J. (1965). *Jensen's History and Trends in Professional Nursing* (5th ed.). St. Louis: C.V. Mosby.

Kalisch, P.A., & Kalisch, B.J. (1986). *The Advance of American Nursing*. Boston: Little, Brown.

Longfellow, H.W. (1868). The lady with the lamp. In Williams, M. (1975), *How Does a Poem Mean?* Boston: Houghton Mifflin.

Mayer, S. (1994). Amelia Greenwald: Pioneer in international public health nursing. *Nursing and Health Care, 15*(2), 74–78.

Nightingale, F. (1859). *Notes on Nursing: What It Is and What It Is Not*. Reprinted 1992. Philadelphia: J.B. Lippincott.

Roberts, M. (1937). Florence Nightingale as a nurse educator. *Am J Nurs, 37*(7), 775.

Sanger, M. (1938). *Margaret Sanger: An Autobiography*. New York: W.W. Norton.

Schuyler, C.B. (1992). Florence Nightingale. In commentary, *Notes on Nursing: What It Is and What It Is Not*. Philadelphia: J.B. Lippincott.

CHAPTER 15

Nursing Today

OBJECTIVES
After reading this chapter, the student will be able to:

◆ Identify methods nurses can use to project a positive nursing image.
◆ Compare and contrast historical and current definitions of nursing.
◆ Describe the characteristics considered indicative of a true profession.
◆ Evaluate nursing based on the criteria established for the profession.
◆ Differentiate between the various programs that offer nursing education.

What image comes to mind when the word "nurse" is mentioned? Why do most nurses continue to feel unappreciated by the public, physicians, administration, and their coworkers? Why is it still so difficult to define what nursing really is?

Lack of a clear definition of the profession, control of nursing by institutions and physicians, and the role of American women in society have all influenced nursing as it developed in the United States. Many of these influences continue today, as nursing moves toward the achievement of a clearer identity and acceptance as a true profession.

■ *The Public's Image of Nursing*

Although television programs featuring nurses are more realistic than they were a decade ago, nurses are still depicted as handmaidens who carry out physician orders. In addition, nurses' contributions to health care are often underestimated and sometimes ignored by the media. Over a 3-month period, a review of 423 published articles about health care cited nurses only 1.1% of the time, yet nursing constitutes the largest healthcare profession in terms of numbers (Buresch, 1993).

■ *Communicating Nursing's Role*

The TriCouncil (a joint effort of several professional nursing organizations) recently organized a campaign designed specifically to communicate the significant contributions of nurses. Three areas in particular were emphasized (Swirsky, 1993):

1. *Nurses as resource people* available to interpret technical health information for consumers
2. *Nurses as healthcare coordinators* who assist consumers in identifying and using appropriate healthcare services
3. *Nurses as expert practitioners* in the provision of health care

Collectively, nurses have more potential power and influence than they currently exhibit. To be able to use this power, nurses need to become more aware of it and more skilled in its use.

To improve their confidence, Hess (1993) suggests that nurses think of themselves as "special agents" who have the following responsibilities:

1. **Carry your license.** The strongest legitimate power that nurses have is the exclusive license to provide the kind of care that the public sees as vitally important. This license provides nurses with intimate access to those entrusted to their care. Your license should also be advertised in the professional appearance that you maintain. Although you may believe that people should not be judged by their appearance, they often are. Think, for example, of how you would feel at a restaurant if the person serving you had dirty hair or fingernails!
2. **Use your special training and experience.** Only nurses know what they know. No one else in health care has their broad specialized education and skills. Be both self-confident and respectful to others when sharing your knowledge and skills with others.
3. **Become a double agent.** Use your personal knowledge and experience to form professional and personal coalitions, both at work and outside of work.
4. **Network and empower your colleagues.** Extend your knowledge of caring to other nurses. Nurses can help each other increase their skills and advance their careers. Empowerment is defined as "the enabling of people and groups of people to act and make decisions where an equitable distribution of power exists" (Mason, Backer, & Georges, 1993). Focusing on consensus building and group decision making will assist nurses in becoming empowered.
5. **Eliminate the enemy within.** The greatest enemy is the colleague with self-defeating thoughts and behaviors. Mobilize yourself and others to positively plan for change. Destructive at-

titudes, criticism, and manipulation of others will not foster a spirit of group collectivity and equality.

6. **Focus on operations.** At whatever level you are, participate. Instead of focusing on the problem, become part of the solution. For example, be a positive infiltrator of relevant hospital committees and professional associations.

The future of nursing depends on nurses' ability to organize as a group, recognize and accept the differences among us, and develop the skills necessary to negotiate within the changing healthcare system.

■ *Nursing Defined*

· · · · · · · · · · · · · · · · · · · ·

DEFINITIONS FROM NURSING LEADERS

The changes that have occurred in nursing are reflected in the definitions of nursing that have been developed since the time of Florence Nightingale.

1859 Nightingale

Nightingale defined the goal of nursing as putting the client "in the best possible condition for nature to act upon him" (Nightingale, 1959, p. 79)

1950 Henderson

Virginia Henderson focused her definition on the uniqueness of nursing: "The unique function of the nurse is to assist the individual, sick or well, in the performance of those activities contributing to health or its recovery (or to peaceful death) that he would perform unaided if he had the necessary strength, will or knowledge. And to do this in such a way as to help him gain independence as rapidly as possible" (Henderson, 1966, p. 21).

1963 Rogers

Martha Rogers defined nursing practice as "the process by which this body of knowledge, nursing science, is used for the pur-

pose of assisting human beings to achieve maximum health within the potential of each person," (Rogers, 1988, p. 100). Rogers emphasized that nursing is concerned with all people, only a segment of whom are ill.

1980 American Nurses Association

The American Nurses Association (ANA) published a social policy statement on the nature and scope of nursing practice (Fig. 15–1). The statement was intended to promote unity and allow members of the profession to develop a common approach to practice. The issues addressed in the ANA's social policy statement (ANA, 1995) include:

1. **The social context of nursing.** Nursing is a part of our society and should be seen as serving the interests of society. Nursing plays an integral part in identifying the current social concerns and influencing the direction of health care. Nursing practice continues to be health-oriented and is concerned with identifying the working relationships necessary to carry out these health-oriented responsibilities.

2. **The nature and scope of nursing practice.** The ANA defined nursing as "the diagnosis and treatment of human responses to actual or potential health problems" (ANA, 1980, p. 9). This definition was later altered to include the four essential features of contemporary nursing practice listed under the third bulleted item in Figure 15–1.

3. **Specialization in nursing practice.** Specialization in nursing practice began to appear in the 1950s. By 1980, it was firmly entrenched in nursing practice. Specialists in nursing practice hold graduate degrees in advanced clinical practice and are eligible to obtain certification in their speciality. The graduate nurse just entering practice is expected to have certain minimum competencies; the specialist is expected to be an expert.

4. **Regulation of nursing practice.** Nurses are legally accountable for their actions as defined by statues and regulations within state nurse practice acts. The nursing profession also regulates

Nursing's Social Policy Statement

- The authority for the practice of nursing is based on a social contract that acknowledges professional rights and responsibilities as well as mechanisms for public accountability.
- The nursing profession remains committed to the care and nurturing of both healthy and ill people, individually or in groups and communities.
- Since 1980, nursing philosophy and practice have been influenced by a greater elaboration of the science of caring and its integration with the traditional knowledge base for diagnosis and treatment of human responses to health and illness. As such, definitions of nursing more frequently acknowledge four essential features of contemporary nursing practice:
  - ○ Attention to the full range of human experiences and responses to health and illness without restriction to a problem-focused orientation
  - ○ Integration of objective data with knowledge gained from an understanding of the patient or group's subjective experience
  - ○ Application of scientific knowledge to the processes of diagnosis and treatment
  - ○ Provision of a caring relationship that facilitates health and healing.
- Nursing is a scientific discipline as well as a profession.
- Nursing involves practices that are restorative, supportive, and promotive in nature.
- The extent to which individual nurses engage in the total scope of nursing practice is dependent on their educational preparation, experience, roles, and the nature of the patient populations they serve.
- Nursing, like other professions, is responsible for ensuring that its members act in the public interest in the course of providing the unique service society has entrusted to them.
- All nurses are legally accountable for actions taken in the course of nursing practice as well as actions delegated by nurses to others assisting in the delivery of nursing care.

FIGURE 15–1   American Nurses Association Social Policy Statement. (From American Nurses Association [1995]. *Nursing's Social Policy Statement*. Washington, D.C.: ANA Publishing, with permission.)

itself through the Code for Nurses (see Appendix 1) and the Standards of Clinical Nursing Practice (see Appendix 2). In addition, credentialing examinations provide opportunities for nurses to document other expertise. For example, a nurse may become a certified medical-surgical or home health nurse through the ANA's credentialing examinations.

As technology continues to advance, nurses will need to redefine their roles clearly to healthcare providers and to the public. The old idea that "a nurse is a nurse is a nurse" does not ensure the level of expertise and safety necessary today.

■ *Characteristics of a Profession*

• • • • • • • • • • • • • • • • •

There is probably more agreement on what a profession is than on what occupations qualify as professions. The term "professional" is used in describing college professors, rock stars, and athletes, all with very different occupations. A number of scholars have tried to identify the benchmarks of a profession (Box 15–1).

Many nursing experts talk about the "art and science of nursing." Martha Rogers, for example, saw nursing as a science developed through scientific research and analysis en-

Box 15–1 Characteristics of a profession

- Systematic body of knowledge
- Mastery of knowledge and an ability to problem-solve
- Specialized, formal education based in colleges and universities
- Unique, distinct role and autonomy
- Standards of practice and a code of ethics
- Legal enforcement and professional accountability
- Motivated by commitment to the community
- Creation of a professional culture

Source: Adapted from Flexner, A.: Is social work a profession? *Scholastic Society, 1(20)*, 901; and Bixler, G.K., & Bixler, R.W. (1959). The professional status of nursing. *Am J Nurs, 59(8)*, 1142–1147.

hanced by the imagination and creativity used by nurses in applying this knowledge to client care (Rogers, 1988). Can this unique service to humanity be defined as a profession? How similar is nursing to the more traditional professions of medicine, law, and the ministry? We will look at each of these characteristics of a profession in terms of the degree to which nursing has met them.

SYSTEMATIC BODY OF KNOWLEDGE

Does nursing have its own unique, systematic body of knowledge? Those who say no argue that nursing has borrowed from other disciplines such as the social sciences, biologic sciences, and medicine. These same critics believe that knowledge from these other disciplines, technical skills, intuition, and experience have been combined to become what we call nursing knowledge.

Those who say yes argue that nursing theorists and nursing researchers have identified and described a unique body of knowledge. As the results of their work are used in practice, the unique body of knowledge will become more widely recognized.

MASTERY OF KNOWLEDGE AND AN ABILITY TO PROBLEM SOLVE

In a true profession, members use their knowledge in a systematic, rational way. The nursing profession uses its knowledge through application of the nursing process to clinical situations. The nursing process is a systematic, problem-solving approach that involves assessment, diagnosis, planning, implementation, and evaluation.

In recent years, emphasis has also been placed on the use of critical thinking. According to Paul (1993, p. 21), critical thinking is purposeful thinking in which the individual systematically and habitually does the following:

- Imposes the criteria of solid reasoning such as precision, relevance, depth, and accuracy
- Becomes aware of all assumptions and points of view in an argument
- Continually assesses the process of thinking
- Determines strengths and limitations and implications of the thinking

Critical thinking is an important aspect of the nursing process because the nurse must continually analyze assumptions, weigh evidence, discriminate between possible decisions, evaluate conclusions, and verify beliefs, actions, and conclusions.

SPECIALIZED FORMAL EDUCATION

One of the biggest threats to the recognition of nursing as a profession is the multiple ways in which a person can pursue preparation to become a registered nurse. As far back as 1965, the ANA published a paper recommending the following:

The education for all of those who are licensed to practice nursing should take place in institutions of higher education; minimum preparation for beginning professional nursing practice should be a baccalaureate degree; minimum preparation for beginning technical nursing practice should be an associate degree in nursing; education for assistants in health service occupations should be short, intensive preservice programs in vocational education rather than on-the-job training. (ANA, 1965, p. 107)

Similar recommendations continue to emanate from the ANA. In 1978, the ANA House of Delegates adopted a resolution that "by 1985, the minimum preparation for entry into professional nursing practice would be the baccalaureate in nursing and . . . ANA would work with state nurses associations to identify and define two categories of nursing practice by 1980" (ANA, 1987). This deadline was not met.

In 1984, the ANA established a goal for implementation of baccalaureate education by 1995 (ANA Cabinet on Nursing Education, 1983). This deadline has also not been met. As we write this section, graduates from all types of nursing programs—diploma, associate degree, and baccalaureate degree—are still taking the same licensure examination. Associate degree graduates make up the largest number of new graduates entering nursing each year.

In addition, many nurses who return to the university for an advanced degree are still encouraged by employers and even by fellow nurses to obtain the baccalaureate or master's degree in a field other than nursing. This is not a common practice in other professions. In fact, the ANA has also issued a statement about this practice:

> Requirement of the baccalaureate for entry into professional practice, of advanced learning [master's degree] for specialty practice, administration, and teaching, and of doctoral education that includes focus on research capabilities emerges as necessary to fulfillment of nursing's social responsibility. (ANA, 1980, p. 22)

UNIQUE, DISTINCT ROLE AND AUTONOMY

Are nurses independent and autonomous in their implementation of nursing actions? In some institutions, nursing practice is heavily controlled by medicine or health service administration. Simple decisions such as whether a client can get out of bed to sit in a chair or go to the bathroom must still be determined by a physician. Even in situations in which nurses are allowed to make

independent decisions, the protocols may be written and approved by physicians or healthcare administrators. However, in many areas in the country, nursing practice has progressed in the developing of a distinct, autonomous role and independent decision making.

STANDARDS OF PRACTICE AND CODE OF ETHICS

The ANA has provided the nursing profession with Standards of Clinical Nursing Practice (see Appendix 2). Standards of practice have been developed for all areas of nursing for use by nurses, students, faculty, healthcare providers, consumers, and healthcare policy makers.

The Code for Nurses, a code of ethics also written by members of the ANA (1985), serves to inform both nurses and consumers of the nursing profession's acceptance of the trust and responsibility given to it by society. It also provides a mechanism for self-regulation within the profession. In the United States, each state is responsible for having a *nurse practice act* that defines requirements for licensure, endorsement, exemptions, and revocations of licenses. The practice act establishes a board of nursing and outlines the board's responsibilities. Practice acts usually contain a definition of nursing and penalties for practicing nursing without a license as well. The individual boards of nursing collectively compose the National Council of State Boards of Nursing, Incorporated.

LEGAL REINFORCEMENT AND PROFESSIONAL ACCOUNTABILITY

Graduates of nursing programs become licensed when they have successfully completed the NCLEX examination. To be eligible to sit for the NCLEX examination, students must be graduates of a state-approved school of nursing. This license is the legal document provided by the state certifying that the person named on the license has met the minimum standards for practice.

In the past, the NCLEX examination was given on the same day, at the same time, twice a year throughout the United States. However, with the computerized adaptive testing (CAT) used now, students may apply to sit for the examination within weeks of graduation from an approved nursing program by making individual appointments at testing centers approved by their state board of nursing.

The NCLEX examination is based on the ANA Standards of Clinical Nursing Practice. The nursing behaviors tested are categorized within the nursing process: assessment, diagnosis, planning, implementation, and evaluation. Nurses licensed to practice in one state may request permission to practice in another state. This procedure is called *endorsement* and indicates that the state will accept the registered professional for licensure without additional requirement.

Unless a license is revoked for illegal or immoral behavior, licensure is permanent. Registration is usually renewed every 1 to 2 years by paying fees to the state or states in which you desire to remain registered. Some states also require evidence of participation in continuing education for license renewal.

Nurses with licenses from other countries must apply through the state's board of nursing for review of their credentials before receiving permission to take the NCLEX examination. Often these foreign nurses have to return to an approved nursing program to complete additional nursing courses before receiving permission to take the examination.

The board of nursing is formed for the protection of the public, not for the protection of the licensed practitioner. Licensed nurses are responsible for providing safe and competent care. Nurses may be held legally liable for malpractice or for negligence as a result of unsafe or incompetent practice. State boards of nursing review all charges of misconduct and recommend disciplinary actions to the larger state agencies of which they are a part.

COMMITMENT TO THE COMMUNITY

Commitment to the community and altruism (service to others) have been apparent since the early days of nursing. Other professions such as law and medicine have had the same commitment to the community and have received generous economic rewards for their services. These economic rewards have ensured the attractiveness of their professions to new generations of po-

tential professionals. Unfortunately, when nurses seek pay increases, they are frequently confronted by employers who accuse them of lacking altruism and a commitment to serve. It is important to separate these two issues. Competitive salaries and fair working conditions are *not incongruent* with commitment and service to the community. In fact, they increase the profession's ability to attract the best and the brightest students.

Some practitioners think of nursing as a job instead of a career. Those nurses who lack a lifelong commitment to nursing will never achieve full professional status.

PROFESSIONAL CULTURE

Professional organizations have several functions that contribute to the creation of a professional culture. These include establishing and enforcing the profession's code of ethics, development of standards of practice, and continuing education of members of the profession. In addition, professional organizations may represent their members in collective bargaining, establishment of national policies affecting the profession, and protection of the membership's general welfare.

There are over 50 professional nursing organizations of various kinds. Many are related to specialty areas such as maternal/child health, community health, critical care, or rehabilitation. Others serve a special purpose as does Sigma Theta Tau, nursing's national honor society, or the Transcultural Nursing Society. The ANA publishes an updated list of these organizations each April in the *American Journal of Nursing*.

The ANA and the National League for Nursing, the two largest professional organizations, are discussed in the next section.

How else can nursing promote its professional culture? The current emphasis on caring and feminist ideology may assist nursing in defining the characteristics of the professional culture. The focus of feminist theory in nursing is the promotion of an atmosphere of mutual respect, trust, and community. Shared leadership, cooperation, and group process are emphasized (Mason, Backer, & Georges, 1993).

Along with the renewed emphasis on feminism, nursing literature is experiencing a renewed interest in *caring*. Although caring has been viewed as central to nursing, human care and caring are now defined as a personal, social, moral, and spiritual engagement of the nurse with other humans (Moccia, 1993).

Finally, becoming involved in role modeling, mentoring, emotional support, and sharing of the powerful lived experiences of nursing is an example of the means by which we can promote our professional culture.

PROFESSIONAL ORGANIZATIONS

American Nurses Association

In 1896, delegates from 10 nursing schools' alumnae associations met to organize a national professional association for nurses.

The constitution and bylaws were completed in 1907, and the Nurses Associated Alumnae of the United States and Canada was born. The name was changed in 1911 to the American Nurses Association (ANA), which in 1982 became a federation of constituent state nurses associations. Nurses actually join the state nurses associations, which in turn make up the ANA.

The purposes of the ANA are to:

1. Work for the improvement of health standards and the availability of healthcare services for all people.
2. Foster high standards for nursing.
3. Stimulate and promote the professional development of nurses and advance their economic and general welfare.

---

1. Establish standard of nursing practice, nursing education and nursing service.
2. Establish a code of ethical conduct for nurses.
3. Ensure a system of credentialing in nursing.
4. Initiate and influence legislation, governmental programs, national health policy, and international health policy.
5. Support systematic study evaluation, and research in nursing.
6. Serve as the central agency for the collection, analysis and dissemination of information relevant to nursing.
7. Promote and protect the economic and general welfare of nurses.
8. Provide leadership in national and international nursing.
9. Provide for the professional development of nurses.
10. Conduct an affirmative action program.
11. Ensure a collective bargaining program for nurses.
12. Provide services to constituent members.
13. Maintain communication with constituent members through official publications.
14. Assume an active role as consumer advocate.
15. Represent and speak for the nursing profession with allied health groups, national and international organizations, governmental bodies, and the public.
16. Protect and promote the advancement of human rights related to health care and nursing (ANA, 1995, pp.1-2).

FIGURE 15-2 Functions of American Nurses Association. (From American Nurses Assocation [1995]. *American Nurses Association Bylaws as Amended July 2, 1995.* Washington, D.C.: ANA Publishing, with permission.)

ANA's bylaws list 16 functions, which can be found in Fig. 15–2.

These purposes should not be restricted by consideration of age, color, creed, disability, gender, health status, lifestyle, nationality, race, religion, or sexual orientation (ANA, 1991a).

Although more than 2 million people are members of the nursing profession in the United States, only 10 percent of the nation's registered nurses are members of their professional organization, the ANA. The many different subgroups and numerous specialty nursing organizations contribute to this fragmentation, which makes it difficult to present a united front from which to bargain for nursing. As the ANA works on the goal of preparing nurses for the 21st century, it is important that nurses work together in their efforts to identify and promote their unique, autonomous role within the healthcare system.

There are many advantages available to the nurse who joins the ANA. Membership in the ANA offers benefits such as informative publications, group life and health insurance, malpractice insurance, and continuing education courses. The ANA also assists state nurses associations to support their members on workplace and client care issues such as salaries, working conditions, and staffing.

As the major voice of nursing, the ANA lobbies the government to influence laws that affect the practice of nursing and the safety of the consumer. The power of the ANA was apparent when nurses lobbied against the American Medical Association's (AMA) proposal to create a new category of healthcare worker, the registered care technician, as an answer to the 1980s nursing shortage. The registered care technician category was never established despite the AMA's vigorous support.

Finally, the ANA offers certification in various specialty areas. Certification is a formal, voluntary process by which the professional demonstrates knowledge and expertise in a specific area of practice. It is a way to establish the nurse's expertise beyond the basic requirements for licensure and is an important part of peer recognition for nurses. In many areas, certification entitles the nurse to salary increases and position advancement. Some specialty nursing organizations also have certification programs.

National League for Nursing

Another large nursing organization is the National League for Nursing (NLN). Unlike the ANA, the NLN opens its membership to other health professionals and interested consumers, not just nurses.

The NLN participates in accreditation of nursing programs, test services, research, and publication. It also lobbies actively for nursing issues and is currently working cooperatively with the ANA and other nursing organizations on healthcare reform. To do such things more effectively, the ANA, NLN, American Association of Colleges of Nursing, and American Organization of Nurse Executives have formed a coalition called the TriCouncil for the purpose of dealing with issues that are important to all nurses.

■ *Educating Nurses*

As the controversy regarding whether nursing is a profession continues, so does the controversy over the amount and type of education that should be required for entry into the profession. Today there are over 1600 basic programs that prepare beginning registered nurses (NLN, 1993). In 1992, 257,983 students were enrolled in nursing programs: 51 percent in associate degree programs, 40 percent in baccalaureate programs, and 9 percent in diploma programs (NLN, 1993).

PRACTICAL NURSING PROGRAMS

Practical nurses (LPNs or LVNs) are licensed separately and are not considered professional nurses (although they are sometimes called "nurses" in long-term care facilities). Their training is usually 9 months to 1 year in length, after which they are eligible to take the NCLEX-PN examination.

Many practical nurses find employment in long-term care facilities or private-duty home care. In any setting, they are expected to work under the supervision of a registered nurse. Increasing numbers of practical nurses are returning to community colleges to attend LPN-to-RN programs to obtain an associate degree and become eligible to take the NCLEX examination for registered nurses.

DIPLOMA PROGRAMS

Diploma nursing programs have existed in the United States since the late 1800s, when nursing education began as apprenticeship training in hospitals. The number of diploma programs has gradually declined; today there are less than 150 in the United States. The programs are clustered in the northeast, with half of the remaining states having none at all (ANA, 1992).

In the past, students in diploma programs were the primary workforce of the hospital. Most of the instructors were either graduates of the same program or members of the hospital's medical staff. Although they were well versed in nursing or medical skills, they were not necessarily well prepared to teach nursing theory and had no background in other important elements of a professional education: language, mathematics, psychology, sociology, microbiology, and so forth.

Diploma programs have continued to be valuable to hospitals because they generate a pool of new graduates who are easily assimilated into their existing nursing staff. Many have aligned themselves with local colleges or universities so that their students can obtain the necessary general education requirements and earn either an associate or baccalaureate degree on completion of the program.

ASSOCIATE DEGREE PROGRAMS

The establishment of nursing programs in community colleges was first proposed by Mildred Montag in 1951. Her doctoral dissertation, "The Education of Nursing Technicians," proposed an approach that would produce nurses more quickly than the 3 year diploma or 4- to 5-year baccalaureate programs of that time. The graduates would be "technical nurses" who worked at the bedside. They would have less autonomy than the baccalaureate graduate but more than the LPN had.

Montag envisioned the associate degree as a terminal degree that students could complete in 2 years and then enter the job market. Approximately half of the coursework would be related to nursing, and the other half would be related to general education courses.

Associate degree nursing programs grew rapidly. However, some of Montag's original concepts have been abandoned. The degree is no longer considered a terminal one but a step toward the baccalaureate degree. Many of the programs also have had difficulty meeting the NLN's recommendation of a maximum of 72 credit hours in the nursing program.

Fueled by the high birth rates of the 1940s (the early "baby boomers"), the community college movement of the 1960s flourished, and their nursing programs flourished along with them. Community colleges promoted equal opportunity, flexible schedules, and improved accessibility to higher education. The married women, men, minorities, and students seeking career changes who were attracted to the associate degree programs in nursing were quite different from the traditional 18-to-25-year-old white women who constituted the majority of nursing students until then.

There are over 800 associate degree programs in the United States today, and the number continues to increase. The NLN (1991) has developed a set of competencies for the graduate of associate degree programs in nursing (see Appendix 3). Although these competencies define the associate degree nurse as a manager of care, additional guidance should be provided for the associate degree nurse to function in the manager role.

Clearly, the questions regarding entry into practice have not yet been resolved. Differentiation among the various educational levels for licensure is still an issue of debate.

BACCALAUREATE DEGREE PROGRAMS

Nursing leaders in the early 1900s felt strongly that nursing education should move from the hospitals into the universities with other professional programs. By this time, nursing education had become firmly entrenched within hospitals despite Nightingale's early opposition to such an arrangement. Universities were reluctant at first to accept nursing as a profession worthy of a university education. However, as nursing leaders such as Nutting continued to press for an equal place in the university, the barriers slowly crumbled, and nursing is now an accepted member of the university community.

Nursing's leaders have continued to emphasize the importance of a solid foundation in science and the humanities as a prerequisite to learning nursing. The debate about the differences between levels of nursing education continues today, 35 years after the ANA's initial position paper recommending baccalaureate education as entry into practice.

Baccalaureate programs today provide nursing education for beginning (generic) students and for registered nurses who have associate degrees or diplomas and wish to earn the BSN (bachelor of science in nursing) degree. Basic programs combine general education and nursing courses in a 4-year curriculum.

In the past, many associate degree and diploma program graduates sought baccalaureate level degrees in non-nursing fields such as health education or business primarily because they did not require any additional clinical courses and so could be completed more quickly. Non-nursing degrees do not provide advanced education in the discipline of nursing. Also, they often do little for the graduate in terms of job promotion or qualification for admission into a master's degree program in nursing.

Recently, many community colleges and universities have established articulation agreements whereby students from the community college receive credit for their associate degree nursing courses so that they do not have to repeat coursework unnecessarily. These cooperative arrangements have made it much easier for graduates of associate degree programs to continue their education and earn a baccalaureate degree.

EXTERNAL DEGREE PROGRAMS

External degree programs grant credit to students for their knowledge and experience, regardless of where they were obtained. Students may obtain credit for life experience, for courses taken at other institutions, or through testing and receive a degree without the traditional coursework required by most institutions.

The best known external degree program in nursing in the New York State Regents External Degree Program, established in 1972. Students in this program are expected to achieve the same competencies as a graduate from an associate degree program in New York and to pass college-level tests in both nursing and general education. The program is accredited by the NLN.

External degree programs have advantages for the nontraditional student:

◆ Reduced commuting time to and from campus.

◆ Reduced child care problems.

◆ Freedom to work at one's own pace and on one's own time.

◆ The stress of returning to a classroom is reduced.

On the other hand, the external degree student must be motivated and self-directed because there are few deadlines and few reminders that there is studying to be done. Although some places arrange for meetings of people pursuing an external degree (somewhat like a support group), it can also be a lonely process in comparison to having a group of classmates with whom to share one's scholastic victories and defeats.

MASTER'S DEGREE PROGRAMS

There are currently over 200 master's degree in nursing programs in the United States (NLN, 1992). Entrance into a master's degree program usually requires a baccalaureate degree in nursing, a minimum grade point average of 3.0 on a scale of 1 to 4, and a satisfactory score on the Graduate Record Examination (GRE) or a similar test. Some programs still require a year of experience in nursing practice as well.

Graduate programs prepare students for advanced clinical practice, teaching, and nursing administration. The most common specialty areas are adult health, child health, community/public health, gerontology, neonatal nursing, nurse anesthesia, nursing administration, nursing education, nurse midwifery, nursing information systems, oncology, and psychiatric/mental health (NLN, 1992). Students receive the degree master of science (MS) or master of science in nursing (MSN) after 1 or 2 additional years of study beyond the baccalaureate level.

As with the baccalaureate degree, students seeking advanced degrees should be encouraged to pursue a degree in nursing rather than in another discipline. Many times the master's degrees in a related field will not allow for the advancement that a nursing degree provides.

DOCTORAL PROGRAMS

Doctoral programs in nursing are comparatively new. As late as the 1970s, many nurses were still pursuing doctoral degrees in other fields than nursing. Currently there are about 60 doctoral programs in nursing in the United States (NLN, 1993). Most offer either the doctor of philosophy (PhD) or the doctor of science in nursing (DNSc) degree. The doctor of nursing science degree is a practice-oriented degree that emphasizes clinical research. The doctor of philosophy degree is considered more academically oriented, preparing scholars for the pursuit of research and theory development. Doctorally prepared nurses are in great demand in both university and community settings.

CONTINUING EDUCATION

In some states, participation in continuing education is required for licensure renewal. In other states, it is required only for advanced practice nurses. Licensed nurses need to be aware of the requirements of the board of nursing in their own state. Continuing education programs provide an avenue for nurses to update and expand their knowledge and skills. The time spent in obtaining continuing education should be viewed as valuable to one's professional growth.

■ Conclusion

• • • • • • • • • • • • • • • • • • •

The public image of nursing has not always done justice to the unique combination of art and science that is truly nursing. Nurses need to take the lead in the movement to-

ward a clearer identity and role delineation of the profession. Paramount to achieving these goals is the recognition of the value of nursing and acceptance of its professional status. The importance of viewing nursing as a profession with a systematic body of knowledge, formal college-based education, unique roles, standards of practice, professional accountability, professional culture, and community commitment will continue to move nursing into the twenty-first century.

? Study Questions

1. How can you portray the profession of nursing in a positive manner in the workplace?

2. Discuss the characteristics of nursing that indicate that nursing is a profession.

3. What are the advantages for a nurse of belonging to the American Nurses Association?

4. What is the purpose of the board of nursing? What impact do the ANA Standards of Clinical Nursing Practice have on decisions made by the board of nursing?

5. Evaluate yourself based on the NLN competencies (see Appendix 3) for the associate degree nurse at graduation. Based on these competencies, what do you see as your strengths? Your weaknesses?

Critical Thinking Exercise

Part I. Ms. P. recently graduated from the local community college and received an associate degree in nursing. On obtaining her registered nurse license, she was hired on a busy pediatric floor of a large local hospital. She was responsible for delegating patient assignments to the LPN and nursing assistant who were assigned with her. She often felt uneasy about her decisions because of her inexperience in this area. When she joined the ANA, she received a copy of the Code for Nurses and Standards of Clinical Nursing Practice. How might these two documents guide her in making decisions about delegating patient assignments?

After a few weeks, she told her nurse manager that she had seen Ms. A., the LPN, discontinuing IVs and hanging IV medications even though it is not allowed by the board of nursing in their state. The nurse manager replied, "Oh, she's just like an RN. Don't worry, I'll cover for her."

1. Why should Ms. P. feel uneasy about that response?

2. What might happen to the nurse manager, the LPN, and Ms. P. if there is problem with a patient regarding these IVs?

3. What can Ms. P. do about this situation?

REFERENCES

Ahern, J. (1993). Healthcare issues of the 90's: A challenge for nurses. *Revolution: The Journal of Nurse Empowerment, 3*(1), 73–74.

American Nurses Association (1965). ANA's just position on education for nursing. *Am J Nurs,* 65, 106–111.

American Nurses Association (1980). *Nursing: A Social Policy Statement.* Kansas City, Mo.: ANA Publishing.

American Nurses Association (1985). *Code for Nurses.* Washington, D.C.: ANA Publishing.

American Nurses Association (1987). *Proceedings of the 1987 House of Delegates.* Washington, D.C.: ANA Publishing, p 5.

American Nurses Association (1987). *The Scope of Nursing Practice.* Washington, D.C.: ANA Publishing.

American Nurses Association (1991). *Nursing's Agenda for Health Care Reform.* Washington, D.C.: ANA Publishing.

American Nurses Association (1991). *Standards of Clinical Nursing Practice.* Kansas City, Mo.: ANA Publishing.

American Nurses Association (1995). *Nursing's Social Policy Statement.* Washington, D.C.: ANA Publishing.

American Nurses Association (1995). *American Nurses Association Bylaws as Amended July 2, 1995.* Washington, D.C.: ANA Publishing.

Bixler, G.K., & Bixler, R.W. (1959). The professional status of nursing. *Am J Nurs, 59*(8), 1142–1147.

Buresch, B. (1993). Media watch: Television coverage of healthcare—Can nurses break in? *Revolution: The Journal of Nurse Empowerment, 3*(2), 14–15, 104–105.

Chally, P.S. (1992). Empowerment through teaching. *J Nurs Educ, 31*(3), 117–119.

Chandler, G. (1992). Nurses in the news: From invisible to visible. *J Nurs Adm, 22*(2), 11–12.

Craver, D., & Hutcherson, K. (1994). Defining nursing excellence. *Revolution: The Journal of Nurse Empowerment, 4*(1), 34–39.

DeTornyay, R. (1992). Reconsidering nursing education: The report of the Pew Health Professions Commission. *J Nurs Educ, 31*(7), 296–301.

Flexner, A. (1915). Is social work a profession? *Scholastic Society, 1*(20), 901.

Hammer, R., & Tufts, M. (1985). Nursing's self image. *J Nurs Educ, 24*(7), 280–283.

Hanner, M.B., Heywood, E.J., & Kaye, M.K. (1993). The curriculum revolution: Implications for associate degree nursing education. In Simmons, J. (Ed.), *Prospectives: Celebrating 40 Years of Associate Degree Nursing Education.* New York: National League for Nursing (NLN).

Henderson, V. (1966). *The Nature of Nursing.* New York: Macmillan.

Hess, R. (1993). In nursing as in life—No risks, no rewards. *Revolution: The Journal of Nurse Empowerment,* (3(1), 84–86, 111-112.

Hull, M. (1993). Your nursing image: Tending the flame. *Nursing 93, 23*(5), 116–118.

Inlander, C. (1993). Bouquets: Ask a nurse. *Revolution: The Journal of Nurse Empowerment, 3*(3), 92–97.

Jeffreys, M. (1994). A vision of professional nursing in 2020. *Revolution: The Journal of Nurse Empowerment, 4*(1), 75–76.

Mancriek, M.A. (1993). The cultural revolution: Transforming barriers to education for registered nurses. *Nurse Educator, 18*(4), 13–17.

Mason, D., Backer, B., & Georges A. (1993). Toward a feminist model for the political empowerment of nurses. *Revolution: Journal of Nurse Empowerment, 3*(1), 63–71, 106–108.

Moccia, P. (1993). Nursing education in the public's trust. *Nursing and Health Care, 14*(9), 472–474.

National League for Nursing. (1991). *ADN Competencies.* New York: National League for Nursing.

National League for Nursing. (1993). *A Vision for Nursing Education* (Publication No. 14–2581). New York: National League for Nursing.

Nightingale, F. (1959). *Notes on Nursing* (Facsimile of the First Edition). Philadelphia: J.B. Lippincott.

Pande, J. (1994). Graduate nursing education: An innovative experiment. *J Nurs Educ, 33*(6), 279–280.

Paul, R. (1993). *Critical Thinking.* California: Foundations for Critical Thinking.

Pillitteri, A. (1994). One nursing curriculum 100 years ago: A retrospective view as a prospective necessity. *J Nurs Educ, 33*(6), 286–287.

Rather, M. (1994). Schooling for oppressions: A critical hermeneutical analysis of the lived experience of the returning RN student. *J Nurs Educ, 33*(6), 263–271.

Resnick, S. (1993). Twenty something nurses. *Revolution: The Journal of Nurse Empowerment, 3*(2), 18–26.

Rogers, M.E. (1988). Nursing science and art: A prospective. *Nursing Science Quarterly, 1,* 99–102.

Swirsky, J. (1993). Exclusive interview with Virginia Trotter Betts, President of the American Nurses Association. *Revolution: The Journal of Nurse Empowerment, 3*(1), 41–48.

Tanner, C. (1991). What nurses of America are all about. *Nurse Educator, 16*(5), 36–37.

Tanner, C. (1993). Nursing education and health care reform. *J Nurs Educ, 29*(7), 295–299.

CHAPTER 16

· ·

Looking to the Future

OBJECTIVES *After reading this chapter, the student will be able to:*

   ◆ Make some predictions about the delivery of health care in the 21st
     century.
   ◆ Describe the changes occurring in the delivery of health care and their
     effect on client outcomes and on nursing.
   ◆ Discuss the positive and negative effects of cost-containment efforts.

What Will Health Care Be Like in the Future?

• • • • • • • • • • • • • • • • • •

The following story is one version of how health care may be delivered in the future:

Arriving at the surgical center of the future, the client is directed to a walk-up window that resembles a present-day automatic teller. The client is instructed to place the appropriate health insurance card into the slot. A computerized voice then directs the client:

"Press 1 if you are having surgery. Press 2 if you are having diagnostic tests. Press 3 if you are here to have a postoperative evaluation. Press 4 if you need further assistance. A qualified healthcare person will be with you shortly."

The client is then instructed to choose the appropriate surgical procedure that is listed across the computer screen. After this is verified and approved, the client receives directions from the electronic voice:

"You may now enter through the double doors to your right. The doors will open automatically. Please step carefully onto the moving platform. The platform is traveling at the same speed as the treatment vehicle. Kindly enter the first treatment vehicle as it approaches. Place the second finger of your left hand into the yellow circle for a blood test. A blood pressure cuff will encircle your left upper arm. Do not pull on the bar or belts. The safety bars and seat belts will lock automatically as the back of your vehicle reclines and the foot rest rises to the forward position. Your vital signs and other appropriate information will be monitored by highly sophisticated computer technology throughout your entire stay with us.

"As you pass through Station 1, please place your right arm through the designated opening for the placement of your intravenous line. This will be inserted by an automated sensor robot. Through the use of infrared sensors and sonography, the sensor robot locates an appropriate vessel with greater skill than an actual nurse. You may feel a slight burning at this time. Do not pull your arm away. We repeat, do not pull your arm away.

"You are now approaching Station 2. Please place your right hand through the designated opening to receive the appropriate medication. The computerized vehicle in which you are traveling has automatically calculated the accurate dosage of medication based on your body weight and metabolism. The medication you will receive has been determined by an analysis of your blood drawn at Station 1. This eliminates any possibility of human error. However, if at any time you feel any itching, tingling, or tightness in your throat or lungs, please press the red button on the left side of your vehicle. Our computers will automatically institute emergency measures for your health and safety. This action precludes the possible delays that can occur in the human decision-making process.

"You have reached Station 3, your assigned surgical suite. Please observe the screen in front of the vehicle. Meet your surgeon, Dr. I.M. Yourfuture, from Houston, Texas. Through the use of computer technology and robotics, she will be performing seven of these procedures simultaneously in different geographic locations. Anesthesia will be administered through the mask moving toward your face. Please remain still while the robot arm securely fastens the straps around your neck. Take several slow deep breaths when the blue light on the console begins to flash. Your anesthetic dose has been predetermined through a highly sophisticated mathematical formula. Pleasant dreams. We hope you enjoy your surgery while at 21st Century Surgical Center, saving healthcare dollars for a better tomorrow."

Compare the experience of the 21st Century Surgical Center to this alternative view of the future of health care:

Arriving at the New Age Health Center, the client walks into a central atrium, is offered a cool drink, and is encouraged to "choose a comfortable seat in the center, where you can enjoy the musical fountain or meditate in one of our quiet corners, whichever you prefer." After relaxing awhile in the atrium, the client walks down the hall to the consultation rooms. The client notices that one of the center's animal healers (a big, friendly Labrador) has joined him and is accompanying him down the hall.

Guides along the walkway ask the client if he knows the way or would like some assistance in choosing a healer to consult. "I'm feeling very stressed at work lately," answers the client. "Having trouble sleeping, which is unusual for me."

"We have several ways to approach your concerns," says the guide. "You could try our stress-reducing exercise path, our yoga path, the medicinal consultation, the sleep consultation, or all four if you'd like."

"I already have a good exercise program and prefer not to use medicinal therapies unless they're necessary, so I think I'll try that sleep consultation. I really need to get more sleep than I have lately."

The guide nods and directs the client toward the sleep center. "Ralph (the Labrador) would be happy to go with you, if you'd like." Ralph wags his tail in agreement.

At the end of the consultation, the client walks to the door with his sleep tapes and a video explaining how to use them as he has been shown by the sleep consultant. His sleep consultant bids him "a good night's rest tonight," and Ralph walks him back to the atrium, leaving him with a quiet "woof."

What is your preferred view of future healthcare delivery? Do you prefer the high-tech approach of the 21st Century Surgical Center or the high-touch approach of the New Age Health Center? Which would your clients choose? Is there a way to combine the best of both approaches? Which one do you think will prevail in the future?

We don't know for sure how health care will be delivered in the future or what nurses' roles will be in the healthcare system of the future. However, we can look at the current trends in our society, their effect on today's healthcare system, and what they may tell us about the future. By doing this, we may find some clues to the future of health care and of the nursing profession.

■ *Current Trends*

A number of general trends in our society appear to be influencing the direction of health care. Of these, some of the most important are the effects of technology, the survival of greater numbers of people with high-risk conditions, and an increasing tendency to evaluate worth in economic terms.

EFFECTS OF TECHNOLOGY

On the whole, Americans value innovation, invention, and aggressive approaches to solving problems, all in the name of progress, efficiency, and productivity (Postman, 1992). In minutes, computers can complete highly complex calculations that would take days or weeks if done by hand. Sophisticated monitors, microsurgery, laser printers, cellular phones, satellite positioning, space exploration, and a whole wonderful array of technical advances have made it possible to do things faster, cheaper, and more accurately.

Yet there may be some disadvantages to all this progress. One of the major concerns about the increasing influence (if not dominance) of technology on our lives is that it may be destructive and dehumanizing. Technological progress may come at a high price, especially to our increasingly stressed natural environment. It may also cause us to neglect the emotional and spiritual aspects of the human experience.

Postman (1992), for example, has commented on the "chilling" use of computer-related metaphors to describe human behavior, especially thinking. He uses the story of the introduction of the stethoscope to illustrate how a piece of equipment can come between the client and the physician. Before the stethoscope was developed, a physician had to place his or her ear right on the client's chest or depend on the client's description of symptoms to understand the problem. When stethoscopes became available, this was no longer necessary.

While a stethoscope hardly seems like a major barrier between client and caregiver, consider adding x-rays, laboratory tests, electrocardiograms, computed tomography scans, magnetic resonance imaging, and so forth to the list. The importance of the client's experience seems to diminish each time another piece of equipment is put into use. Each piece of equipment is thought to supply more "objective" information than the words of the client or the eyes, ears, and hands of the caregiver can supply.

Today we even have computerized client interviews, which can be used in place of taking a client history. Before long, it may be possible to monitor our clients without seeing or touching them at all.

Contrast this highly technological scenario to the philosophy that caring is an essential element of health care, that knowing, being with, doing for, and enabling (Watson, 1988) the individual should be part of any encounter with a healthcare professional. In a machine-oriented healthcare environment, talking with a client and family could become superfluous, but in a caring environment, it would be a priority (Locsin, 1995). The difference between the two is illustrated by the two scenarios at the beginning of the chapter.

Clients define quality of nursing care as a combination of technical competence and caring behaviors. Even in this time of confusion and change in health care, nurses can retain their commitment to caring and quality of care for the clients we serve. Miller (1996, p. 32) suggests ways to keep caring in nursing practice Box 16–1.

Box 16–1 Keeping caring in your nursing practice

- Analyze your own caring skills. Become more aware of your caring abilities throughout the work day.

- Understand that caring is an important part of all types of nursing practice: clinical, advance practice, administration, education, and research. Learn to appreciate how other nurses use caring skills in their unique practices.

- Think of caring as a set of skills that can be improved: showing kindness, preserving dignity, explaining with empathy, being patient, staying emotionally present, enabling another's life transitions, sustaining faith in another's life transitions, recognizing another's humanity weakness and strength, doing for another as you yourself would want. Practice these—become expert.

- Be a role model for caring. If caring skills can be enhanced, they can be taught. Be a teacher to all around you.

- Do not let anyone diminish the importance of the caring actions that you direct toward nurses and others in your organization. Support caring actions of clinical nurses toward patients and families, even when care giving is focused on the technological tasks of nursing.

- Patients do not equate time with caring. Make sure nurses understand the value of their caring actions to patients and families and to you.

- Let caring "civilize" the not-so-civilized current healthcare industry. Remind yourself every day that without caring, we would be like every other business. Patients, families, and colleagues need us and our caring skills.

- Lastly, and importantly, *use your caring skills on each other*. Especially when stress is high, we all need to be cared for.

Source: From Miller, K. L. (1995). Keeping the care in nursing care: Our biggest challenge. *J Nurs Adm, 25(11)*, 29–32. Used with permission of Lippincott-Raven Publishers, Philadelphia, Pa.)

SURVIVAL OF VULNERABLE INDIVIDUALS

From high-risk newborns to accident victims to the critically ill elderly, advances in health care have made it possible for many to survive who would not have survived in years past. The result is that we have both very high expectations of our healthcare system and larger numbers of people in need of care, especially of rehabilitation, long-term care, and home health care. The "baby boomers" are entering their 50s. As they move into their later years, their demands for health care will increase. Continued advances in technology will not only provide more options but also keep people alive longer. A great deal of concern has been expressed recently as to whether we will have sufficient resources to provide adequate care to all of these survivors.

The belief that everyone has a right to the best possible health care, no matter how much it costs, has been weakened by this concern that our resources are limited and could be exhausted unless some restraints are put into place (Drew, 1990).

EMPHASIS ON ECONOMICS

Concern about cost has led us on a quest for the highest level of efficiency possible in the delivery of health care. The result is a whole range of changes designed to minimize the time and money spent on a patient and maximize the profit gained. The danger is that this may result in a serious decline in the quality of health care and eventually pose a threat to the health of the population, especially the most vulnerable members of our society (Ritzer, 1993).

The April 8, 1996 issue of *Business Week* identified a number of large employers, such as Xerox, USAIR, GTE, and Marriott, who had been instrumental in pushing for lower health costs. By the end of 1995, corporations had convinced 71 percent of their employees to move into less costly managed care plans (Magnusson, 1996, p. 104). In the past, neither patients nor insurers nor the government were likely to question a medical decision or the cost of implementing that decision. Today, the final decision may rest with a representative of an insurance company or HMO who does not even have a healthcare background, unless the client is able to pay out of his or her own pocket.

In some cases, the decision is made primarily on the basis of cost rather than the need of the client, and accusations of unnecessary harm and even death resulting from cost-based decisions have been made. There is some evidence that the healthcare consumer is beginning to rebel against these cost-driven decisions, in some cases by taking the issue to the courts (Felsenthal, 1996). In addition, some states are adopting laws to better define a client's rights in cases where needed care is not made available.

In the next section, we describe some of these changes in more detail.

■ *Changes in the Healthcare System*

What has been the response to these attempts to improve the efficiency and cost-effectiveness of health care? Leah Curtin (1996, p. 7) has described the response eloquently:

> A coward dies a thousand deaths, a brave man dies but once . . . but once is enough. So goes the new twist on an old proverb. It is particularly apropos today when fear rules—if not the land, then at least the health care system and almost all of the 10 million people it employs. Administrators fear loss of influence, status and income. Physicians fear loss of autonomy, control, and income. Nurses fear loss of professional standing, job and income. And just about everyone with two live brain cells and a functioning conscience fears for the safety of patient care.

It is important that we clearly separate fact from fiction as we respond to the current trends in health care. Let's begin with some background information.

HISTORICAL PERSPECTIVE

Before 1965, the year Medicare was enacted, nurse vacancy rates in hospitals ran between

20 and 25 percent. Once Medicare was enacted, hospitals were able to shift much of the cost of nursing salaries onto Medicare, and the nursing shortages decreased.

When the diagnostic-related groups (DRGs) were introduced in the 1980s, the number of hospital admissions and average length of stay were reduced. Clients admitted to hospitals were more acutely ill and were discharged more quickly (the "quicker and sicker" movement). At this time, hospitals realized that the registered nurse was best able to provide the care needed to move these clients safely and quickly through the hospital stay. Although hospitals began questioning physicians about their practice patterns, the use of registered nurses to provide most of the client care was not questioned.

However, in the 1990s, hospitals were unable to shift costs any further, managed care became far more popular, and uncertainty over healthcare reform lingered in the air (Buerhaus, 1995, p. 10), raising questions about the role of nurses and other healthcare professionals in the healthcare system of the future.

Today, Medicare and Medicaid absorb roughly 18 percent of the federal budget every year. At the end of 1995, the Congressional Budget Office estimated the accumulated federal deficit to be $3617 trillion. Another 16 percent of the federal budget has to be used to pay the interest on this debt. It is projected that by the year 2005, the federal deficit will be close to $6757 trillion. Healthcare costs are projected to reach $16 trillion by the year 2030 (Buerhaus, 1996b, p. 15; Richards, 1996, p. 13). With the demand for health care increasing, the federal budget deficit growing, and public support for decreasing the debt ongoing, cost-containment measures in health care are certain to continue.

MANAGED CARE

Managed care is "a coordinated approach to providing necessary health services with an ultimate goal of low-cost, quality care" (Richards, 1996, p. 13). The most common type of managed-care organization is the health maintenance organization, or HMO. Physicians are also organizing groups to offer managed care through preferred provider organizations (PPOs).

Consumers in a managed-care system select a primary care physician provider from an approved list. Each provider is paid a predetermined (capitation) rate for each client, usually on a monthly basis. The primary care physician is seen as the "gatekeeper" because the client cannot consult specialists without a referral from the primary care physician. Using out-of-plan providers is not allowed in many plans. If out-of-plan providers are allowed, the client is often charged the full cost or a large part of the cost of services for this referral.

The theory behind managed care is that stressing preventive health care, including yearly physicals, immunizations, and health education, is an effective way to avoid illness and future hospitalizations, thereby reducing cost (Richards, 1996, p. 13). If clients do become ill, the physicians within the plan are often given powerful incentives to control costs (Buerhaus, 1996a, p. 21) by limiting the number of diagnostic tests done, for example, or by avoiding a hospital stay altogether if possible.

Criticism of the way managed-care plans actually operate has been considerable. The concerns include physician gag rules (the inability of the physician to disclose restrictions or options for the client), overly short maternity hospital stays, qualifications of providers, difficult access to specialists, and the influence of financial incentives given to physicians to reduce costs. In addition, many critics fear that Medicaid, often considered the last resort for people unable to pay for their own health care, will be threatened and that many areas of the country, such as rural areas, may not be well served under managed care (Pierce & Luikart, 1996, p. 28; Rovner, 1996, p. 1).

Proponents of managed-care organizations respond by stating that the criticism is mostly from physician specialists and medical societies who are unhappy with losing their piece of the healthcare pie (Grimaldi, 1996, p. 12).

SUBACUTE CARE

Another way to reduce cost is to shift people out of the expensive acute-care hospital as quickly as possible into less costly settings such as subacute-care units. Subacute units can offer round-the-clock nursing care to stable clients with a variety of diagnoses. Subacute care may be offered in a variety of settings; freestanding skilled nursing facilities, hospital-based skilled nursing units, swing bed units, and rehabilitation hospitals or units can all be used as subacute units.

Many subacute-care providers have developed programs for specific populations, such as people in need of wound care, oncology treatment, or rehabilitation. Nurses skilled in these areas can significantly decrease the cost of providing care. Many believe that the subacute setting will continue to grow as a viable alternative to more costly acute care (Masso, 1995). Associate-degree prepared nurses are in great demand in subacute units. Their expertise in the essentials of nursing care for the relatively stable client will assist the managed-care provider in offering cost-effective, quality care (Browne & Biancolillo, 1996, p. 23).

COMMUNITY-BASED CARE

Another alternative to the acute-care setting is to provide care in ambulatory settings and in the home. Many types of surgery can be done on an outpatient basis, and many therapies once considered too complex to do at home (intravenous therapies and dialysis, for example) are now being done safely and effectively in clients' homes. Buerhaus (1996a, p. 14) lists characteristics of the past

and future healthcare delivery system (Table 16–1).

CHANGING HEALTHCARE INSTITUTIONS

You are probably well aware of the fact that many changes have occurred in healthcare institutions recently and that much of the change has been in response to pressure to restrain spending for health care. Employers who pay their workers' health insurance costs, insurance companies themselves, and state and federal agencies have all contributed to this pressure.

These pressures have forced healthcare institutions to make a number of changes designed to keep costs under control. It is still not clear if they will be successful in their attempts to provide quality care while holding down costs (Curtin, 1994). Healthcare institutions have been busy re-engineering, restructuring, and redesigning jobs. Let's define each of these terms first.

Re-engineering involves changing the processes by which things are accomplished. The use of critical pathways in directing client care is a form of re-engineering. Often the term *re-engineering* is used erroneously for what is actually restructuring. *Restructuring* alters the architecture of the organization. Promoters of restructuring usually suggest a smaller number of managerial levels, decentralization, and allowing first-line care-

---

TABLE 16–1

COMPARISON OF THE PAST AND FUTURE HEALTH CARE DELIVERY SYSTEMS

Past/Traditional	Future Managed Health Care System
Episodic illness-focused	Wellness and prevention-oriented
Insurance-based payment	Managed care
Inpatient care	Ambulatory and community-based
Hospitals as profit centers	Hospitals as cost centers
Specialist providers	Primary care providers
Independent solo physicians	Multispecialty group practices
Fee for-service payments	Predetermined capitated fee
Heavily regulated environment	Highly competitive environment
Provider-driven system	Cost-driven system
Presumption of high quality	Systematic evaluation of quality indicators

Source: Adapted from Buerhaus, P.I. (1996). A heads up on capitation. *Nursing Policy Forum, 2(3),* 21.

givers to make more decisions. *Job redesign* is focused on who does what and how the work can be accomplished more efficiently. To accomplish this, cross-training is frequently used (Curtin, 1994).

In an effort to maximize service with the least number of staff members possible, many hospitals have undertaken *cross-training*. This often involves training healthcare professionals from other disciplines to perform some nursing functions such as dispensing medications or starting IVs. At the same time, nurses are being taught the skills of other healthcare providers, such as doing electrocardiograms or basic laboratory tests.

As you can see, cross-training is part of a movement away from having many different specialists and toward making everyone more of a generalist. Many healthcare professionals have concerns about these efforts to change the way in which care is given and by whom (Strasen, 1994). In fact, when faced with these changes, some staff have exhibited anger, foot-dragging, and active resistance (del Bueno, 1995). This has created morale problems in some institutions. It also presents a problem for the new graduate who needs assistance in adapting to the new working environment.

■ *Effect on Nursing*
• • • • • • • • • • • • • • • • • • • •

The profession of nursing has evolved along with the healthcare system. One of the few things we can say for certain is that it will continue to evolve:

> Looking back through the cloudy lenses of time, we see the nurse as the comforter and assistant to the physician healer. She took our temperature, measured our pulse, read our blood pressure, held our hands—and, in places like emergency rooms and far-off battlefields, got her hands bloody as she nursed. That nurse, though nobly remembered, is far removed from today's reality. (Alliance for Health Care Reform, 1996, p. 1)

Before considering how the profound changes occurring within the healthcare system will affect individual nurses and the pro-

fession as a whole, let's review the current status of the profession in the United States (Alliance for Health Reform, 1996; Wunderlich, Sloan, & Davis, 1996):

◆ There are 2.2 million registered nurses in the United States; 1.9 million are actively employed.

◆ There are four times as many nurses as physicians in the United States.

◆ Hospitals are still the largest employer of nurses, employing two-thirds of all nurses.

◆ In 1983, hospitals employed 698,000 registered nurses, 874,000 in 1993.

◆ In 1993, there were 755 nurses per 100,000 population. This compares to 292 per 100,000 in 1960.

◆ Most nurses are women (96 percent), although the number of men in nursing is increasing.

◆ Seventy percent of all practicing nurses spend at least half their time in direct client care.

◆ Nurses' salaries increased faster than the rest of the economy in the late 1980s and early 1990s.

Several additional facts about nursing provide us with some clues to future trends (Alliance for Health Reform, 1996; Wunderlich, Sloan, & Davis, 1996):

◆ Although most newly licensed nurses are still employed by hospitals, the number is declining and the number employed by long-term care facilities is increasing.

◆ Although still a relatively small percentage of nurses, the number of nurses employed in ambulatory care and home health is increasing.

◆ Although unemployment rates for nurses have been rising, statistics through 1994 indicate that they were still consistently lower for nurses than for other professions, including teachers.

Given an aging and increasingly ethnically diverse population, continued pressure to contain costs, and increasing concern about the quality of care, how will nurses be affected by the changes in the healthcare system? How will the profession as a whole change? The following are a few predictions:

- More nurses will be employed in ambulatory care settings and home health care.
- Nurses will increasingly be called on to provide care across the continuum of care. For example, instead of planning the care for a client in the hospital who had a hip replacement, a nurse will be expected to plan the client's care from home to hospital to rehabilitation center, then back home with home health, and finally, at home functioning independently.
- Advanced practice skills will be expected of an increasing number of nurses.
- As the number of technical or ancillary staff members increases, nurses will need more leadership and management skills than ever (Wunderlich, Sloan, & Davis, 1996).
- The nursing workforce will become increasingly diverse in terms of gender, race, and ethnic group membership.

In 1995, the Pew Health Professions Commission predicted that there could be a 200,000 to 300,000 surplus of nurses as acute-care hospitals downsize and close. They also predicted that registered nurses will move into different settings to provide health care. Members of the commission suggested that nursing education programs reduce the size of their basic programs and increase the number of master's degree-level nurse practitioner programs. They also discussed the possibility of consolidating allied health professional roles into one multiskilled provider (Pew Health Professions Commission, 1995).

Although the Pew Health Professions Commission's recommendations are controversial and certainly not universally accepted, it is imperative that nurses be aware that such recommendations are being made to policy makers. All nurses need to be involved in educating consumers, policy makers, and colleagues on the importance of the professional nurse in this new era in health care.

ELIMINATION OF POSITIONS

Forced to contain costs, hospitals have merged departments and units. This elimination of services has also resulted in the loss of nursing positions. Nurse managers may be responsible for two or three units instead of just one. Staffing levels may be reduced to the minimum necessary to provide safe care. This results in too few nurses for too many clients, often causing stress for the staff (Curtin, 1994).

SHORTER STAYS

In addition, clients are sent home as soon as possible to keep down the cost of an inpatient stay. The result is that the remaining clients are more critically ill and in need of more time and care. Only the flexible and productive nurse will survive these changes.

STAFFING RATIOS

Alternating cycles of shortage and oversupply have been common in nursing history. These cycles cause fluctuations in both the production (education) and hiring of nurses. The recent decline in the number of inpatient hospital days has reduced the need for staff nurses in acute-care institutions. At the same time, many hospitals have hired unlicensed assistive personnel to fill some of the gaps (Aiken, 1995). These people need supervision and may be viewed as an added responsibility for an already stretched nursing staff. On the other hand, unlicensed personnel are able to perform some basic care functions, freeing the professional nurses to focus their efforts on those aspects of care that only nurses can deliver competently.

■ *Unanswered Questions*
• • • • • • • • • • • • • • • • • • • •

Some of the questions yet to be answered about the future of health care and nursing's role in particular are as follows:

- Do re-engineering and restructuring really reduce costs? Will quality of care be sacrificed in the name of cost-effectiveness?

◆ What effect will the new staffing patterns have on the morbidity (illness) and mortality (death) of clients?

◆ What will be the public's response to these changes in healthcare delivery?

◆ Will blurring of the distinctions between the different health-related disciplines (e.g., physical therapy, respiratory therapy, nursing) increase? How will this affect the delivery of health care?

◆ Will both high-tech and high-touch care be important in the future, or will just one of these prevail?

◆ How will the role of the associate-degree nurse expand and evolve as much of health care moves into subacute, long-term, and community settings?

This is the time for nursing to demonstrate what it has to offer. Consider these changes to be positive, and realize that to gain satisfaction from your chosen profession, you must be proactive within it. Anticipate the future with excitement and remember that "a nurse is never finished" (Nightingale, 1859).

■ *Responding to the Changes in the Healthcare System*

• • • • • • • • • • • • • • • • • • •

Do most nurses understand what is happening in health care? Are they prepared to respond to these massive changes? A study of nurse managers in four teaching hospitals indicated that the nurse managers felt better prepared to deal with problems that occur on their unit than with organization-wide concerns or with pressures from the external environment (Edwards & Roemer, 1996). The researchers expressed concern that the nurses participating in the study did not recognize the importance of the changes occurring in the external environment.

The following are some suggestions for coping with all of these changes that are taking place. They are based on a set of "rules for successful redesign" developed by Porter-O'Grady (1996).

1. Remember that everyone is affected in some way by these changes. No one is exempt. Don't be like the proverbial ostrich that buries its head in the sand. Look up; look around at what's happening, and prepare to respond effectively.

2. Watch for those clues (the ones in the statistics listed earlier, for example) that indicate what trends are occurring. Use your own insight and experience to analyze these trends. Listen to what others are saying, especially the leaders of the profession, and read the news reports and professional literature to keep abreast of what is expected to happen.

3. Follow your vision. What is it about nursing that is especially important to you? What are your values? Hold onto what is most meaningful, and continue to work toward accomplishing your vision.

4. Empower yourself and others. Actually, as Porter-O'Grady notes, there is "precious little real empowerment" of employees in most healthcare organizations (1996, p. 50). Some of the suggestions in Chapter 6 on power and organizations may help you develop your own sense of empowerment.

5. Understand how your own goals fit with your employer's goals. Your personal goals and vision for nursing may or may not agree with your employer's. It is important that you recognize whatever differences exist and decide how you can reconcile them, if necessary.

6. Look past today. When changes come at you fast and furiously, it is very difficult to step back and evaluate the effect of those changes and to decide how to respond to them. You need to keep in mind your own long-term career plan and to evaluate how you can accomplish them in a changing environment.

Although some of these changes may be disturbing, there are positive aspects to what is happening in health care. These changes provide an opportunity for nursing to emerge as a positive force in the midst of a revolution. Nursing offers caring in a system that appears to have forgotten its importance to people and their well-being.

What does all this mean to the graduate nurse entering the healthcare system? Healthcare institutions will expect the new nurse to be flexible and use skills that may not have been included in their basic education. Graduate nurses will need to be open to learning new information and developing different skills. The demands on the new graduate will be greater, and client outcomes will be observed more closely. Nurses will also find opportunities in a variety of health settings, particularly in the community (Lescavage, 1995).

Earlier chapters discussed client care management techniques, communication skills, and teamwork. Now is the time to put all these ideas together and develop your leadership role in the working environment. If you maintain a positive attitude as you gain experience, you will become more comfortable in this challenging environment.

❓ *Study Questions*

1. What are the major forces affecting the healthcare system today? What kinds of changes have occurred in response to these changes?

2. Explain how the implementation of managed care, subacute care, and cross-training are responses to cost-containment pressures.

3. Describe the current employment picture for nurses. What changes do you expect in the future?

Critical Thinking Exercise

Read the two scenarios at the beginning of this chapter a second time. Then create your own futuristic scenario for an episode of client care. If you can, share your scenario with your classmates.

1. What do you think are the most promising characteristics of these imaginary healthcare systems?

2. What characteristics concern you the most?

3. Explain why you find some characteristics promising and others troublesome.

4. What is your vision of an ideal healthcare system?

REFERENCES

Aiken, L.H. (1995). Transformation of the nursing workforce. *Nurs Outlook, 43*(5), 201–209.

Alliance for Health Reform. (1996). *The Twenty-First Century Nurse*. Washington, D.C.: Alliance for Health Reform.

Browne, R., & Biancolillo, K. (1996). The integral role of nursing in managed care. *Nursing Management, 27*(4), 22–24.

Buerhaus, P.I. (1995). Economics and reform: Forces affecting nurse staffing. *Nursing Policy Forum, 1*(2), 8–14.

Buerhaus, P.I. (1996a). A heads up on capitation. *Nursing Policy Forum, 2*(3), 21.

Buerhaus, P.I. (1996b). Quality and cost: The value of consumer and nurse partnerships. *Nursing Policy Forum, 2*(2), 12–17.

Curtin, L. (1994). Restructuring: What works—and what does not. *Nursing Management, 25*(10), 7–8.

Curtin, L. (1996). Editorial: Other people's lives. *Nursing Management, 27*(5), 7.

del Bueno, D.J. (1995). Ready, willing, able? Staff competence in workplace redesign. *Nurs Adm, 25*(9), 14–16.

Drew, J.C. (1990). Health maintenance organizations: History, evolution & survival. *Nursing & Health Care, 11*(3), 145–149.

Edwards, P.A., & Roemer, L. (1996). Are nurse managers ready for the current challenges of healthcare? *Nurs Adm, 26*(9), 11–17.

Felsenthal, E. (1996, May 17). When HMO's say no to health coverage, more patients are taking them to court. *Wall Street Journal*.

Grimaldi, P. (1996). Protection for patients or providers? *Nursing Management, 12*(3), 127–128.

Lescavage, N. (1995). Nurses, make your presences felt: Taking off the rose-colored glasses. *Nursing Policy Forum, 1*(1), 18–24.

Locsin, R. (1995). Machine technologies and caring in nursing. *Image, 27*(3), 201–203.

Magnusson, P. (1996, April 8). Health care: The quest for quality. *Business Week*, pp. 104–106.

Masso, A. (1995). Managed care and alternative-site health care delivery. *Journal of Care Management, 1*(1), 45–51.

Miller, K. (1996). Keeping the care in nursing care. *Nurs Adm, 25*(11), 29–38.

Nightingale, F. (1859). *Notes on Nursing*. Reprinted 1992. Philadelphia: J.B. Lippincott.

Pew Health Professions Commission (1995). *Primary Care Workforce-2000-Federal Policy Paper*. San Francisco: UCSF Center for the Health Professions.

Pew Health Professions Commission. (1995). *Critical Challenges: Revitalizing the Health Profession for the Twenty-First Century*. San Francisco: UCSF Center for the Health Professions.

Pierce, S., & Luikart, C. (1996). Managed care: Will the health care needs of rural citizens be met? *Nurs Adm, 26*(4), 28–32.

Porter-O'Grady, T. (1996). The seven basic rules for successful redesign. *Nurs Adm, 26*(1), 46–53.

Postman, N. (1992). *Technopoly: The Surrender of Culture to Technology*. New York: Vintage Books.

Richards, S. (1996). Managed care 101. *Nursing Policy Forum, 2*(3).

Ritzer, G. (1993). *The McDonaldization of Society*. Thousand Oaks, Calif.: Pine Forge Press.

Rovner, J. (1996). The safety net: What's happening to health care of last resort? *Advances, 1*, 16–17.

Strasen, L. (1994). Reengineering hospitals using the function follows form model. *Nurs Adm, 24*(12), 59–63.

Watson, J. (1988). *Human Science and Human Care*. Norwalk, Conn.: Appleton-Century-Crofts.

Wunderlich, G.S., Sloan, F.A., & Davis, C.K. (1996). *Nursing Staff in Hospitals and Nursing Homes: Is It Adequate?* Washington, D.C.: National Academy Press.

APPENDIX 1*

American Nurses Association Code for Nurses

1. The nurse provides services with respect for human dignity and the uniqueness of the client, unrestricted by considerations of social or economic status, personal attributes, or the nature of health problems.

2. The nurse safeguards the client's right to privacy by judiciously protecting information of a confidential nature.

3. The nurse acts to safeguard the client and the public when health care and safety are affected by the incompetent, unethical, or illegal practice of any person.

4. The nurse assumes responsibility and accountability for individual nursing judgments and actions.

5. The nurse maintains competence in nursing.

6. The nurse exercises informed judgment and uses individual competence and qualifications as criteria in seeking consultation, accepting responsibilities, and delegating nursing activities to others.

7. The nurse participates in activities that contribute to the ongoing development of the profession's body of knowledge.

8. The nurse participates in the profession's effort to implement and improve standards of nursing.

9. The nurse participates in the profession's efforts to establish and maintain conditions of employment conducive to high quality nursing care.

10. The nurse participates in the profession's effort to protect the public from misinformation and misrepresentation and to maintain the integrity of nursing.

11. The nurse collaborates with members of the health professions and other citizens in promoting community and national efforts to meet the health needs of the public.

*From American Nurses Association (1985). *Code for Nurses*. Washington, D.C.: ANA Publishing, with permission.

APPENDIX 2*
. . . .

Standards of Care

Standard I. Assessment
THE NURSE COLLECTS CLIENT HEALTH DATA.

Standard II. Diagnosis
THE NURSE ANALYZES THE ASSESSMENT DATA IN DETERMINING DIAGNOSES.

Standard III. Outcome Identification
THE NURSE IDENTIFIES EXPECTED OUTCOMES INDIVIDUALIZED TO THE CLIENT.

Standard IV. Planning
THE NURSE DEVELOPS A PLAN OF CARE THAT PRESCRIBES INTERVENTIONS TO ATTAIN EXPECTED OUTCOMES.

Standard V. Implementation
THE NURSE IMPLEMENTS THE INTERVENTIONS IDENTIFIED IN THE PLAN OF CARE.

Standard VI. Evaluation
THE NURSE EVALUATES THE CLIENT'S PROGRESS TOWARD ATTAINMENT OF OUTCOMES.

■ Standards of Professional Performance
. . . .

Standard I. Quality of Care
THE NURSE SYSTEMATICALLY EVALUATES THE QUALITY AND EFFECTIVENESS OF NURSING PRACTICE.

Standard II. Performance Appraisal
THE NURSE EVALUATES HIS/HER OWN NURSING PRACTICE IN RELATION TO PROFESSIONAL PRACTICE STANDARDS AND RELEVANT STATUTES AND REGULATIONS.

Standard III. Education
THE NURSE ACQUIRES AND MAINTAINS CURRENT KNOWLEDGE IN NURSING PRACTICE.

Standard IV. Collegiality
THE NURSE CONTRIBUTES TO THE PROFESSIONAL DEVELOPMENT OF PEERS, COLLEAGUES, AND OTHERS.

Standard V. Ethics
THE NURSE'S DECISIONS AND ACTIONS ON BEHALF OF CLIENTS ARE DETERMINED IN AN ETHICAL MANNER.

Standard VI. Collaboration
THE NURSE COLLABORATES WITH THE CLIENT, SIGNIFICANT OTHERS, AND HEALTH CARE PROVIDERS IN PROVIDING CLIENT CARE.

Standard VII. Research
THE NURSE USES RESEARCH FINDINGS IN PRACTICE.

Standard VIII. Resource Utilization
THE NURSE CONSIDERS FACTORS RELATED TO SAFETY, EFFECTIVENESS, AND COST IN PLANNING AND DELIVERING CLIENT CARE.

*From American Nurses Association (1991). Standards of Clinical Nursing Practice. Kansas City: ANA Publishing, with permission.

APPENDIX 3*

NLN Competencies: Educational Outcomes of Associate Degree Nursing Program Roles and Competencies

Since 1952, the goal of associate degree nursing programs has been to prepare the graduate for the role of registered nurse. In the initial research on associate degree education, both Montag (1951) and Matheney

*Reproduced with permission of National League for Nursing, from *Educational Outcomes of AD Nursing Program Roles and Competencies,* pp 10–17, by NLN © copyright 1991, New York: National League for Nursing Press.

(1972) describe the majority of the functions of the registered nurse as falling in a middle range between job categories more circumscribed on the one hand and more expansive on the other. Associate degree nursing curricula have been and continue to be planned, developed, and studied systematically in light of this belief.

The goal of associate degree nursing programs continues to be preparation of registered nurses to provide direct client care. Although associate degree nursing students receive preparation to provide care for clients across the life span, the majority of the graduates are employed in settings where the focus of care is on adult clients.

This document describes the anticipated educational outcomes of associate degree nursing programs. These outcomes encompass competencies expected of the graduate at graduation from the program, and those that may be anticipated following six months of practice as a registered nurse. These statements describe behaviors which demonstrate that the graduate has acquired the knowledge, skills, and attitudes inherent in the three roles basic to associate degree nursing practice: provider of care, manager of care, and member within the discipline of nursing.

of the graduate from an associate degree nursing program encompasses preparation for practice in both acute and long-term care settings where policies and procedures are specified and guidance is available.

To develop the cognitive, psychomotor, and affective abilities necessary to make sound nursing decisions and to practice competently, it is essential that the nurse has current knowledge in nursing concepts, principles, processes, and skills. Supportive of that knowledge is an understanding of health; acute and chronic health deviations; nutrition; pharmacology; communication; human development; teaching-learning principles; current technology; humanities; and biological, social, and behavioral sciences.

■ *Role As Provider of Care*

The practice of a graduate from an associate degree nursing program is characterized by critical thinking, clinical competence, accountability, and a commitment to the value of caring. This practice applies to clients across the life span, with emphasis on adults who have health needs and require assistance to maintain or restore their optimum states of health or support to die with dignity. Because the aged comprise an increasing proportion of nursing's clients, the nurse with an associate degree is prepared to address the acute and chronic health care needs of this population. The nurse is concerned with individual clients and their relationships within their families, groups, and communities.

The nursing process is used as a basis for decisions. The nurse establishes and analyzes a data base, identifies health care needs, selects nursing diagnoses, sets client-centered goals, plans and implements care to achieve the goals, and evaluates client outcomes.

The nurse's commitment to client-centered care is reflected through a collaborative approach involving the client, family, significant others, and members of the health care team. The provider of care role

■ *Competencies at Graduation*

ASSESSMENT. Upon graduation, the associate degree nurse demonstrates the following competencies in assessment:

- Obtains data through assessment of the client.

- Collects additional data relative to the client from family, significant others, health records, health care team members, and other resources.

- Identifies changes in health status that affect the client's ability to meet needs.

- Contributes the information to a data base.

DIAGNOSIS. Upon graduation, the associate degree nurse demonstrates the following competencies in diagnosis:

- Identifies actual or potential health care needs on the basis of assessment.

- Selects nursing diagnoses on the basis of analysis and interpretation of data.

PLANNING. Upon graduation, the associate degree nurse demonstrates the following competencies in planning:

◆ Participates with the client, family, significant others, and members of the health care team to establish client-centered goals directed toward promoting and restoring the client's optimum state of health, preventing illness, and providing rehabilitation.

◆ Establishes priorities for care with recognition of client's diagnoses and needs.

◆ Develops care plan incorporating data related to the client's cultural and spiritual beliefs and physiological, psychosocial, and developmental needs and strengths.

◆ Collaborates with other health care workers in the development of individualized teaching plans that include health counseling, discharge planning, and implementation of a therapeutic regimen.

◆ Supports client's right to make decisions regarding care.

IMPLEMENTATION Upon graduation, the associate degree nurse demonstrates the following competencies in implementation:

◆ Implements a care plan according to priority of goals.

◆ Initiates nursing interventions in response to client's needs.

◆ Adjusts priorities for nursing interventions as client situations change.

◆ Uses current technology to enhance client care.

◆ Demonstrates safe performance of nursing skills.

◆ Provides for physical safety of the client.

◆ Promotes an environment conducive to maintenance or restoration of the client's ability to carry out activities of daily living.

◆ Promotes the rehabilitation potential of the client.

◆ Administers and monitors the prescribed medical regimen for the client undergoing diagnostic tests and/or therapeutic procedures.

◆ Promotes psychological safety of the client.

◆ Demonstrates caring behavior in providing nursing care.

◆ Utilizes communication techniques that assist the client, family, and significant others to cope with and resolve problems.

◆ Communicates verbally and in writing client behaviors, responses to nursing interventions, and responses to medical regimen.

◆ Implements teaching plans that are specific to the client's level of development, knowledge, and learning needs.

◆ Provides for continuity of care in the management of chronic health care needs.

◆ Makes referrals on the basis of identified client needs and knowledge of available resources.

EVALUATION. Upon graduation, the associate degree nurse demonstrates the following competencies in evaluation:

◆ Determines the effects of nursing interventions on the status of the client.

◆ Participates with the client, family, significant others, and members of the health care team in the evaluation of client's progress toward goals.

◆ Revises care plan as needed.

■ *Anticipated Competencies Following Six Months of Practice as a Registered Nurse*

Following six months of practice as a registered nurse, the associate degree graduate demonstrates the following competencies:

◆ Develops, implements, and evaluates individualized plans of care.

◆ Uses the nursing process as a basis for decision making.

◆ Establishes and maintains effective communication with clients, families, significant others, and health team members.

◆ Promotes participation by the client, family, significant others, and members of the health care team in the plan of care.

◆ Demonstrates clinical competence when providing client care.

◆ Makes decisions and takes actions that are consistent with standards for nursing practice and licensing laws.

■ *Role as Manager of Care*

The practice of a graduate from an associate degree nursing program is characterized by collaboration, organization, delegation, accountability, advocacy, and respect for other health care workers. As a manager of care, the nurse with an associate degree provides and coordinates care for a group of clients who have health care needs.

In organizing nursing care, the nurse may delegate aspects of care to licensed and unlicensed personnel commensurate with their educational backgrounds and experience. The nurse is accountable for care delegated to other workers and for knowing legal parameters of their practice as well as their roles and responsibilities. Consultation with other members of the health care team is initiated when the situation encountered is beyond the nurse's knowledge and experience. The nurse participates in evaluation of the client care delivery system, contributes to change, and promotes an environment that fosters team relationships.

The nurse is manager of care in acute and long-term care settings where policies and procedures are specified and guidance is available.

To be competent in the role as a manager of care, the nurse must possess the knowledge and skills necessary to make decisions regarding priorities of care, to delegate some aspects of nursing care and direct others, to efficiently use time and resources, and to know when to seek assistance. Supporting

this knowledge is an understanding of the principles of client care management, communication and delegation, legal parameters of nursing practice, and roles and responsibilities of members of the health care team.

■ *Competencies at Graduation*

Upon graduation, the associate degree nurse demonstrates the following competencies:

◆ Establishes priorities for nursing care for a group of workers commensurate with their educational preparation and experience.

◆ Is accountable for nursing care delegated to other workers.

◆ Assists other nursing personnel to develop skills in providing nursing care.

◆ Interacts with other members of the healthcare team in a collegial manner.

◆ Utilizes appropriate channels of communication to accomplish goals related to delivery of client care.

◆ Provides for continuity of care within the employing institution.

◆ Serves as an advocate for clients.

◆ Seeks assistance from other members of the health care team when the situation encountered is beyond the nurse's knowledge and experience.

◆ Utilizes current technology to increase efficiency of management of client care and resources.

◆ Practices in a cost-effective manner.

■ *Anticipated Competencies Following Six Months of Practice as a Registered Nurse*

Following six months of practice as a registered nurse, the associate degree graduate demonstrates the following competencies:

- Manages an environment that promotes clients' self-esteem, dignity, safety, and comfort.

- Manages care for a group of clients in a timely and cost effective manner.

- Follows the policies and procedures of the employing institution.

- Promotes effective team relationships.

- Provides direction and guidance to other health care workers.

- Is accountable for performance of nursing activities delegated to other workers based upon the nurse's knowledge and experience.

- Utilizes appropriate channels of communication within the organizational structure.

- Promotes continuity of client care by utilizing appropriate channels of communication external to the organization.

- Participates in evaluation of the client care delivery system.

■ Role as Member within the Discipline of Nursing

The practice of a graduate from an associate degree nursing program is characterized by a commitment to professional growth, continuous learning, and self-development. The nurse with an associate degree practices within the ethical and legal framework of nursing and is responsible for ensuring high standards of nursing practice.

The nurse contributes to the improvement of nursing and nursing practice through participation on committees of the employing institution, attendance at conferences, and membership in nursing organizations.

To be a contributing member within the discipline of nursing and to practice quality nursing care, it is essential that the nurse understand ethical standards and the legal framework for practice; the importance of nursing research; rules and regulations governing the practice of nursing; roles of the professional organizations; political, economic, and societal forces affecting practice;

and lines of authority and communication within the work setting.

■ Competencies at Graduation

Upon graduation, the associate degree nurse demonstrates the following competencies:

- Practices within the ethical and legal framework of nursing.

- Maintains confidentiality of information regarding clients.

- Communicates truthfully in verbal and written form the client's behavior and responses to interventions.

- Reports concerns regarding quality of care to the appropriate person.

- Values nursing as a career and values own practice.

- Supports peers and other workers in the delivery of client care.

- Recognizes and reports ethical dilemmas encountered in practice.

- Serves as a role model to members of the nursing team.

- Uses information from current literature to provide safe nursing care.

- Uses resources for continuous learning and self-development.

- Uses constructive criticism and suggestions for improving nursing practice.

■ Anticipated Competencies Following Six Months of Practice as a Registered Nurse

Following six months of practice as a registered nurse, the associate degree graduate demonstrates the following competencies:

- Practices within the ethical and legal framework of nursing.

- Fosters high standards of nursing practice.
- Participates in learning activities to maintain safe practice.
- Constructs a course of action when confronted with ethical dilemmas in practice.
- Seeks assistance for colleagues whose behaviors indicate a potential impairment.

- Participates in self-evaluation and peer review.
- Participates in committees and conferences of the employing institution.
- Participates in professional organizations.
- Participates in research conducted at the employing institution.

Guidelines for the Registered Nurse in Giving, Accepting, or Rejecting a Work Assignment

Registered nurses, as licensed professionals, share the responsibility and accountability along with their employer to ensure that safe nursing care is provided at an acceptable level of quality. This accountability is both a legal responsibility as specified in the Nurse Practice Act and an ethical one as indicated in the American Nurses' Association's (ANA) *Code for Nurses*. In addition, there are employer requirements as outlined in the health care facility personnel policies and clinical guidelines/procedures.

The ANA *Code for Nurses* states, "The nurse exercises informed judgment and uses individual competence and qualifications as criteria in seeking consultation, accepting responsibilities, and delegating nursing activities to others." The nurse's decision regarding accepting or making work assignments is based on the legal, ethical and professional obligation to assume responsibility for nursing judgment and action.

■ **Scenarios**

◆ Suppose you are asked to care for an unfamiliar patient population or to go to a unit for which you feel unqualified—what do you do?

*Reproduced with permission of Florida Nurses Association, 1989, Orlando, Florida.

◆ Suppose you are approached by your supervisor and asked to work an additional shift. Your immediate response is that you don't want to work another shift—what do you do?

Such situations are familiar and emphasize the rights and responsibilities of the registered nurse to make informed decisions. Yet all members of the health care team, from staff nurses to administrator, share a joint responsibility to ensure that quality patient care is provided. At times though, differences in interpretation of legal or ethical principles may lead to conflict.

This document endeavors to facilitate strategies for problem solving as the staff nurse, nurse manager, chief nurse executive and administrator operationalize practice within the complex environment of the health care system.

■ *Guidelines for Decision Making*

• • • • • • • • • • • • • • • • • • •

The complexity of the delivery of nursing care is such that only professional nurses with appropriate education and experience can provide nursing care. Upon employment with a health care facility the nurse contracts or enters into an agreement with that facility to provide nursing services in a collaborative practice environment.

It is the nurse's responsibility to:

◆ provide competent nursing care to the patient;

◆ exercise informed judgment and use individual competence and qualifications as criteria in seeking consultation, accepting responsibilities and delegating nursing activities to others;

◆ clarify assignments, assess personal capabilities, jointly identify options for patient care assignments when he/she does not feel personally competent or adequately prepared to carry out a specific function. The nurse has the right to refuse an assignment that he/she does not feel prepared to assume.

It is the nursing management's responsibility to:

◆ ensure competent nursing care is provided to the patient;

◆ evaluate the nurse's ability to provide specialized patient care;

◆ organize resources to ensure that patients receive appropriate nursing care.

◆ collaborate with the staff nurse to clarify assignments, assess personal capabilities, jointly identify options for patient care assignments when the nurse does not feel personally competent or adequately prepared to carry out a specific function. The facility has the right to take appropriate disciplinary action according to facility policies.

◆ communicate in written policies to the staff the process to make assignment and reassignment decisions.

◆ provide education to staff and supervisory personnel in the decision-making process regarding patient care assignments and reassignments, including patient placement and allocation of resources.

It is the health care facility's responsibility to:

◆ ensure competent nursing care is provided to the patient;

◆ plan and budget for staffing patterns based upon patients' requirements and priorities for care;

◆ provide a clearly defined written mechanism for immediate internal review of proposed assignments, that includes the participation of the staff involved, to help avoid conflict.

Issues Central to Potential Dilemmas are:

◆ the right of the patient to receive safe professional nursing care at an acceptable level of quality;

◆ the responsibility for an appropriate utilization and distribution of nursing care services when nursing becomes a scarce resource; and

◆ the responsibility for providing a practice environment that assures adequate nursing resources for the facility, while meeting the current socioeconomic and political realities of shrinking health care dollars.

■ *Legal Issues*

Behaviors and activities relevant to giving, accepting, or rejecting a work assignment that could lead to the disciplinary action include:

◆ practicing or offering to practice beyond the scope permitted by law, or accepting and performing professional responsibilities which the licensee knows or has reason to know that he or she is not competent to perform; performing, without adequate supervision, professional services which the licensee is authorized to perform only under the supervision of a licensed professional, except in an emergency situation where a person's life or health is in danger.

◆ abandoning or neglecting a patient or client who is in need of nursing care without making reasonable arrangements for the continuation of such care;

◆ failure to exercise supervision over persons who are authorized to practice only under the supervision of the licensed professional.

Of the above, the issue of abandonment or neglect has thus far proven the most legally devastating. Abandonment or neglect has been legally defined to include such actions as insufficient observation (frequency of contact), failure to assure competent intervention when the patient's condition changes (qualified physician not in attendance), and withdrawal of services without provision for qualified coverage. Since nurses at all levels most frequently act as agents of the employing facility, the facility shares the risk of liability with the nurse.

■ *Application of Guidelines for Decision Making*

The following are some specific examples of how a nurse may apply the guidelines for decision making and the legal concepts as have been outlined in this document.

SCENARIO—A QUESTION OF COMPETENCE

An example of a potential dilemma is when an evening supervisor pulls a psychiatric nurse to the coronary care unit because of a lack of nursing staff. The CCU census has risen and there is no additional qualified staff available.

Suppose you are asked to care for an unfamiliar patient population or to go to a unit for which you feel unqualified—what do you do?

1. CLARIFY what it is you are being asked to do.
   ● How many patients will you be expected to care for?
   ● Does the care of these patients require you to have speciality knowledge and skills in order to deliver safe nursing care?
   ● Will there be qualified and experienced RNs on the unit?
   ● What procedures and/or medications will you be expected to administer?
   ● What kind of orientation do you need to function safely in this unfamiliar setting?
2. ASSESS yourself. Do you have the knowledge and skill to meet the expectations that have been outlined to you? Have you had experience with similar patient populations? Have you been oriented to this unit or a similar unit? Would the perceived discrepancies between your abilities and the expectations lead to an unsafe patient care situation?
3. IDENTIFY OPTIONS and implications of your decision.
   a) If you perceive that you can provide safe patient care you should accept

the assignment. You would now be ethically and legally responsible for the nursing care of these patients.

b) If you perceive there is a discrepancy between abilities and the expectations of the assignment, further dialogue with the nurse supervisor is needed before you reach a decision. At this point it may be appropriate to consult the next level of management, such as the House Supervisor or the Chief Nurse Executive.

In further dialogue, continue to assess whether you are qualified to accept either a portion or the whole of the requested assignment. Also point out options which might be mutually beneficial. For example, obviously it would be unsafe for you to administer chemotherapy without prior training. However, if someone else administered the chemotherapy perhaps you could provide the remainder of the required nursing care for that patient. If you feel unqualified for the assignment in its entirety, the dilemma becomes more complex.

At this point it is important for you to be aware of the legal rights of the facility. Even though you may have legitimate concern for patient safety and your own legal accountability in providing safe care, the facility has legal precedent to initiate disciplinary action, including termination, if you refuse to accept an assignment. Therefore, it is important to continue to explore options in a positive manner, recognizing that both you and the facility have a responsibility for safe patient care.

4. POINT OF DECISION/ IMPLICATIONS.

If none of the options are acceptable, you are at your final decision point.

a) Accept the assignment, documenting carefully your concern for patient safety and the process you used to inform the facility (manager) of your concerns. Keep a personal copy of this documentation and send a copy to the Chief Nurse Executive.

Courtesy suggests that you also send a copy to the manager(s) involved. Once you have reached this decision it is unwise to discuss the situation or your feelings with other staff or patients. Now you are legally accountable for these patients. From this point withdrawal from the agreed upon assignment may constitute abandonment.

b) Refuse the assignment, being prepared for disciplinary action. Document your concern for patient safety and the process you used to inform the facility (manager) of your concerns. Keep a personal copy of this documentation and send a copy to the Nurse Executive. Courtesy suggests that you also send a copy to the manager(s) involved.

c) Document the steps taken in making your decision. It may be necessary for you to use the facility's grievance procedure.

SCENARIO—A QUESTION OF AN ADDITIONAL SHIFT

An example of another potential dilemma is when a nurse who recognizes his/her fatigue and its potential for patient harm, is required to work an additional shift.

Suppose you are approached by your supervisor and asked to work an additional shift. Your immediate response is that you don't want to work another shift—what do you do.

1. CLARIFY what it is you are expected to do.

For example, would the additional shift be with the same patients you are currently caring for, or would it involve a new patient assignment?

- Is your reluctance to work another shift because of a new patient assignment you do not feel competent to accept? (If the answer is yes, then refer to the previous example, "A Question of Competence.")
- Is your reluctance to work due to fatigue, or do you have other plans?
- Is this a chronic request due to poor scheduling, inadequate staffing, or chronic absenteeism?

- Are you being asked to work because there is no relief nurse coming for your present patient assignment? Because your unit will be short of professional staff on the next shift? Because another unit will be short of professional staff on the next shift?
- How long are you being asked to work—the entire shift or a portion of the shift?

2. ASSESS yourself.

Are you really tired, or do you just not feel like working? Is your fatigue level such that your care may be unsafe? Remember, you are legally responsible for the care of your current patient assignment if relief is not available.

3. IDENTIFY OPTIONS and implications of your decision.
   a) If you perceive that you can provide safe patient care and are willing to work the additional shift, accept the assignment.
   b) If you perceive that you can provide safe patient care but are unwilling to stay due to other plans or the chronic nature of the request, inform the manager of your reasons for not wishing to accept the assignment.
   c) If you perceive that your fatigue will interfere with your ability to safely care for patients, indicate this fact to the manager.

If you do not accept the assignment and the manager continues to attempt to persuade you it may be appropriate to consult the next level of management, such as the House Supervisor or the Nurse Executive.

In further dialogue continue to weigh your reasons for refusal versus the facility's need for an RN. If you have a strong alternate commitment, such as no child care, or if you seriously feel your fatigue will interfere with safe patient care, restate your reasons for refusal.

At this point, it is important for you to be aware of the legal rights of the facility. Even though you may have legitimate concern for patient safety and your own legal accountability in providing safe care, or legitimate concern for the safety of your children or other commitments, the facility has legal precedent to initiate disciplinary action, including termination, if you refuse to accept an assignment. Therefore, it is important to continue to explore options in a positive manner, recognizing both you and the facility have a responsibility for safe patient care.

4. POINT OF DECISION/ IMPLICATIONS.
   a) Accept the assignment, documenting your professional concern for patient safety and the process you used to inform the facility (manager) of your concerns. Keep a personal copy of this documentation and send a copy to the Nurse Executive. Courtesy suggests that you also send a copy to the manager(s) involved. Once you have reached this decision it is unwise to discuss the situation or your feelings with other staff and/ or patients.
   b) Accept the assignment, documenting your professional concerns for the chronic nature of the request and possible long term consequences in reducing the quality of care. Documentation should follow the procedures outlined in (a).
   c) Accept the assignment, documenting your personal concerns regarding working conditions in which management decides the legitimacy of employee's personal commitments. This documentation should go to your manager. You may wish to request a meeting with your manager to discuss the incident and your concerns regarding future requests.
   d) Refuse the assignment, being prepared for disciplinary action. If your reasons for refusal were patient safety or an imperative personal commitment, document this carefully including the process you used to inform the facility (nurse manager) of your concerns. Keep a personal copy of this documentation and send a copy to the Chief Nurse Executive. Courtesy suggests that you also send a copy to the manager(s) involved.

e) Document the rationale for your decision. It may be necessary to use the facility's grievance procedure.

◼ *Summary*

• • • • • • • • • • • • • • • • • •

Some specific examples of how a nurse may apply the guidelines for decision making in the actual work situation have been presented. Staffing dilemmas will always be present and mandate that active communication between staff nurses and all levels of nursing management be maintained to assure patient safety. The likelihood of a satisfactory solution will increase if there is prior consideration of the choices available. This consideration of available alternatives should include recognition that professional nurses are intelligent adults who should be involved in the decision-making process. Professional nurses are accountable for nursing judgements and actions regardless of the personal consequences. Providing safe nursing care to the patient is the ultimate objective of the professional nurse and the health care facility.

◼ *Resources*

• • • • • • • • • • • • • • • • • •

To maintain current and accurate information on accountability of registered nurses for giving, accepting or rejecting a work assignment, the following resources are suggested:

◆ **Health Care Facility:** Nurses are encouraged to seek consultation with their nurse manager/executives to discuss the facility's missions and goals as well as policies and procedures.

◆ The **Florida Nurses Association,** the largest statewide organization for registered nurses, represents nursing in the governmental, policymaking arena and maintains current information and publications relative to the nurse's practice environment. Contact FNA, P.O. Box 536985, Orlando, FL 32853-6985/407/ 896-3261 for the benefits and services of membership, as well as priorities and activities of the Association.

◆ The **American Nurses Association** serves as a national clearing-house of information and offers publications on contemporary issues, including standards of practice, nursing ethics, as well as legal and regulatory issues. Contact ANA for a complimentary copy of the Publications Catalogue: ANA, 2420 Pershing Road, Kansas City, MO 64108, or phone (800) 821-5834.

◆ **Board of Nursing:** 4080 Woodcock Drive, Suite 202, Jacksonville, FL 32207, or phone (904) 858-6940. A complimentary copy of the Nurse Practice Act is available to each registered nurse upon request.

The **Florida Nurses Association Labor and Employment Relations Commission** acknowledges:

◆ the work of the **North Carolina Nurses Association ad hoc Committee on RN Work Assignments** for their initial work in developing the concepts for this publication:

> **Elizabeth A. Trought, M.N., R.N., Chairman**
> Betty Baster, B.S., R.N., C.N.A.
> Betty Benton, R.N.
> Charlotte Hoelzel, M.S., R.N.
> Joyce H. Monk, B.S.N., R.N.
> Eldean Pierce, M.S.N., R.N.
> Loucille Swain, R.N.
> Gladys Warlick, R.N.

◆ the **Florida Organization of Nurse Executives** for input and collaboration in the development of the 1989 edition of this document.

◆ the **Florida Nurses Association ad hoc Committee on Safe Nursing Practice** for final preparation of the revised 1989 edition of this document:

> **Frank Moore, R.N., Chairman**
> Richard Bednar, R.N.
> Phyllis Connerley, R.N.
> Gina Giovinco, R.N.
> Sandra Janzen, R.N.
> Pamela Erb, R.N.
> Katherine Mason, R.N.
> Paula Massey, R.N.

APPENDIX 5*

Patient's Bill of Rights

1. The patient has the right to considerate and respectful care.

2. The patient has the right to obtain from his physician complete and current information concerning his diagnosis, treatment, and prognosis in terms the patient can be reasonably expected to understand. When it is not medically advisable to give such information to the patient, the information should be made available to an appropriate person in his behalf. He has the right to know by name the physician responsible for coordinating his care.

3. The patient has the right to receive from his physician information necessary to give informed consent prior to the start of any procedure and/or treatment. Except in emergencies, such information for informed consent, should be included but not necessarily be limited to the specific procedure and/or treatment, the medically significant risks involved, and the probable duration of incapacitation. Where medically significant alternatives for care or treatment exist, or when the patient requests information concerning medical alternatives the patient has the right to such information. The patient also has the right to know the name of the person responsible for the procedures and/or treatment.

4. The patient has the right to refuse treatment to the extent permitted by law, and to be informed of the medical consequences of his action.

5. The patient has the right to every consideration of his privacy concerning his own medical care program. Case discussion, consultation, examination, and treatment are confidential and should be conducted discreetly. Those not directly involved in his care must have the permission of the patient to be present.

6. The patient has the right to expect that all communications and records pertaining to his care be treated as confidential.

7. The patient has the right to expect that within its capacity a hospital must make

reasonable response to the request of a patient for services. The hospital must provide evaluation, service, and/or referral as indicated by the urgency of the case. When medically permissible a patient may be transferred to another facility only after he has received complete information and explanation concerning the needs for and alternatives to such a transfer. The institution to which the patient is transferred must first have accepted the patient for transfer.

8. The patient has the right to obtain information as to any relationship of his hospital to other health care and educational institutions insofar as his care is concerned. The patient has the right to obtain information as to the existence of any professional relationships among individuals by name, who are treating him.

9. The patient has the right to be advised if the hospital proposes to engage in or perform human experimentation affecting his care or treatment. The patient has the right to refuse to participate in such research projects.

10. The patient has the right to expect reasonable continuity of care. He has the right to know in advance what appointment times and physicians are available and where. The patient has the right to expect that the hospital will provide a mechanism whereby he is informed by his physician or a delegate of the physician of the patient's continuing health care requirements following discharge.

11. The patient has the right to examine and receive an explanation of his bill regardless of source of payment.

12. The patient has the right to know what hospital rules and regulations apply to his conduct as a patient.

Index

A "b" following a page number indicates a box; an "f" indicates a figure; a "t" indicates a table.